Resisting Extortion

Criminal extortion is an understudied, but widespread and severe problem in Latin America. In states that cannot or choose not to uphold the rule of law, victims are often seen as helpless in the face of powerful criminals. However, even under such difficult circumstances, victims resist criminal extortion in surprisingly different ways. Drawing on extensive fieldwork in violent localities in Colombia, El Salvador and Mexico, Moncada weaves together interviews, focus groups, and participatory drawing exercises to explain why victims pursue distinct strategies to resist criminal extortion. The analysis traces and compares processes that lead to individual acts of everyday resistance; sporadic killings by ad hoc groups of victims and police; institutionalized and sustained collective vigilantism; and coordination between victims and states to co-produce order in ways that both strengthen and undermine the rule of law. This book offers valuable new insights into the broader politics of crime and the state.

Eduardo Moncada is an Assistant Professor in the Department of Political Science at Barnard College, Columbia University. He is the author of Cities, Business and the Politics of Urban Violence in Latin America (2016) and co-editor of Inside Countries: Subnational Research in Comparative Politics (2019). His research has been supported by the American Council of Learned Societies, the Ford Foundation Fellowship Program and the National Academy of Sciences.

CAMBRIDGE STUDIES IN COMPARATIVE POLITICS

GENERAL EDITOR

KATHLEEN THELEN *Massachusetts Institute of Technology*

ASSOCIATE EDITORS

CATHERINE BOONE *London School of Economics*
THAD DUNNING *University of California, Berkeley*
ANNA GRZYMALA-BUSSE *Stanford University*
TORBEN IVERSEN *Harvard University*
STATHIS KALYVAS *University of Oxford*
MARGARET LEVI *Stanford University*
MELANIE MANION *Duke University*
HELEN MILNER *Princeton University*
FRANCES ROSENBLUTH *Yale University*
SUSAN STOKES *Yale University*
TARIQ THACHIL *University of Pennsylvania*
ERIK WIBBELS *Duke University*

SERIES FOUNDER

PETER LANGE *Duke University*

OTHER BOOKS IN THE SERIES

Continued after the index

Resisting Extortion

Victims, Criminals, and States in Latin America

EDUARDO MONCADA

Barnard College, Columbia University

CAMBRIDGE
UNIVERSITY PRESS

CAMBRIDGE
UNIVERSITY PRESS

University Printing House, Cambridge CB2 8BS, United Kingdom

One Liberty Plaza, 20th Floor, New York, NY 10006, USA

477 Williamstown Road, Port Melbourne, VIC 3207, Australia

314–321, 3rd Floor, Plot 3, Splendor Forum, Jasola District Centre,
New Delhi – 110025, India

103 Penang Road, #05–06/07, Visioncrest Commercial, Singapore 238467

Cambridge University Press is part of the University of Cambridge.

It furthers the University's mission by disseminating knowledge in the pursuit of
education, learning, and research at the highest international levels of excellence.

www.cambridge.org
Information on this title: www.cambridge.org/9781108843386
DOI: 10.1017/9781108915328

© Eduardo Moncada 2021

First published 2021

A catalogue record for this publication is available from the British Library.

Library of Congress Cataloging-in-Publication Data
NAMES: Moncada, Eduardo, 1977– author.
TITLE: Resisting extortion : victims, criminals and states in Latin America / Eduardo Moncada,
Barnard College, Columbia University.
DESCRIPTION: New York, NY : Cambridge University Press, 2021. | Series: Cambridge studies
in comparative politics | Includes bibliographical references and index.
IDENTIFIERS: LCCN 2021027340 (print) | LCCN 2021027341 (ebook) | ISBN 9781108843386
(hardback) | ISBN 9781108915328 (ebook other)
SUBJECTS: LCSH: Extortion – Latin America. | Offenses against property – Law
and legislation – Latin America. | Crime prevention – Latin America. | Vigilantism – Latin
America. | BISAC: POLITICAL SCIENCE / American Government / General
CLASSIFICATION: LCC HV6604.L29 M66 2021 (print) | LCC HV6604.L29 (ebook) | DDC 364.16/
5098–dc23
LC record available at https://lccn.loc.gov/2021027340
LC ebook record available at https://lccn.loc.gov/2021027341

ISBN 978-1-108-84338-6 Hardback
ISBN 978-1-108-82470-5 Paperback

For my family

Contents

Figures, Tables, and Maps

Acknowledgments

It is an understatement to say that 2020 was a very strange year to finish a book project. But this difficult period of time also made me even more appreciative of the support, encouragement, and guidance that I received for this project from brilliant and courageous people over the past several years. There is simply no way that I can adequately express my gratitude in this section to everyone who has contributed to the development of this book. But I would be remiss if I did not highlight some of the people to whom I am deeply indebted. I am most thankful to the many people in my field sites who agreed to be interviewed, participated in focus groups, introduced me to friends and family, invited me to observe meetings, and shared with me their difficult experiences. And I am indebted to my research assistants in Colombia and Mexico and two informal interlocutors in El Salvador. All were crucial in my ability to navigate complex and insecure environments. More importantly, they all helped me to see the ways in which victimization is inherently political. *Gracias.*

An early version of this manuscript benefited significantly from detailed and extensive feedback provided by Enrique Desmond Arias, Angelica Durán-Martínez, Beatriz Magaloni, David Skarbek, and Richard Snyder. I was also fortunate to receive insightful and helpful comments on ideas and parts of the manuscript over the years from Jorge Antonio Alves, Matthew Amengual, Ana Arjona, Regina Bateson, Allyson Benton, Hannah Baron, Nicholas Barnes, Rebecca Bell-Martin, Christopher Carter, José Miguel Cruz, Christian Davenport, Cecilia Farfán-Méndez, Albert Fishlow, Gustavo Flores-Macías, Janice Gallagher, Omar García-Ponce, Yanilda González, Jonathan Hartlyn, Alisha Holland, Evelyne Huber, Philip Johnson, Oliver Kaplan, Jana Krause, Paul Lagunes, Romain Le Cour Grandmaison, Sandra Ley, Zachariah Mampilly, Mary Fran Malone, Lindsay Mayka, Benjamin Lessing, Juan Masullo, Vicky Murillo, Jennifer Pierce, Alison Post, Logan Puck, Jonathan Rosen, Ben Ross Schneider, Erica Simmons, Hillel Soifer, Paul Staniland, Guillermo Trejo, Megan Turnbull, William Reno, Livia Schubiger, Nicholas Rush Smith, Rodrigo Soares, Mark Ungar, Federico Varese, Erik Wibbels, Michael Weintraub, Phil Williams, Michael Jerome Wolff,

Deborah Yashar, Lauren Young, and Jessica Zarkin. Sarah Parkinson provided helpful advice on methodological questions. Scott Straus and Kendra Koivu shared valuable feedback on the some of the overarching concepts and typologies.

An excellent conference at Harvard University organized by Dara Kay Cohen and Danielle Jung on lynchings and vigilantism was a productive space in which to learn from a diverse group of scholars and receive feedback that also made its way into the book. I also benefited from the questions and suggestions that I received on parts of the manuscript from participants in a number of workshops, conferences, and seminars over the last few years, including at Barnard College, the City University of New York, Columbia University, Cornell University, the University of Connecticut, Duke University, Florida International University, the University of Georgia, the University of Gothenburg, University of North Carolina at Chapel Hill, Ohio University, the University of Pennsylvania, the University of Pittsburgh, Princeton University, Stanford University, the University of Wisconsin-Madison, and Yale University.

I began this project shortly before joining the faculty at Barnard College. There I found a collegial department of supportive colleagues who have contributed to my development as both a scholar and a teacher. I also thank Vicky Murillo at Columbia University for her engagement and support.

I want to acknowledge the vital institutional support for different parts of this project that I received from the American Council of Learned Societies, Barnard College, and the Institute for Latin American Studies at Columbia University. I was fortunate to be able to finish a first draft of the full manuscript while a Visiting Fellow at the Program in Latin American Studies at Princeton University, where Gabriela Nouzeilles built and led a welcoming and intellectually stimulating environment.

The manuscript benefited from Amanda Pearson's detailed editing and suggestions. Rudy Leon crafted the index. Deepu Raghuthaman and Mathivathini Mareesan effectively coordinated the copyediting. At Cambridge University Press, Cameron Daddis, Jadyn Fauconier-Herry and Becky Jackaman helped to move the manuscript along smoothly. Sara Doskow has been a wonderful and encouraging editor. Two anonymous reviewers provided detailed and excellent feedback that greatly improved the manuscript. I am grateful to Kathleen Thelen and a reader for inviting this book to be part of the Cambridge Studies in Comparative Politics Series. Parts of Chapters 2 and 3 draw on material from my 2020 article, "The Politics of Criminal Victimization: Pursuing and Resisting Power," *Perspectives on Politics* 18(3): 706–721. I use this article with permission from Cambridge University Press, and I am grateful to the anonymous reviewers who offered incisive comments and suggestions on it.

I dedicate this book to my family. There were moments when I lost myself in this work, and moments when I nearly lost so much more. I am grateful that my family kept me rooted.

Abbreviations

APHIS	Animal and Plant Health Inspection Service
ARENA	Alianza Republicana Nacionalista (Nationalist Republican Alliance)
Barrio 18	Eighteenth Street Gang
CJNG	Cartel Jalisco Nueva Generación (Jalisco Cartel New Generation)
CUSEPT	Cuerpo de Seguridad Pública de Tancítaro (Public Security Force of Tancítaro)
DTO	Drug Trafficking Organization
FGR	Fiscalía General de la República de El Salvador (Attorney General of the Republic of El Salvador)
FMLN	Frente Farabundo Martí para la Liberación Nacional (Farabundo Martí National Liberation Front)
Iduhca	Instituto de Derechos Humanos de la Universidad Centroamericana (Institute for Human Rights of the Central American University)
JLSV	Junta Local de Sanidad Vegetal (Plan Health Board)
MS-13	Mara Salvatrucha
NAFTA	North American Free Trade Agreement
ODIN	Organización Delincuencial Integrada al Narcotráfico (Criminal Organizations Integrated with Drug Trafficking)
OVA	Oficina del Valle de Aburrá (Office of the Aburrá Valley)
PAN	Partido Acción Nacional (National Action Party)
PDDH	Procuraduría para la Defensa de los Derechos Humanos de El Salvador (Office of the Human Rights Ombudsman of El Salvador)
PNC	Policía Nacional Civil de El Salvador (National Civil Police of El Salvador)

PRD	Partido de la Revolución Democrática (Party of the Democratic Revolution)
PRI	Partido Revolucionario Institucional (Institutional Revolutionary Party)
SAGARPA	Secretaría de Agricultura, Ganaderia, Desarrollo Rural, Pesca y Alimentación (Secretariat of Agriculture, Livestock, Rural Development, Fisheries, and Food)
SPS	Sanitary and Phytosanitary
USDA	United States Department of Agriculture
WHO	World Health Organization

PART I

RESISTANCE TO CRIMINAL EXTORTION

I

Introduction

In the southwestern Mexican state of Michoacán, Raul recounted the procedures that he and other members of the avocado sector in the municipality of Tancítaro followed at the stone barricade they constructed in 2013 on the road leading into their community:[1]

One rifle shot meant everyone should grab their guns and be alert for anything. Two rifle shots meant come with your weapons to the barricade because the Templarios [referring to the Knights Templar drug trafficking organization, or DTO] were coming. And three shots meant that everyone, even kids, had to come to the barricade. But this was only if the [municipal] police were approaching. Because imagine what things were like before we rose up in arms: the [municipal] police had a checkpoint down the road from us, and two kilometers down from that one there was a checkpoint run by the Templarios! And the Templarios could just walk through the police checkpoint – like they were common citizens, without a worry – and into our community to insult us and demand money from us.[2]

Armed *autodefensas* (self-defense groups) appeared in dozens of municipalities across Michoacán starting in 2013 (Fuentes Díaz and Paleta Pérez 2015). Raul and several hundred avocado sector actors formed one such self-defense group to stop the Knights Templar's extortion, popularly referred to as *derecho* or *cuota*. Collectively they planned, coordinated, and enacted lethal and nonlethal practices of *collective vigilantism* against the DTO.[3] As a local journalist explained to me: "The most important thing was for there to be organization in

---

[1] I use pseudonyms for all of the individuals who were interviewed or participated in focus groups for this project. With the exclusion of Tancítaro in Mexico and Medellín in Colombia, I also use pseudonyms for the localities where I conducted field research. I discuss the security protocol that I followed in more detail in both Chapter 2 and the Appendix.

[2] Interview with Raul (MCN950), avocado producer, Tancítaro, July 2018.

[3] DTOs are not cartels because they do not control the pricing market for their products through collusion with each other (Thoumi 2003, 6). Additionally, because the term "cartel" itself is politically contentious (Grillo 2011), I refer to them as DTOs except where the term appears in the

the communities. There was no other group of persons in Tancítaro that was more organized than the *aguacateros* (avocado producers). So they had the advantage that they could organize people very quickly once things began here."[4] But in the municipality of La Unión also in Michoacán, mobilization to end criminal extortion looked very different.

In La Unión, producers and exporters in the municipality's lucrative berry sector had also been extorted by the Knights Templar and, as in Tancítaro, the municipal police force was captured by the criminal organization. Berry producers repeatedly shared stories of local police looking the other way as trucks of armed men from the Knights Templar cruised the municipality's streets, or of police who "arrested" berry producers and delivered them to the DTO for failure to pay the criminal tax. Moreover, it was widely known in both Tancítaro and La Unión that municipal presidents were handing over money from the municipal budgets to the DTO every year in order for the criminals to allow the local government to continue operating. Yet, despite these similarities in the two cases, collective mobilization to end extortion unfolded in very different ways. Unlike the centralized nature of collective vigilantism in Tancítaro's avocado sector, where victims of extortion coordinated with each other, victims in La Unión's berry sector fragmented into several autonomous armed groups, used varying practices to contest their victimization that often functioned at cross-purposes, and struggled to coordinate with each other. The multiple groups of victims in La Unión engaged in violence against the DTO to end extortion, but strikingly also against each other, including armed clashes in the streets as well as targeted violence against each other's members.

But while collective mobilization in Michoacán took place in settings where police were actively complicit with criminals and governing authorities were providing criminals with public resources, state actors are not always threats to victims' extralegal efforts against criminal actors. In El Salvador, the country's two main gangs, the Mara Salvatrucha (MS-13) and the Barrio 18 (Eighteenth Street Gang),[5] are infamous for extortion in which they force victims to regularly pay informal taxes called *la renta* (the rent). In two municipalities – El Pilar in the country's western region near the capital of San Salvador and Cienfuegos in the hot and humid eastern Pacific coast – small groups of victims of extortion in rural communities located within municipalities called *cantones* (cantons) assassinated several gang members from 2014 through 2016. These groups consisted of handfuls of small-scale farmers from the dominant agricultural economies of basic grains and vegetables in each municipality. But both groups also included a few individual local police from the lower

---

title of existing works, in the names of particular criminal organizations, or is used by an interview subject or focus group participant.

[4] Esperanza (MCN201), journalist, Tancítaro, electronic communications, May 2018.

[5] In 2005 the Barrio 18 gang split into two factions: the *Revolucionarios* (Revolutionaries) and *Sureños* (Southerners).

ranks of the country's Nacional Civil Police (*Policía Nacional Civil*, PNC). The farmers and police agents shared weapons, information, and other resources to target and kill individual gang members in periodic acts of what I term *piecemeal vigilantism*. For example, in 2014 several farmers wore police uniforms lent to them by a local police officer as they shot an MS-13 gang member who oversaw the local collection of extortion rents. While the farmers killed the gang member in a house, another police officer kept watch outside in case police that was not privy to the group's extralegal activities happened to pass by.[6] Unlike the military and police death squads that methodically disappeared and killed political opponents under the direction and with the support of El Salvador's government during the civil war (Arnson 2000), the two groups engaging in piecemeal vigilantism were founded and directed by civilian victims of crime who enlisted individual police to support their occasional acts of violence in part to help them evade elements of the state that attempted to enforce the rule of law.

Yet, confronting criminals does not always entail victims carrying out extralegal violence. In the localities in Michoacán as well as in western and eastern El Salvador where I conducted field work, before pursuing extralegal violence, victims used rhetorical tricks and other subtle subversive tactics when interacting with the criminals that were extorting them. This strategy was particularly evident in another one of my field sites: a large informal market in Medellín, Colombia, where several hundred *recicladores* (recyclers) – informal vendors who scour trash bins and landfills for goods to clean, repair, and sell – paid the criminal tax known there as the *vacuna* (vaccination). The criminal group that taxed the recyclers, called a *Convivir,* worked for a powerful criminal organization that was based in one of the city's peripheral neighborhoods and which coordinated a range of criminal markets, including drug trafficking. The vendors – who faced both local police captured by the Convivir and municipal authorities who they perceived as tolerant of extortion in the city center – did not mobilize collectively to end their victimization. Instead, they relied on individual and sporadic acts of *everyday resistance* (Scott 1985, 1990) that entailed calibrated, but contentious, verbal jousting with members of the Convivir. Although this repertoire of practices did not end extortion and only offered vendors marginal reductions in material taxation, it did enable them to reclaim a sense of dignity as workers and citizens despite ongoing victimization at the hands of a powerful criminal group.

Finally, victims' resistance to extortion can remarkably extend beyond verbal sparring and extralegal violence to include the threat and use of violence to shape electoral outcomes and governance. In the wake of collective vigilantism in Tancítaro and La Unión in Michoacán, victims mobilized to influence local elections in 2015 and 2018. This mobilization

---

[6] Case M, El Pilar, judicial files. See the Appendix for a description of the individual legal cases that I analyze in El Salvador.

was part of what I call the *coproduction of order* wherein victims, governing authorities, and police jointly build order in ways that strengthen parts of the rule of law while weakening others. The coproduction of order accomplishes this by strengthening the ability of local governments and police to enforce the law, while also enabling victims to retain informal privileges that violate the law, ranging from carrying restricted firearms in public to infringing on the authority of local police.

These contrasting cases of *resistance to criminal victimization* are puzzling. Popular media depicts victims of organized crime as being resigned to their fates at the hands of the powerful armed criminal groups that operate in Latin America and other parts of the developing world. The violence that criminal groups generate is undoubtedly substantial and tragic with long-lasting effects. But victims are not always helpless, even when at first glance they seem submissive in the face of armed criminal actors. Sometimes victims use indirect tactics that are difficult for observers to discern without first comprehending how victims understand criminal victimization and the power dynamics it entails, as in the case of everyday resistance by the recyclers in Medellín. At other times, victims resist in clearly observable ways, using forms of violence that mimic those they experience at the hands of organized crime, including beatings, disappearances, and lethal violence. Moreover, the manner in which extralegal violence by victims against criminals unfolds can range from occasional acts of violence that take place across months to weeks-long waves of intense coordinated violence. Thus, in contesting their victimization, civilians can contribute to the very violence and insecurity that we normally attribute only to organized crime or state–criminal conflict.

Growing academic research shows that crime influences the political behavior of victims in contrasting ways, including effects on whether and how they vote (Ley 2018; Trelles and Carreras 2012) as well as civic engagement (Bateson 2012; Dorff 2017). But this tells us little about the ways in which victims engage and confront armed criminal groups. In shifting the focus to precisely this phenomenon, this book joins with and extends an emerging line of study on the political origins and consequences of victims' responses to crime (Bateson 2013; Curry 2020; Jung and Cohen 2020; Mattiace, Ley, and Trejo 2019; Moncada 2017; Osorio, Schubiger, and Weintraub 2021; Phillips 2017; Smith 2019).

In settings where the state is unable or unwilling to enforce the rule of law, why do victims resist similar forms of criminal victimization in contrasting ways? By resistance I mean observable strategies outside of the rule of law that victims direct at criminals to negotiate, end, or prevent their victimization. I use the widespread, but understudied, phenomenon of criminal extortion in Latin America to introduce resistance to criminal victimization as a novel phenomenon in the emerging research on the politics of crime. To explain the different ways in which victims resist criminal extortion, my argument centers on three variables: the time horizons of criminals; the nature of local political economies; and the criminal capture of the police. Using ethnographic data collected during field research in Colombia, El Salvador, and Mexico, I identify and trace pathways and mechanisms to the following strategies of resistance: individual-level acts of everyday resistance; the sporadic killings by ad hoc groups of victims and police that characterize piecemeal vigilantism; institutionalized and sustained forms of collective vigilantism; and coordinated efforts between victims and states to co-produce order in ways that both fortify and undermine the rule of law.

1.1 KEY CONTRIBUTIONS

Latin America provides fertile terrain in which to analyze resistance to criminal extortion. Criminal violence in the region threatens economies, institutional stability, and social development (Moncada 2013). As shown in Figure 1.1, levels of lethal violence in both Central and South America tower above those in other world regions, with average intentional homicide rates between 2003 and 2018 of 22.1 and 22.7 per 100,000 population, respectively. Today Latin America accounts for 8 percent of the world's population, but nearly one-third of the

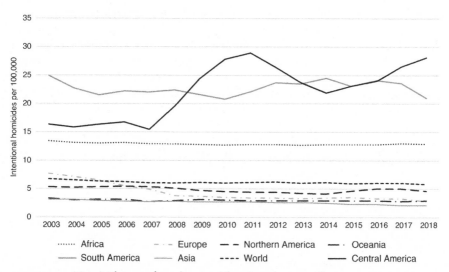

FIGURE 1.1 Homicide rates for select world regions (2003–18)
Note: Central America refers to Belize, Costa Rica, El Salvador, Guatemala, Honduras, Mexico, Nicaragua, and Panama. South America refers to Argentina, Bolivia, Brazil, Chile, Colombia, Ecuador, French Guiana, Guyana, Paraguay, Peru, Uruguay, and Venezuela.
Source: UNODC (https://public.tableau.com/views/Homicide-Estimate/Homicide-Estimate?:showVizHome=no)
Accessed on May 26, 2020.

world's annual homicides.[7] This violence prematurely ends lives; inflicts lasting psychological and emotional scars on victims, families, and communities; and constrains development.[8]

The intense criminal violence in Latin America has catalyzed a growing body of research that provides valuable insights into the dynamics of the illicit drug trade (Arias 2006; Durán-Martínez 2017; Lessing 2017; Snyder and Durán-Martínez 2009; Trejo and Ley 2020).[9] But most people in the region experience organized crime not through spectacular and lethal acts of drug violence, but instead through the everyday victimization associated with criminal extortion. As Magaloni et al. (2020, 1165) state: "Lethal violence is not the only or most pervasive danger for the general population. Citizens are trapped in networks of extortion and coercion where DTOs prey on them, often with the acquiescence or direct collaboration of local states and law enforcement agents." Criminal groups in the region oversee a range of lucrative illicit markets beyond the drug trade that have been insufficiently scrutinized empirically or theoretically. Extortion is one such illicit market wherein criminal actors extract rents by threatening and/or using force in exchange for the promise of protection from others and themselves.[10] One of this book's main contributions is therefore to broaden our understanding of the politics of crime by shifting the analytical focus onto criminal extortion.

Figure 1.2 provides a comparison of rates of extortion as documented in official government statistics in the three countries where I conducted research for this book. Because extortion often goes underreported (Del Fratte 2004, 151–152), however, the figures in Figure 1.2 most certainly underestimate the prevalence of extortion in the region. In Mexico alone, for example, an estimated 97.4 percent of extortion cases are never reported to government authorities.[11] Whereas it is difficult – though not impossible – to hide the bodies of the people killed in drug-related violence, accurately tallying extortion places the responsibility on victims to report the crime to authorities. But fear of punishment by criminals or the state – or sometimes both – provides strong disincentives for doing so. Moreover, the available evidence indicates that extortion disproportionately affects businesses

---

[7] Tom Phillips, "Breathtaking Homicidal Violence: Latin America in Grip of Murder Crisis," *Guardian* (US edition), April 26, 2018.

[8] During the first decade of the twentieth century, for example, sharp growth in homicides in Mexico reversed the trend of the previous six decades of increased life expectancy (Aburto et al. 2016).

[9] Bergman (2018) analyzes contraband and smuggling economies in Latin America.

[10] I am not implying that researchers have exhausted the study of the illicit drug trade. To the contrary, studies continue to unpack important dimensions of the drug trade that we are only just beginning to understand, including the nature and strategic use of lethal violence (Durán-Martínez 2017; Lessing 2017; Osorio 2015; Ríos 2013; Shirk 2010; Snyder and Durán-Martínez 2009; Trejo and Ley 2018) and the complex relations between criminal actors involved in different aspects of the drug trade, the state, and social groups (Arias 2017; Leeds 1996; Penglase 2014; Willis 2015; Wolff 2015).

[11] Parker Asmann, "Underreporting Helps Extortion Thrive in Mexico, Latin America," InSight Crime, November 1, 2018.

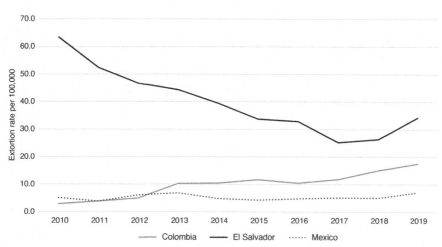

FIGURE I.2 Extortion rates in Colombia, El Salvador and Mexico (2010–19)
Sources: Data for Colombia is from the Ministry of National Defense of Colombia. Available at: www.mindefensa.gov.co/irj/go/km/docs/Mindefensa/Documentos/descargas/ estudios_sectoriales/info_estadistica/Logros_Sector_Defensa.pdf. Accessed on July 15, 2020. Data for El Salvador is from the Policía Nacional Civil de la República de El Salvador. Available at: www.transparencia.gob.sv/institutions/pnc/. Accessed on May 2, 2020. Data for Mexico is from the Secretariado Ejecutivo del Sistema Nacional de Seguridad Pública. Available at: www.gob.mx/sesnsp/acciones-y-programas/datos-abiertos-de-incidencia-delictiva?state=published. Accessed on May 3, 2020.

relative to the general population. Based on a unique victimization survey of businesses in Mexico conducted by the Instituto Nacional de Estadística y Geografía (National Institute of Statistics and Geography), Figure 1.3 shows that the rate of extortion for Mexican business firms is much higher than for the general population. Remarkably, across the five waves of victimization surveys represented in Figure 1.3, an average of 95 percent of the cases of extortion of business firms were not reported to public authorities.[12]

Yet, extortion generates both direct and indirect costs for victims, societies, and states (Frye and Zhuravskaya 2000; Gambetta 1996; Varese 2014). Rough estimates suggest that the economic consequences of extortion in Latin America are substantial. In El Salvador extortion by gangs costs the country's economy at least USD 4 billion annually, or approximately 15 percent of the national annual gross domestic product.[13] In downtown Medellín alone criminal extortion

---

[12] The survey specifically asks firms the following question: "Did the owner, a legal representative or employee go to the Public Ministry to report the crime?" Available at: www.inegi.org.mx/contenidos/ programas/enve/2020/doc/modulo_delitos_enve2020.pdf. Accessed on October 1, 2020.

[13] Molly O'Toole, "Micro-extortion by Gangs Is Costing El Salvador Millions of Dollars a Year, $10 at a Time," *Quartz*, June 17, 2017.

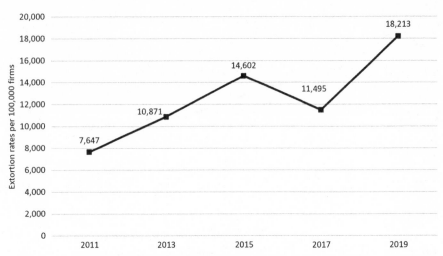

FIGURE 1.3 Extortion rates for business firms in Mexico (select years)
Sources: Instituto Nacional de Estadística y Geografía (INEGI). Encuesta Nacional de Victimización de Empresas 2012, 2014, 2016, 2018, and 2020. Available at www.inegi.org.mx/programas/enve/2020/. Accessed on October 1, 2020.

generates nearly USD 250,000 every month for criminal actors.[14] However, when we conceive of criminal extortion as a onetime physical act rather than a dynamic relational process that includes but extends beyond its material costs, we risk overlooking its important social and political dimensions. My focus on the process of criminal extortion therefore invites us to complicate how we study the nature and consequences of relations between criminals and victims.

Research often shifts from victims experiencing criminal acts to assessing whether this makes it more or less likely that the victims will either engage with or disengage from the state via conventional channels of participation. This makes it difficult to see and study the iterative nature of relations between victims and criminals. Not all crimes are onetime acts. Victimization can consist of a series of acts and reactions that together shape the process of victimization. The nature of victim–criminal relations can thus vary across different types of crimes as well as across space and time. I find that the extraction of criminal rents is embedded within contentious power relations between victims and criminals that are analogous to those between subordinate and dominant actors. I detail and build on this finding to bridge the study of the politics of crime and broader research on relations between the ruled and rulers (Migdal 1988; Migdal, Kohli, and Shue 1994; Scott 1990). For example, scholars of state–society relations (Migdal, Kohli, and Shue 1994), state-

---

[14] "Miembros de 'Convivir' de Medellín Ganan un Millón de Pesos Mensuales," *El Tiempo*, August 11, 2014.

building (Boone 2003), authoritarianism (Blaydes 2018; Wedeen 1999), capital–labor relations (Scott 1977), and colonization (Lawrence 2013) show that seemingly asymmetric power relations are often more contested than we suspect. Recent civil war studies similarly complicate the assumption of civilian submission to rebels and other armed political actors (Arjona 2017; Kaplan 2017a; Krause 2018; Mampilly 2012; Masullo 2020; Metelits 2009). I find analogous dynamics in my research on criminal extortion showing that it is more than a material transaction and instead a relationship in which victims and criminals contest material and non-material forms of *power*. This insight gleaned through in-depth fieldwork in multiple localities enables us to extend research on relations between subordinate and dominant actors into a new empirical terrain.

This book also brings business into the study of the politics of crime. Scholars analyze how economic actors shape the trajectories of civil wars (Wood 2000) and post-conflict peace-building (Rettberg 2008). But the role of business in the growing literature on crime is comparatively underdeveloped.[15] Meanwhile scholars analyze how crime affects productivity and capital investment (BenYishay and Pearlman 2014; Gaviria 2002), while others assess how businesses' demands for order fuel the private security industry (Abrahamsen and Williams 2010; Ungar 2007) or preferential treatment by police (Becker and Müller 2013; Davis 2013; Samara 2011). These studies are partly motivated by the fact that businesses are often disproportionately the victims of crimes relative to individuals and households. But our understanding of the victimization of business is limited given that with rare exceptions, such as that presented in Figure 1.3, victimization surveys disproportionately focus on individuals and households (Mugellini 2013).[16]

I tackle this empirical gap not by enumerating the incidence of criminal extortion, but by collecting and analyzing ground-level data to generate a fresh analytical perspective into how business firms experience and react to criminal extortion. This approach provides a powerful vantage point from which to study the repeated, face-to-face interactions between business owners and the criminals who extort them. By doing so, this book reveals the ways in which criminal actors not only extract money, but also strategically use other aspects of the identities of business owners to facilitate victimization, including offending victims' status as entrepreneurs *and* citizens of the state. Throughout my fieldwork business owners highlighted these nonmaterial dimensions of extortion in discussing how they both experience and resist criminal victimization.[17] Discovering this led me to approach victimization under extortion as a more complex phenomenon than a coerced transaction

---

[15] See Flores-Macías (2014) on how insecurity shapes the tax preferences of the private sector.

[16] A business is defined as "a company, public corporation, partnership or individual which sells goods and/or services with the intention of generating a surplus from its trading activities for its owners" (Grant 1987, 3).

[17] This aligns partially with Loveman's (1998) argument that collective action against repressive actors is driven by a combination of material incentives and "purposive motivations." See also Wood (2003) on how "pleasure in agency" drives participation in rebellion.

and instead explore it as an intense and layered experience where both victims and criminals invoke multiple aspects of each other's identities in order to contest power between them.

Relatedly, this book shows how dialogue between emerging studies of the politics of crime and the established literature on the political economy of development can contribute to both lines of research. I engage with the rich literature on state–business relations (Doner and Schneider 2000; Evans 1979; Maxfield and Schneider 1997) that shows how businesses mobilize in response to state policies that affect their economic interests. This business mobilization weighs on the substance and trajectory of a range of issues, including economic liberalization, land reform, labor protections, and privatization, among others (Bartell and Payne 1995; Durand and Silva 1998; Fairfield 2015; Kingstone 1999; Schneider 2004). But we know comparatively less about how businesses respond to the informal policies of criminal actors who wield authority within territory and intervene in everyday life in ways that directly and indirectly impact their economic interests. I show how the types of organizational arrangements that govern economic sectors and that emerge out of state–business relations affect the ways in which businesses later mobilize to resist victimization.

1.2 PREVIEWING THE ARGUMENT

This book advances theory-building about the phenomenon of resistance to criminal victimization. I therefore unpack and describe the different strategies of resistance that victims pursue, and then I trace, analyze, and compare the dynamic processes and mechanisms that can lead to these distinct strategies. To develop my argument, I combine inductive and deductive strategies. I use process tracing (Bennett and Checkel 2015; Collier 2011) to interrogate diverse forms of data that I collected during my field research in Colombia, El Salvador, and Mexico. Process tracing that triangulates multiple types of data is particularly well suited for generating theory and making legible the processes and mechanisms associated with distinct outcomes. I leverage variation in resistance to criminal extortion to carry out cross-case and within-case comparisons of processes and mechanisms. I find that three factors help us to better understand the observed variation in strategies of resistance: the time horizons of criminals; the nature of local political economies; and whether there is criminal capture of the police.

Building on classic analyses of state formation (Olson 1993; Tilly 1982) and agenda-setting research on governance by armed non-state actors (Arias 2017; Arjona 2017; Magaloni, Franco-Vivanco, and Melo 2020; Mampilly 2012; Metelits 2009), I argue that the time horizons of criminal actors influence the nature of their interactions with victims. But while existing studies focus on how shifts in time horizons impact the behaviors of armed non-state actors, I consider how criminals' time horizons impact the behavior of victims. When criminal actors have long time horizons, victims are more likely to opt for everyday resistance that contests, but does not end, victimization. This is because under long time horizons criminal actors not only provide victims with goods and services – notably protection and order – but also enjoy a position of strength given a lack of external challengers. Victims thus prefer negotiating with criminal actors in order to reduce the level and/or frequency of material taxation, and because they deem the risk associated with attempting to end victimization as too high. By contrast, criminal actors with short time horizons provide fewer goods and services and use more predatory behaviors because they face challenges from either the state and/or criminal rivals that threaten their positions by generating uncertainty and stress on their resources. Under these circumstances victims prefer to end their victimization. But while it is necessary to consider how the time horizons of criminal actors influence victims' preferences, it is not sufficient. I find that even when faced with criminals who all have short time horizons, the structures, practices, and trajectories of resistance vary across my cases. To explain this variation, we also need to consider the capacity of victims to mobilize collective action.

Local political economies shape whether and how businesses mobilize collectively to resist criminal victimization. Following work on subnational political economies (Herrigel 2000; Locke 1995), I conceptualize local political economies as consisting of two dimensions: relations among business firms on the one hand and between firms and local governing authorities on the other hand. I differentiate between three ideal-type local political economies: atomized, segmented, and encompassing. The first refers to political economies where ties among firms and between them and governing authorities are nearly nonexistent. Here victims will struggle to mount sustained collective resistance and instead are limited to individual or sporadic practices among small groups. By contrast, victims in encompassing political economies will mobilize and enact resistance as a single group because they harness the bonds of trust and familiarity, robust decision-making structures, and pooled assets contained within a single central preexisting organization that encompasses all relevant business actors. This single coordinating organization in an encompassing political economy also serves as the primary institutional channel between firms and political authorities. Having this single channel of communication with political authorities enables victims to work with governing authorities to jointly advance particular strategies of resistance. Finally, segmented political economies feature multiple groups of victims organized under competing organizations who fight against the criminal actor but, despite their shared grievances, also among themselves as they compete for resources, like money and authority. Here the absence of a single central channel to government officials further fuels competition between subsets of victims who use violence to also seek out legitimacy, political power, and informal control over politicians and governing institutions as part of resistance to criminal victimization. My focus on how victims repurpose business organizations to enact resistance to criminal extortion aligns with diverse literatures that examine the role that associational organizations play in a range of outcomes, including democracy (Berman 1997; Putnam, Leonardi, and Nanetti 1994), development (Tsai 2007), and ethnic conflict (Varshney 2003), as well as civilian mobilization in the face of repressive states (Chenoweth and Stephan 2011; Zald and McCarthy 1987) and rebel insurgencies (Arjona 2017; Kaplan 2017a; Mampilly 2012). By analyzing how these organizations serve as critical links between victims and the state, I draw from and contribute to research on the role of business organizations in the political economy of development (Doner and Schneider 2000; Fairfield 2015; Herrigel 2000; Kingstone 1999; Locke 1995; Maxfield and Schneider 1997; Schneider 2004).

The third factor that influences resistance by victims is whether there is criminal capture of the police. A defining feature of the state is having a monopoly on the legitimate use of force (Weber 1946). Theoretically the police embody this feature in their role as "street level bureaucrats" (Lipsky 1980) that provide order while adhering to the rule of law. But across much of Latin America, the police lack the capacity to provide order while concurrently adhering to the rule of law (Ungar 2002, 2011). Efforts to strengthen their abilities to do so confront the reality of criminal capture of the police across much of the region (Yashar 2018). By criminal capture I am referring to instances in which criminal actors use a combination of bribes and threats to obtain police complicity in their illicit activities. This complicity can range from passive practices, such as looking the other way in the face of criminal activities, to the active participation of police in crimes in support of criminal actors, including extralegal acts. In contexts of criminal capture, victims are confronted by police who are theoretically responsible for upholding the rule of law but who in practice are complicit in criminal victimization.[18] Here victims will avoid incorporating the police into their resistance and, in some instances, will target police as part of their mobilization.

But what about when the police have limited institutional capacities, but they are not captured by criminal actors? The conventional wisdom under these conditions is that victims still have no recourse to end their victimization. But as I show in this book, if the police are autonomous from criminal actors but lack institutional capacity to impose order within the constraints imposed on them by the rule of law, I find that both police and victims have incentives to work together. Low-capacity, but autonomous, police have incentives to join with victims in extralegal violence to ensure their own survival in contexts where criminal actors threaten them. Since even low-capacity police can still offer some valuable inputs for extralegal practices, including protection from other parts of the state for their extralegal activities, victims have incentives to incorporate police into their

---

[18] Note that this is distinct from settings where police coordinate, direct, and are the primary beneficiaries of the extortion of civilians (see Tellez, Wibbels and Krishna 2020).

efforts to resist victimization. My analysis shows that providing order, in other words, can result from processes that either contribute to or weaken the rule of law. This should dissuade us from viewing groups of victims who engage in extralegal practices as part of resistance as "lesser evils" relative to criminals, but instead as complex efforts to reshape order and reconfigure modalities of local governance.

1.3 STRUCTURE OF THE BOOK

This book is divided into three sections. Part I builds the argument of resistance to criminal extortion. In Chapter 2 I discuss the key concepts that readers will encounter throughout this book. I then develop the argument to explain variation in the strategies of resistance that victims pursue in the face of criminal extortion. Here I expand on why a focus on criminals' time horizons, the nature of local political economies, and criminal capture of the police can help to account for this variation. I show that the confluence of these factors yields distinct strategies of resistance that vary in their structures, practices, and trajectories. I label these ideal-type strategies *everyday resistance, piecemeal vigilantism, collective vigilantism,* and the *coproduction of order.* Part I concludes with a discussion of the argument's scope conditions, case selection, and strategies of data collection and analysis.

Parts II and III present the empirical case studies. Part II begins by drawing on evidence from across my cases to show how when criminal actors enjoy long time horizons victims are relegated to everyday resistance regardless of variation in the nature of their political economies and status of the police. This part of the book then analyzes and contrasts cases in Colombia and El Salvador where victims operated in atomized political economies with weak ties among them on the one hand and between them and governing authorities on the other hand, but faced varying types of police. Police in the case of the informal vendors in Medellín were captured by the criminal group carrying out extortion, making the police unavailable to assist the vendors in resisting victimization. Vendors thus pursued everyday resistance consisting mainly of rhetorical practices meant to negotiate the material aspect of victimization but also to contest the strategies that criminals used to impose social and political domination over the vendors as part of sustaining extortion. Chapter 4 then turns to the case of small-scale farmers extorted by gangs in El Salvador and who also operated in atomized political economies. But unlike the informal vendors in Medellín, the small-scale farmers faced police that were not captured by the gangs but were instead autonomous from them. Here farmers thus pursued piecemeal vigilantism wherein they worked in coordination with handfuls of police to carry out sporadic acts of extralegal violence against gang members responsible for extortion. Part II of the book ends with a discussion of how these cases illuminate the crucial role that the status of the police plays in shaping victims' strategies of resistance despite shared conditions of criminal actors with short time horizons and atomized political economies.

Part III turns to the cases in Mexico. The case of Tancítaro has recently garnered international media attention as a locality where the avocado sector finally reached a breaking point with continued extortion and violence at the hands of a DTO and so took up arms against it.[19] I delve deeper into the case to show how the encompassing political economy in the avocado sector, wherein victims counted on a single robust sectoral organization to coordinate among themselves and between them and governing authorities, unleashed a particular process and activated specific mechanisms that led to a centralized form of collective vigilantism. This entailed sustained collective mobilization in which victims carried out a range of practices closely coordinated by a group of leaders. I then contrast the case with that of the berry sector in a nearby municipality that I call La Unión, where a segmented political economy featured a plurality of competing sectoral organizations that precluded victims' abilities to coordinate with each other as part of a unified self-defense group or with local governing authorities. This led to decentralized collective vigilantism in which multiple self-defense groups engaged in a range of both complementary and contradictory practices against criminals and simultaneously jockeyed against each other for power and resources. Chapter 6 continues the comparative analysis of the two municipalities in Michoacán by leveraging within-case shifts in the availability of police as allies for victims' resistance efforts. In both Tancítaro and La Unión the variants of collective vigilantism produced "bottom-up" purges of the local police who had been captured by criminal actors. Victims responded to this shift in strategic conditions by pursuing the coproduction of local order. Yet the projects of coproduction varied in their structures and practices in ways that reflected the enduring differences in the nature of the local political economies and the legacies of differing forms of collective vigilantism. In Tancítaro victims employed their robust sectoral organization and joined with governing authorities to jointly shape local order, whereas in La Unión the legacy of decentralized collective vigilantism and weak ties to governing authorities resulted in violent competition between coalitions of armed victims and politicians to obtain political power. Chapter 7 concludes by exploring the theoretical extensions of the argument, tasks for future research, and the policy implications derived from the analysis and findings.

Collecting the data necessary to trace these processes, identify mechanisms, and compare strategies of resistance to criminal victimization required repeated stints of field research in multiple localities. Each of the field sites posed complex and different challenges in terms of security for participants, research assistants, and me. In the Appendix I discuss the research process and how each method

---

[19] Katy Watson, "The Avocado Police Protecting Mexico's Green Gold," *BBC*, November 28, 2017.

generated different types of data that I then triangulated to study processes and mechanisms leading to strategies of resistance. I do not use all of the data that I collected – doing so would pose risks for some of the people who put their trust in me by accepting invitations to discuss sensitive topics. I state this to underscore the dangerous conditions and difficult choices that the people who accepted these invitations face on a daily basis. Thus, in addition to contributing to our scholarly understanding of the politics of crime through the unique focus on resistance to criminal extortion, my hope is that this book is also able to convey to readers a small part of these lived realities in settings of insecurity and crime.

2

Explaining Variation in Resistance to Criminal Extortion

In this chapter I develop my argument to explain variation in the processes and mechanisms that lead to distinct strategies of resistance to criminal extortion. First, I define the core concepts that we will encounter throughout the book. Second, I explain the logic of the argument to show how the intersection between the time horizons of criminal actors, the nature of local political economies, and the existence of criminal capture of the police shapes the strategies of resistance that victims pursue. I then outline the parameters under which I expect the argument to hold, and discuss how my study builds on existing research. I conclude by discussing the research design, case selection, and the methodologies that I used to collect and analyze data.

2.1 KEY CONCEPTS

2.1.1 Criminal Extortion

Criminal extortion refers to situations in which an actor threatens or uses violence to extract rents from a population in return for the promise of protection from external threats.[1] Providing protection from physical harm in exchange for tribute is central to classic theories of Western European state formation (Tilly 1990).[2] Scholars have examined forms of extortion perpetrated by state actors as part of informal modes of governance in Africa (Shaw 2016), Asia (Wilson 2015), Europe (Gans-Morse 2012; Stephenson 2015), and Latin America (Dewey 2018; Snyder and Durán-Martínez 2009). This phenomenon, however, is not unique to the state. Tilly (1982, 169) situates states and non-state actors on a continuum and argues that if "protection

---

[1] For a conceptual analysis of extortion, see Varese (2014).
[2] Centeno (2002) critiques the portability of this argument outside of the European historical context.

rackets represent organized crime at its smoothest, then war making and state making – quintessential protection rackets with the advantage of legitimacy – qualify as our largest examples of organized crime." As Gambetta (1996) made clear, the sale of protection is central to the operation of mafias (see also Blok 1975; Campana 2011; Frye 2002; Konrad and Skaperdas 1998; Reuter 1983; Schelling 1971; Skaperdas 2001; Varese 2001; Volkov 2002). But it is equally crucial to the operations of a range of non-state armed groups, including Islamist jihadists (Ahmad 2017), rebels (Peceny and Durnan 2006), paramilitary groups (Misse 2007; Zaluar and Conceição 2007), as well as the criminal actors that I analyze in this book.

Criminal extortion can vary in its modality. Extortion can be a onetime occurrence whereby a victim pays the criminal actor once and never again sees them. Alternatively, the criminal actor can regularly tax the victim. Extortion does not necessarily have to take place in person. A growing phenomenon in Latin America is "virtual extortion," whereby victims receive threats via anonymous text messages or phone calls demanding money under threat of physical harm.[3] My focus is on extortion that is recurring and happens face-to-face between victims and criminals. It is here where we can best unpack dynamic relations among victims, criminals, and states.

Criminal extortion is not always predatory (Volkov 2000, 725). As Frye (2002, 574) argues, assuming that extortionists are thieves "prejudges their behavior by excluding the distinct possibility that they provide services to their subjects." At times the populations that criminal actors extort receive reliable protection from external threats, such as occurred during Russia's market liberalization when criminal groups provided businesses with fairly reliable security services (e.g., property rights and contract enforcement) (Frye 2002; Varese 2001; Volkov 2002). But the "double-edged" (Tilly 1982) nature of protection becomes apparent when populations must pay for protection from the very actors who are taxing them rather than from external threats. Of course, this is not a zero-sum issue. Beneath the provision of "legitimate" protection there always lurks the threat of violence against the population being taxed for failing to adhere to the rules of the game. This is why we can consider those paying taxes even when they receive benefits from criminals to still be victims.

My focus in this book is on extortion directed and carried out by criminal actors. To be clear, this does not rule out state participation in extortion, such as by offering criminals protection from reprisal by other parts of the state or helping criminals punish victims that fail or refuse to pay criminal taxes. But unlike the extortion rackets found in urban Brazil run by former and current police agents and other state actors (Cano 2013; Zaluar and Conceição 2007), in the cases that I examine in this book it is criminal actors that direct the scope,

---

[3] Meribah Knight, "Families Fear Phone Call from Mexico's Cartels," *New York Times*, July 31, 2010.

practices, and modalities of extortion. Similarly, my empirical focus on extortion by criminal actors departs from civil war studies that focus on pro-government militias that coordinate with states to safeguard government interests (Carey, Mitchell, and Lowe 2013), such as the paramilitaries in Colombia (Romero 2000).[4] It is likely that resistance to extortion directly perpetrated by the state or its allies would pose additional barriers to resistance by victims given the role of government authorities in facilitating extortion and benefitting politically from its continuation.

2.1.2   Criminal Victimization

The terms "crime" and "victimization" are often used interchangeably. But parsing the two can help us to better observe and theorize criminal victimization. A crime is an *act* that violates a formal law and whose violation is punishable by the state.[5] Victimization is a *process* that encompasses the criminal act, but it can also include other interactions between victims and criminal actors. These interactions vary in length and nature, but they all entail the negotiation of material and nonmaterial resources. Attention to the relational aspects of criminal victimization reveals contentious power dynamics that get overlooked when we think about crimes – particularly violent crimes – solely as onetime physical offenses.

The time it takes for a crime to occur and the extent of the interaction between a victim and a criminal actor can overlap substantially. Consider a carjacking: here the interaction between the criminal and the victim is limited to the time that it takes for the criminal to force the victim out of the vehicle and flee. Mapping the frequency of carjacking across space and time would therefore be analytically fruitful to understand both the act and the process of victimization. But the degree of overlap between the criminal act and the process of victimization varies across different types of crime.

For example, kidnapping is the act of taking or detaining someone by force, often for a ransom. But the process of victimization features other interactions in which power between the victim and victimizer is contested and negotiated. Stockholm syndrome is a bond of dependence and even affection that victims develop for their kidnappers over time, but which victims may strategically cultivate in order to obtain improved treatment (Ochberg 1978). Kidnappers engage in calculated practices beyond physically detaining their victims, including sensory deprivation, name-calling, and humiliation, but also "positive experiences for victims" in the form of "the provision of newspaper and radios . . .

---

[4] Jentzsch, Kalyvas, and Schubiger (2015) argue that militias can either have links to states or operate autonomously from them.

[5] Because laws are derived from social norms and the distribution of power within society, states' definitions of crimes reflect the predominant categorization of what is acceptable and unacceptable to those in power in particular places at particular points in time rather than impartial interpretations of right and wrong.

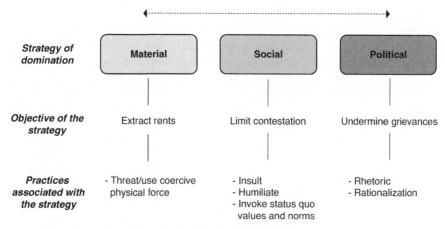

FIGURE 2.1 Strategies of domination by criminal actors

food, books, and television" and "clean clothes" (Phillips 2011, 846–847; 865).[6] Decoupling crime and victimization therefore makes visible the intriguing dynamics of victimization beyond – but intimately linked to – the criminal act. To analyze these dynamics, we can theorize relations between criminals and victims as analogous to those between dominant and subordinate actors.[7] This reveals that fundamental power dynamics between dominant and subordinate actors found in a range of settings, including authoritarian regimes (Fu 2018; O'Brien 1996; Wedeen 1999), colonial rule (Lawrence 2013), racial subjugation (Kelley 1993), neoliberalism (Bayat 2000), civil wars (Arjona 2016; Mampilly 2012), and capital-labor politics (Gaventa 1980; Scott 1977), are also evident in relations between victims and armed criminal groups.

Like all dominant actors, criminal actors that control territory use different practices to subordinate populations for varied objectives, as summarized in Figure 2.1. Material domination is the use or threat of coercive force to extract material rents from subordinates. But extortion is more than the use of violence to extract money because coercive force is necessary, but insufficient, to sustain taxation (Levi 1988, 13). I find that criminal actors thus maintain material extraction by employing practices of social and political domination alongside, and sometimes in lieu of, coercive force.[8]

---

[6] Human trafficking is another example of how decoupling the act and the process of victimization can yield new insights. Here, the act of physically relocating a person for the purposes of having them perform certain acts, ranging from forced labor to commercial sex, is embedded in a broader set of power dynamics between victims and criminals (Shelley 2010).

[7] See Arjona (2017) for an analogous approach to the study of civilian–rebel group relations.

[8] As Tilly (2003, 36) argues in discussing the "violent specialists" who play critical roles in the politics of collective violence: "The genuinely effective specialist deploys threats of violence so persuasively that others comply before the damage begins."

Social domination is an effort to dissuade subordinates from raising issues that threaten the power of dominant actors.[9] The "symbolic taxes" of social domination include "humiliation, disprivilege, insults, [and] assaults on dignity" to elicit "deference, demeanor, posture, verbal formulas and acts of humility" (Scott 1990, 188). For example, Auyero (2012) finds that state bureaucracies force marginalized citizens to endure long and uncertain waits for access to social services as a way to reaffirm social control and political power.[10] Petersen (2001, 83) concludes that the Russian Empire sought to avert resistance to its annexation of Lithuania by replacing the native Latin alphabet with Cyrillic: "Lithuanians came to experience the day-to-day feeling of subordination by being told what language, and alphabet, to use, among other humiliations." Wedeen (1999) found that authoritarian rule persists in Syria partly because the regime forces citizens to engage in mundane but repeated political rituals that foster compliance. I find that criminal actors, too, invoke symbolic taxes to elicit compliance from victims. Using a range of practices, including insults and physical acts intended to humiliate, criminal actors attempt to convince victims that it is irrational and futile to openly contest the criminals' authority to impose informal taxation. As an analysis of domestic abuse contends: "Victimization works best when the perpetrator produces a sense of immobilization and helplessness and a loss of self-respect" (Boss 2002, 161).

Criminal actors also use practices of political domination as part of victimization. Unlike social domination, political domination aims to prompt subordinates to question the legitimacy of their grievances and, in turn, "accept their role in the existing order of things" (Lukes 2004, 11). The intent here is to shape how subalterns understand their political subjectivity and, in turn, what is possible or not possible within the political arena to advance their interests. For example, Gaventa's (1980) study of seeming quiescence among impoverished populations in the US Appalachia finds that local economic elites had reconfigured norms and values to erode the weight of views that would challenge their authority. Similarly, "rape myths," defined as "attitudes and beliefs that are generally false but are widely and persistently held, and that serve to deny and justify male sexual aggression against women" (Lonsway and Fitzgerald 1994), deny victims their rights, undermine the perceived legitimacy of the violation of those rights, and legitimize continued victimization (Burt 1980). I find that criminal actors use rhetorical tools to encourage victims to question the authority and legitimacy of the state, consequently solidifying the idea of the criminal as an alternative ruler. But analyzing victimization as a dynamic process also challenges us to consider how victims exercise agency through resistance to criminal victimization.

---

[9] See Bachrach and Baratz (1962), who drawing on Schattschneider's (1960, 69) notion of the "mobilization of bias," call this the "second face of power."

[10] Soss (2002) identifies similar dynamics in the operation of welfare programs in the United States.

2.1.3 Resistance to Criminal Extortion

I define resistance as observable strategies outside of the rule of law that victims direct at criminals to negotiate, end, or prevent their victimization. At its foundation, resistance entails challenging criminal authority, though how victims accomplish this depends on the particular type of resistance that they pursue. This feature of resistance sets it apart from concepts such as resilience, which has been applied to territorial units as well to individuals, families, and communities who face forms of adversity originating in nature (e.g., earthquakes) or human behavior (e.g., climate change).[11] Resilience is the ability to survive and overcome adverse phenomena (Meerow, Newell, and Stults 2016). Unlike resistance, however, resilience does not require challenging the authority of the sources of that adversity. This brings us to the second feature of resistance: the practices through which victims challenge criminal victimization.

Resistance involves victims undertaking practices that violate or are in tension with the rule of law. This sets resistance as a concept apart from conventional responses to crime, such as filing a report with the police.[12] Resistance instead largely circumvents traditional institutional channels. It entails practices such as extralegal violence or knowingly allowing criminal activities to take place in hopes that this will elicit leniency from criminal actors. Researchers have analyzed how victims navigate judicial institutions in pursuit of justice (Epp 1998; Gallagher 2017; Gauri and Brinks 2008; Michel and Sikkink 2013), pursue civic mobilization in response to victimization (Bateson 2012), and channel their responses through the ballot box (Ley 2018; Visconti 2019). But resistance, as I analyze it in this book, is about victims targeting criminals in bids to negotiate, end, or prevent their victimization in ways that sit uneasily with or violate the rule of law. To be clear, this conceptualization does not mean that resistance is mutually exclusive of traditional responses to crime, such as engaging legal channels for redress. Nor does it preclude victims from engaging with the state as part of resistance.[13] As I theorize subsequently and show empirically in Parts II and III of the book, under certain conditions the incentives of victims and parts of the state align to coordinate with each other to enable, execute, and sustain resistance, including its extralegal practices.[14]

Table 2.1 presents a typology of resistance to criminal victimization. While the four types of resistance summarized in the table share the aforementioned

---

[11] See Koonings and Kruijt (2015) for a discussion of urban resilience in violent cities.

[12] Many victims decline to initiate formal legal demands precisely because they view the police as being complicit in their victimization or unable to provide order while adhering to the rule of law (Sanguinetti et al. 2015, 23; Tankebe 2013).

[13] For example, Cooper-Knock and Owen (2015) find that victims of crimes in South Africa and Nigeria first file official reports with the police – despite knowing that the police lack the capacity to act on their cases – because doing so generates an official record of an offense that they paradoxically later invoke to legitimize extralegal violence.

[14] It is worth noting that victims can also respond to criminal victimization by migrating within their countries or emigrating (Bada and Feldmann 2019; Cantor 2014; Marston 2020).

TABLE 2.1 *Typology of strategies of resistance to criminal victimization*

Conceptual dimensions	Strategies of resistance			
	Everyday resistance	Piecemeal vigilantism	Collective vigilantism	Coproduction of order
Intent	Negotiate victimization	End victimization	End victimization	Prevent victimization
Social organization	Individual	Ad hoc group	Institutionalized group	Institutionalized group
Frequency	Sporadic	Sporadic	Sustained	Sustained
Repertoire of practices	Noncoercive rhetoric	Extralegal violence	- Extralegal violence - Informal justice	- Extralegal violence - Strengthen rule of law
State involvement	No	Yes (individual-level)	Yes (individual-level)	Yes (institutional-level)

core features (i.e., challenging criminal authority, involving measures that violate or conflict with the rule of law, and targeting criminal actors), they vary along specific conceptual dimensions that can help us to better differentiate strategies of resistance: intent, social organization, frequency, repertoire of practices, and state involvement.

The concept of *everyday resistance* to criminal victimization draws on James Scott's (1985, 1990) seminal work on the nuanced ways in which subaltern populations resist subordination. It entails a repertoire of individual-level practices, including discourses, rhetoric, and other noncoercive actions. Victims sporadically use these practices to negotiate the material aspect of their victimization (i.e., the extent of their financial losses), but also to contest the nonmaterial dimensions of extortion (i.e., the social and political strategies of domination that criminal actors use). As Scott (1989, 37) argues: "For every form of appropriation there is likely to be one – or many – forms of everyday resistance devised to thwart that appropriation." Though everyday resistance does not end victimization, I show in Chapter 3 that at particular points in time in each of my empirical cases, everyday resistance enabled victims to not only obtain some marginal material dividends, but also nonmaterial benefits, including a sense of self-worth and dignity.

Vigilantism is the "use or threat of extra-legal violence in response to an alleged criminal act" (Moncada 2017, 408).[15] *Piecemeal vigilantism* entails an ad hoc group of victims and police who carry out sporadic acts of extralegal violence against criminal actors in an attempt to end victimization. Here ad hoc means that the individuals who engage in piecemeal vigilantism do not represent a consistent and coherent group who readily engage in extralegal violence, but instead come together as needed in a haphazard fashion. These ad hoc groups lack clear structures for decision-making and have minimal, if any, specialized roles under which participants repeatedly fulfill the same functions for the group. The ad hoc nature of piecemeal vigilantism can also be evident in the hasty ways in which individual acts of extralegal violence are conceived and executed. State involvement in piecemeal vigilantism entails individual-level participation of police that enable and/or participate in the extralegal practices. Unlike other forms of resistance detailed in the subsequent text, state participation in piecemeal vigilantism does not take place at the institutional level in the form of entire governments or police institutions. This conceptualization of piecemeal vigilantism recognizes that the state is far from a cohesive entity and instead enables us to explore how its fragmented nature can be leveraged by victims as part of resisting criminal extortion, but also how other parts of the state may stand against and attempt to stop victims from engaging in resistance.

Collective vigilantism differs from piecemeal vigilantism, as shown in Table 2.1. Unlike the ad hoc nature of piecemeal vigilantism, the social organization of

---

[15] This aligns with other conceptual analyses of vigilantism (Abrahams 2020; Bateson 2020; Johnston 1996).

collective vigilantism is institutionalized. Here, victims fulfill specific functions of leadership, management, and labor situated within a recognized organizational hierarchy. The institutionalized nature of collective vigilantism means that the group remains in place over time. As with piecemeal vigilantism, elements of the state can participate in collective vigilantism either directly or indirectly in ways that facilitate and sustain it. However, unlike in piecemeal vigilantism, state actors, including governing authorities and police, can become targets of collective vigilantism alongside criminals. We are particularly likely to see victims targeting elements of the state perceived to be captured by the criminal actors and thus threats to victims' collective mobilization. While both variants of vigilantism entail extralegal violence, collective vigilantism is further distinguished by the additional practice of informal justice that mirrors formal judicial processes, such as victim-organized "trials" and "hearings," during which fellow victims can bring forth grievances and demand punishments for criminal actors as well as amends or reparations from the same.[16]

The *coproduction of order* refers to coordination between victims and state actors to prevent victimization and jointly establish order. In the literatures on development and public goods, coproduction is generally defined as "the process through which inputs used to produce a good or service are contributed by individuals who are not 'in' the same organization" (Ostrom 1996, 1073). Unlike piecemeal or collective vigilantism, coproduction combines practices that both uphold and undermine the rule of law. Under coproduction, victims help to construct the institutional capacity of governing authorities to uphold the rule of law by providing the state with financial resources and information on criminal activities. Police institutions in much of Latin America suffer from limited and uncertain budgets, which inhibit their abilities to carry out basic functions (Ungar 2011) and, in turn, make it difficult to foster trust between themselves and the communities they are theoretically supposed to serve (Arias and Ungar 2009; Moncada 2009). Under coproduction victims provide financial support to police institutions for personnel, training, weapons, vehicles, and other necessities, as well as information to help police prevent or stop crime. But coproduction can also undermine the rule of law when states intentionally refrain from enforcing laws against victims in return for political and economic rents – what Holland (2017) terms "forbearance." Under the coproduction of order, governments and police allow victims to engage in extralegal practices, such as carrying outlawed firearms, usurping functions exclusive to the police, and acts of extralegal violence. In return, politicians and police receive victims' political and economic support, respectively. The coproduction of order is thus coordinated by a constellation of actors arranged in ways that sit uneasily on the border between the legal and extralegal realms.

---

[16] In post-apartheid South Africa, community members in townships held "people's courts" that entailed arresting victimizers, investigating victims' allegations, issuing verdicts, and enacting forms of justice ranging from material restitution to physical punishment (Lee and Seekings 2002).

The typology shown in Table 2.1 provides a new conceptual language to help identify and analyze resistance to criminal victimization. Unpacking the conceptual dimensions of vigilantism also reveals contrasting types of resistance that have distinct outcomes (the focus of this book) and political consequences (the particular focus of Chapter 6). The disaggregation of vigilantism into multiple types goes beyond the tendency in existing literature to treat it as a single outcome. Recognizing how vigilantism and other forms of resistance vary along distinct dimensions underscores the need for greater attention to the specific processes and mechanisms that produce them.

2.2 THE ARGUMENT

In this section I develop my argument to help to explain when we are likely to see distinct processes and mechanisms unfold that lead victims to pursue one of the strategies of resistance conceptualized in the preceding section. The theory draws our attention to three variables: the time horizons of criminal actors, the nature of local political economies, and the existence of criminal capture of the police. Different combinations of these variables make the materialization of different processes and mechanisms more probable. Figure 2.2 summarizes the pathways to contrasting strategies of resistance, and the remainder of this section unpacks the processes and mechanisms.

2.2.1 The Time Horizons of Criminal Actors

Whether a criminal actor has a short or long time horizon is a function of two factors. The first is competition from rival criminal groups, which drives armed actors to discount the future and focus on organizational survival and sustaining territorial control (Arias 2013; Arjona 2017, chapter 3). The second factor is state crackdowns that also compress time horizons by pressuring criminal actors to prioritize organizational survival and territorial control given their uncertain futures (Magaloni et al. 2020). In both instances – rival competition and state crackdowns – criminal actors must invest money, weapons, time, and labor into fending off challengers instead of focusing on their illicit operations. But the time horizons of criminal actors also influence whether victims prefer to negotiate or end their victimization.[17]

Criminal actors with long time horizons operate as "stationary bandits" (Olson 1993) who practice self-restraint toward victims so as to elicit their cooperation in

---

[17] This part of the argument builds on Ana Arjona's (2017) foundational analysis of the implications of variation in the time horizons of rebel groups for the types of social orders that are produced in wartime territories. Arjona focuses on how civilians and rebels negotiate social order when the latter have long time horizons, and argues that under short time horizons the outcome is disorder. My analysis shifts the focus to contexts of criminal rule while also showing how the time horizons of armed actors influence civilians' preferences to produce varied outcomes even when criminal actors have short time horizons.

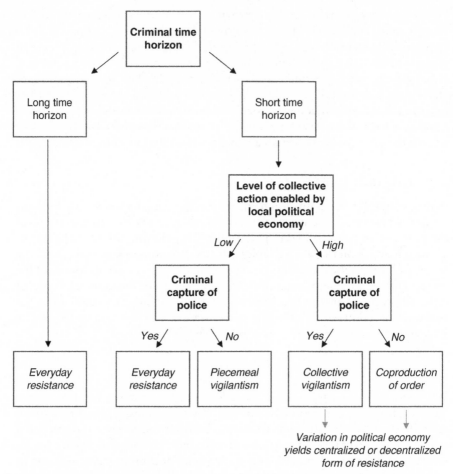

FIGURE 2.2 The argument: Pathways of resistance to criminal extortion

sustaining territorial control. Absent cooperation, criminal actors must forcibly obtain obedience, which can be costly to sustain in the long run. Under long time horizons criminal actors thus provide victims with goods and services to elicit cooperation, including protection from everyday crime, conflict resolution, and order. This tactic by criminals is strategic rather than altruistic – it enhances victims' productivity, which benefits criminal actors by enabling them to continue or increase their informal taxation (Tilly 1982). When criminals have long time horizons, the lack of external challengers means they also operate from a position of strength, leading victims to prefer negotiating their victimization. Here victims favor continued access to the goods and services that criminals provide while remaining cognizant that their attempts to end victimization face a high risk of failure given the criminal actor's ability to marshal their available resources to repel such challenges. Victims under these conditions will instead aim to secure better treatment without risking violent punishment from a dominant criminal actor. Moreover, criminal actors with long time horizons may strategically tolerate victims' noncoercive strategies as a safety valve to prevent the emergence of more threatening forms of resistance – as I illustrate in Chapter 3 – thus reinforcing victims' preferences for everyday resistance.[18]

Conversely, criminal actors with short time horizons resemble "roving bandits" (Olson 1993) that act in a more predatory fashion toward their victims in terms of not only using violence but also strategies of social and political domination. Here criminal actors diminish or altogether stop providing goods and services to victims. Extortion generates sizeable streams of hard cash that criminal actors can use to fund their efforts against rivals and/ or the state, such as paying for foot soldiers and weapons. For example, when the Mexican federal government initiated militarized operations against the drug trade in Michoacán in 2006, the leadership of the Familia Michoacana DTO demanded increased levels of extortion from its ground-level troops to finance the fight against rival criminal groups and the federal government.[19] As challenges from rivals and/or the state strain the internal monitoring capacities of criminal groups, street-level members may also engage in predatory behaviors beyond those approved by criminal leaders in order to benefit themselves (Arjona 2017).[20] Victims see criminal actors that are challenged by competitors and/or the state as embattled and more vulnerable to strategies of resistance intended to end victimization. Victims may therefore deduce that external challengers could be potential allies to support their efforts to end their victimization. But although victims who face criminal actors with short time horizons favor strategies beyond negotiating the terms of their victimization, whether and how they attempt to do so depend on additional factors.

2.2.2 Local Political Economies: Atomized, Encompassing, and Segmented

To assess whether businesses have the capacity to mobilize resistance to extortion, we need to consider the level of collective action that distinct political economies afford them. Political economies structure relations among business actors and

---

[18] States sometimes refrain from outright coercion and instead allow some limited forms of contentious behaviors in order to prevent the radicalization of social groups (Goldstone and Tilly 2001).

[19] Field notes in Tancítaro and La Unión, August 2018.

[20] On principal–agent problems, see Arrow (1986) and Moe (1984). Weakening oversight mechanisms and ambiguity in the macro-level environment can prompt more predatory behaviors by proximate coordinators of criminal extortion. As Elisabeth Wood (2009, 137) argues in analyzing wartime sexual violence, the degree to which an armed group has in place a hierarchical system of internal governance and decision-making influences the capacity of the group's leaders to effectively direct and regulate the forms of violence used by its ground-level units. Part of the ability of the leadership of a criminal organization to do so, however, depends on its capacity to show that it can effectively confront challengers in order to maintain cohesion among ground-level members and groups.

between them and governing authorities. This conceptualization is used in explanations of diverse cross-national developmental outcomes (Doner and Schneider 2000; Fairfield 2015; Kingstone 1999; Maxfield and Schneider 1997; Schneider 2004). However, political economies vary not only across countries, but within them as well (Giraudy, Moncada, and Snyder 2019, 14–16). Locke (1995) traced variances in the fortunes of manufacturing sectors inside Italy to micro-level variation in the sociopolitical networks of local economies. Herrigel (2000) upended the national-level classification of Germany's political economy by mapping and explaining contrasting regional-level political economies. Recent studies build on these insights to analyze subnational variation in developmental outcomes inside countries (e.g., Amengual 2016; Hurst 2009; Rithmire 2015; Sinha 2005). I build on the collective insights generated by these literatures to bring subnational political economies into the study of the politics of crime.

I differentiate between three ideal-type subnational political economies that range in their ability to enable collective mobilization from low to high: atomized, segmented, and encompassing. In atomized political economies relations both among businesses and between them and political authorities are limited. Here firms lack a sectoral organization to coordinate among themselves or oversee and coordinate market transactions. The absence of such a sectoral organization inhibits relations between firms and political authorities. Atomized political economies therefore offer weak grounds for pursuing collective mobilization. By contrast, ties among firms and between them and political authorities in encompassing political economies are comparatively more robust, facilitating a high degree of collective mobilization. Encompassing political economies feature a single organization that encompasses all sectoral actors and thus fosters and sustains horizontal ties among them while serving as the main coordinator of sectoral activities within a particular subnational territory. This core organization is characterized by high membership density, a robust internal decision-making structure to mediate member interests, and the provision of selective benefits to its members (Doner and Schneider 2000). The strong ties between sectoral actors are matched by robust ties between the core organization and political authorities. These authorities include those government agencies and policymakers most directly responsible for the particular economic sector, but also elected officials in the territories where the sector operates. The institutionalized channel of state–business relations is mutually beneficial: businesses benefit from established points of access to the policymaking and political spaces relevant to their economic interests, and governments only have to interface with a single entity from the economic sector (Schneider 2004). Finally, segmented political economies occupy an intermediate position between atomized and encompassing political economies. They feature a plurality of organizations with divisions between them and no core organization to coordinate among them. Firms at the top layer of the sector's commodity chain – where the bulk of the value-added is generated – favor fragmentation because it keeps them in a position of power and limits the abilities of smaller and less resource-rich firms from effectively making claims for greater redistribution of sectoral rents. These vertical divisions within the sector are coupled with horizontal divisions among the firms at the top of the commodity chain as they compete against each other for market share. The organizations in segmented political economies vary in their leadership structure, coercive capacity, and ability to provide members selective benefits. Segmented political economies lack the institutionalized and sector-wide channel of communication with political authorities found in encompassing contexts. Ties between economic actors and political authorities in segmented contexts are instead individualized and particularistic.[21]

Variation in political economies result in part from contrasting histories of state–business relations. States in Latin America organize sectors during periods of economic and/or political flux (Schneider 2004). Under these conditions, the benefits to states of accessing specialized information, coordinating and aggregating individual preferences and priorities (Schmitter and Streeck 1981, 27), and generating political support for state actors and their policies (Schneider 1998; 2002) outweigh the costs of bringing and keeping sectoral actors together as part of encompassing political economies. A corollary is that during relatively more stable periods, states refrain from building sectoral organizations and relations with sectoral actors, and instead outsource the task – and the related costs – to firms. Outsourcing enables the most powerful firms within a sector to then craft the political economy in ways that strengthen their positions vis-à-vis other sectoral actors. This results in segmentation that preserves the relative strength of a handful of individual firms while denying power to other sectoral actors. It also inhibits the formation of enduring sector-wide linkages between firms and the state such as those found in encompassing political economies. In addition, states may resist organization building among firms in sectors that are peripheral or threats to its economic interests and priorities. Here states resist organization building in order to maintain atomized political economies that limit the ability of firms to collectively challenge the state's preferences. Different political economies should yield contrasting structures, practices, and trajectories of resistance via the four mechanisms summarized in Table 2.2.

2.2.3 Cohesion: Enabling High-Risk Collective Action and Preventing Denunciation

Cohesion refers to the bonds of trust and familiarity that are crucial for collective action in places where the probability is high that mobilization will meet with violence. Because cohesion to confront repressive actors is difficult to build in the short term (Taylor 1988), preexisting organizations offer bonds of trust and familiarity that can be harnessed to organize and enact high-risk

---

[21] This segmented political economy is similar to what Locke (1995) describes as "polycentric" and "polarized" local economic orders in Italy.

TABLE 2.2 *Mechanisms linking local political economies and strategies of resistance*

Mechanisms	Atomized political economy	Segmented political economy	Encompassing political economy
Cohesion: *Enable high-risk collective action.*	• Struggle to mobilize beyond individual-level or ad hoc groups	• Formation of multiple autonomous and competing groups	• Formation of single institutionalized group
Decision-making: *Coordinate collective action and prevent intra-group cleavages.*	• No/limited coordination of activities	• Struggle to coordinate collectively across groups • Increased vulnerability to outside intervention	• Effective coordination of collective activities • Reduced vulnerability to outside intervention
Assets: *Increase coercive capacity.*	• Limited assets given inability to pool collectively	• Uneven distribution of coercive capacity across multiple groups	• Concentration of coercive capacity in a single group
Ties to governing authorities: *Coordinate between victims and local government.*	• Lack of ties to governing authorities as part of resistance	• Lack of protection for local authorities from criminal or state reprisal • No coordination between local authorities and victims on collective extralegal violence	• Protection for local governing authorities from criminal or state reprisal • Increased coordination between local authorities and victims to enable collective extralegal violence

collective action (Kramer, Brewer, and Hanna 1996; Laitin 1995; Loveman 1998, 483; McAdam 1986; Petersen 2001; Tarrow 1994).[22] Widespread intra-communal ties in territories under criminal control, particularly when criminals have short time horizons, are likely to be particularly weak as criminal actors constrain the mobility of populations and encourage lookouts and others within the community to denounce potential dissent.[23] As one interview respondent in Michoacán told me: "You didn't know if the person that you were talking to was someone that was also working for the *malandros* (slang for violent criminals)."[24] Stathis Kalyvas (2006, 176–81) identifies an analogous dynamic in wartime settings, where he argues that "it is often overlooked that the sort of fear that is so pervasive in civil wars is not just generic fear of armed actors but often fear of being denounced by one's own neighbors." And Petersen (2001, 18) underscores that those who favor resistance to predatory rulers face the challenge that "informants may have permeated the general population."

Hence victims that pursue resistance are likely to turn to the cohesion within preexisting organizations to limit the probability that their collective efforts will be denounced by individuals outside of their organizations. But cohesion can also reduce the risk of denunciation from *within* preexisting organizations. Organized crime thrives on its ability to penetrate governing institutions (Shelley 2001; Trejo and Ley 2020; Yashar 2018). This logic extends to business organizations attractive to criminal actors seeking to extract rents through extortion. By capturing individuals within such organizations, criminals gain access to detailed information on the scale and scope of production activities that enable it to maximize rent extraction. Here victims can use bonds of trust and familiarity to identify and circumvent those within the organization who have been or are susceptible to overtures from the criminal actor. Petersen (2001, 18) notes that shared histories of interaction "produce knowledge of who can be trusted, who can be persuaded (and what the best means of persuasion might be), and who must be isolated (or liquidated)." Preexisting organizations do not eliminate the potential for denunciation either from outside or inside the organization, but they do offer the lowest-risk vehicle for collective resistance given the availability of already existing bonds of trust and familiarity among their members. Victims limit their mobilization to members of preexisting organizations given that the risk of

---

[22] See Humphreys and Weinstein (2008) and Arjona and Kalyvas (2009) for analyses that show how preexisting social networks influence recruitment patterns among rebel groups.

[23] Arjona (2016) problematizes oft-used notions of civilian "support" or "collaboration" and shows that cooperation can be differentiated by whether the civilian is doing the bare minimum to evade punishment by following a rule imposed by an armed group – termed "obedience" – or is going beyond the bare minimum, from spontaneous forms of support to enlisting in an armed group.

[24] Interview with Gerardo (MCN77), berry producer, La Unión, August 2018.

denunciation increases the further beyond organizational boundaries victims venture in pursuing collective resistance.

In encompassing political economies, the relatively high level of cohesion within a single organization enables victims to organize resistance as a single group. A high level of cohesion allows victims within that single group to identify and circumvent potential sources of denunciation. By contrast, in segmented political economies, victims will form multiple groups that reflect the plurality of organizations in this setting. Here the boundaries of groups will reflect those of individual organizations, and groups will operate autonomously from each other despite the shared objective of resisting victimization. Moreover, the lack of a central coordinating force in segmented political economies increases the probability of inter-group conflict despite their shared grievance, as I explain below. Finally, in atomized political economies the absence of organizational structures to foster and sustain cohesion among business firms will limit the ability of victims to mobilize beyond the level of individual actions or those of ad hoc groups.

2.2.4 Decision-Making Structures: Coordinating Collective Action and Managing Conflict

Institutionalized decision-making structures enable groups to collectively develop mutually agreeable objectives (Ostrom 1990; 1992). Groups with preexisting organizations can use the rules, communications systems, and oversight mechanisms of their decision-making structures to plan and enact collective resistance. Decision-making structures also help prevent intra-group cleavages from becoming intra-group conflicts, an occurrence that is rife among non-state armed actors (Bakke, Cunningham, and Seymour 2012; Parkinson 2016). In contexts of criminal victimization, cleavages make victims' resistance more vulnerable to intervention by actors who can use them to derail or co-opt resistance.[25]

The criminal groups who are the targets of resistance have the most to lose if victims succeed in ending victimization. Such groups will therefore leverage intra-group cleavages to identify "weak links" in victims' efforts, including those who are reluctant to challenge the criminal actor, those who view the status quo as acceptable, or those who seek material rewards from the criminal actor in exchange for information on resistance. Rival criminal actors will exploit intra-group cleavages to capture new territories and illicit rents.[26] A rival criminal group can offer victims support to carry out resistance in exchange for allowing it to establish territorial control once the original

---

[25] In settings of civil war, Kaplan (2017a, 40) finds that "cooperation can mean fewer divisions within a community that armed groups can exploit." I show that states can also leverage such divisions.

[26] Criminal turf wars are often catalyzed by state actions that upend equilibriums between competitors (Phillips 2015; Calderón et al. 2015). My research identifies an additional factor that contributes to dynamics of violence in turf wars: collective resistance by victims.

criminal group is ousted. This enables a rival criminal group to piggyback on victims' efforts without having to assume the full cost of challenging its criminal competitor. In exchange, rivals may commit to not pursuing the type of victimization that prompted resistance in the first place. Parts of the state also have incentives to derail or co-opt collective resistance. At a basic level, extralegal violence by victims challenges the state's theoretical monopoly on the legitimate use of force (Weber 1946). Images of victims engaging in extralegal violence against criminals are a powerful political statement about the state's failure to enforce the rule of law, one that political opponents can harness to paint incumbents as ineffectual. However, using force to bring an end to collective resistance is a politically fraught move for political incumbents in contexts where resistance enjoys popular support. Here states will therefore try to co-opt victims' resistance by transforming subgroups of mobilized victims into auxiliary or paramilitary forces who work as extensions of the state.[27]

Intra-group tensions can predate criminal victimization, such as between capital and labor, ideological rifts, and partisan divides, among others. Tensions can also emerge endogenously as part of resistance, such as disputes over strategy, group practices, targets of violence, and regulations for disciplining the behaviors of the group and its individual members. Regardless of their origins, tensions that morph into full-blown cleavages provide outside actors with leverage to derail or capture victims' resistance.

In an encompassing political economy, victims will use the robust decision-making structure of their single organization to coordinate the group's extralegal activities. The relatively enhanced capacities of organizations in encompassing political economies to resolve intra-group tensions before they harden into fissures enable victims to prevent outside interventions in their collective efforts. By contrast, in segmented political economies, the absence of a decision-making structure across the population of victims inhibits inter-group coordination to end victimization. Each group will instead find itself in a "dual contest" (Bakke, Cunningham, and Seymour 2012; Cunningham, Bakke, and Seymour 2012) in which it is working toward the common goal of ending criminal rule while simultaneously competing against other groups of victims to sustain its own power given the uneven distribution of coercive capacity and resources across groups. In contrast to encompassing contexts, cleavages between groups of victims in segmented contexts provide leverage for outside actors to derail or co-opt individual groups of victims. In atomized political economies, victims struggle to coordinate collectively given the lack of a preexisting organizational structure to provide cohesion or robust decision-making capacity.

---

[27] In the United States during the 1950s and 1960s, for example, some municipal governments transformed vigilante groups into auxiliary police units as a way to monitor them and reduce their abilities to challenge formal political authority (Marx and Archer 1971).

2.2.5   Pooling Assets: Enhancing Coercive Capacity

Criminal actors sustain territorial control by amassing and maintaining foot soldiers, weapons, and surveillance structures. Victims who want to resist their victimization beyond negotiating its terms have to invest in building their own coercive power. Victims can use economic resources to obtain the services of "violence specialists" (Tilly 2003). Informal marketplaces in which a range of actors supply coercive services to the highest bidders thrive in settings where the state has a limited or contested monopoly on coercive force. But enlisting violence specialists is a double-edged sword given the potential for them to turn their coercive power against victims for their own ends. One actor whom victims can enlist with their assets are rival criminal organizations. Here victims provide rival groups with money in return for assistance in ousting their victimizers. Rivals, as noted above, have incentives to collaborate with victims as a way to reduce the costs of capturing new territories and markets. In places where police are autonomous from criminal actors but unable to establish order while adhering to the rule of law, the police have incentives to join with victims in confronting the criminal actors that are also targeting the police. Here victims leverage police protection and assistance for their resistance, including police overlooking victims' extralegal practices. Victims can also use assets to sustain themselves as they engage in collective resistance. The opportunity costs of participating in collective resistance include time not spent engaging in normal productive activities (Bates, Greif, and Singh 2002). Economic assets can enable victims to defray these costs, as well as to obtain weapons, vehicles, and other equipment for the purposes of carrying out resistance. Though victims can use preexisting organizations to pool and invest economic resources, the nature of the local political economy in which they exist shapes the ways in which victims do so and, in turn, their coercive capacities.[28]

In encompassing political economies victims will use the robust decision-making structures of their preexisting organizations to pool and invest collective economic assets so as to increase their groups' coercive capacities. Though victims in this scenario may use funds to enlist violence specialists, the robust nature of their preexisting organization should prevent the eruption of cleavages that violence specialists could use to co-opt collective resistance. By contrast, segmented political economies lack a central organization to coordinate the pooling and use of economic assets across the population of

---

[28] Existing research argues that access to economic assets influences the coercive capacity of armed non-state actors in wartime contexts and, most crucially, the repertoires of violence that these actors utilize. Non-state actors who can readily obtain economic resources, for example, are theorized to be more likely to engage in indiscriminate violence against civilians relative to their resource-poor counterparts (Humphreys and Weinstein 2006; Weinstein 2006). Recent work argues that the effects of resources on armed non-state actors' behaviors are contingent on the organizational structures that shape how a group uses those assets (Staniland 2012, 2014).

victims. Here coercive power will therefore be unevenly distributed among competing groups of victims. External actors can then leverage this unequal distribution as a way to co-opt resistance by widening the cleavages between groups. Rival criminal organizations, for example, may seek to support the relatively powerful groups of victims by helping them eliminate weaker groups and oust criminal competitors. State actors, meanwhile, may entice weaker groups of victims by making them extensions of the state and providing them with resources. Finally, in atomized political economies the absence of a preexisting organization to pool assets across the population of victims will severely inhibit their coercive capacity. Yet, as I discuss below, victims in atomized political economies may be able to increase their coercive capacity by enlisting police depending on whether the latter are autonomous or not from criminal actors.

2.2.6 Ties to Political Authorities

Local political economies shape relations not only among firms, but also between them and political authorities. These ties influence several aspects of resistance to criminal victimization in different ways across distinct local political economies. Criminal actors target and pressure political authorities to acquiesce to their informal authority in settings where criminals exert or covet territorial control. This acquiescence can manifest in different ways, including politicians passively ignoring criminals' operations, actively providing criminals with protection by not enforcing the rule of law, and accepting criminals' demands for payments from public coffers. While these types of behaviors are conventionally deemed to be acts of corruption, the nature of preexisting relations between victims and political authorities – or their absence – actually serves as a lens that victims use to interpret the actions of political authorities and, in turn, how victims think about authorities' potential roles in resistance. More specifically, the nature of relations between victims and governing authorities will influence whether victims perceive the latter to be complicit with criminals or simply obeying criminals to avoid violent punishment.[29] This distinction affects whether victims incorporate governing authorities into their mobilization to resist extortion. Victims that view politicians as having simply obeyed criminals to survive will be more likely to enlist them as allies in resistance. Conversely, victims that view politicians as complicit with criminal actors will circumvent them in their mobilization to resist extortion.

I expect that victims operating in encompassing political economies with strong preexisting ties to local governing authorities will incorporate the latter into their resistance. Here victims will protect governing authorities from two potential threats. The first threat is of reprisal from the criminal actor that may

---

[29] This builds on foundational conceptual and empirical work by Arjona (2017) and Wood (2003) on the need to differentiate and complicate notions of civilian cooperation and noncooperation with rebel groups.

target political authorities to punish them for allowing victims' resistance to take place. The second threat comes from higher levels of government that may oppose victims' mobilization and demand that local political authorities align with them in their opposition. In both instances victims' protection can entail forewarning governing authorities about impending collective mobilization to give them time to flee the area and avoid harm or political reprisal. In return, local politicians can help sustain resistance by erecting bureaucratic barriers against efforts by higher levels of government to constrain victims' mobilization. More broadly, local political authorities can strategically overlook victims' extralegal practices.

By contrast, in segmented political economies the lack of a single institutionalized linkage between the population of victims and local governing authorities means that victims will be more likely to perceive governing authorities as being complicit with criminals. This carries important consequences. Here victims will not protect local governing officials from reprisals by criminal actors and thus will not offer advance warning of their impending mobilization. Similarly governing authorities will refrain from assisting victims in their resistance. Where this resistance entails collective mobilization, we are therefore more likely to see local governing authorities take steps to facilitate intervention by higher levels of government that could serve to constrain, co-opt, or otherwise derail victims' collective mobilization. Finally, in atomized political economies the lack of ties to political authorities will lead victims to perceive governing authorities as complicit in their victimization. Victims in atomized political economies will therefore avoid engaging governing authorities in their resistance.

It is important to note that political economies not only influence whether and how victims are able to mobilize collectively to resist victimization, but that they also affect the ways in which criminals structure extortion. As I discuss in Chapter 3, atomized political economies that lack preexisting organizations force criminals to carry out extortion as a face-to-face transaction with each individual victim. By contrast, in segmented and encompassing political economies, criminal actors adapt the mechanics of extortion to the organizational structures they confront. As I show in Chapter 5, criminals target core organizations in encompassing political economies to obtain detailed information on the economic market in order to increase the efficiency of extortion by clarifying the population of targets and what they can afford to pay. The lack of a core organization that encompasses the entire population of economic actors in segmented political economies, by contrast, prompts criminals to target the top firms in each individual grouping of firms. I find that this leads those top firms to then outsource the cost of extortion to smaller and weaker firms beneath them by deducting the cost of criminal taxation from payments for goods and services. But I show in Chapter 5 that as the time horizons of criminal actors contract this prompts harmonization of the mechanics of extortion wherein criminals shift to more face-to-face interactions with their victims as part of trying to extract as much as they can in the shortest amount of time given uncertainty about the future.

2.2.7 Criminal Capture of the Police

States are bundles of actors and institutions that can have conflicting and even contravening objectives on a range of issues (Migdal, Kohli, and Shue 1994), including extortion. Police are on the frontlines of state efforts to stop crime and uphold the rule of law. In an ideal world, victims of extortion could turn to the police to end their victimization. In reality, the state's uneven and incomplete territorial coverage means that populations in much of the developing world cannot easily access the police and other state institutions (O'Donnell 1993).[30] I set aside the issue of the territorial absence of the police, however, to consider how the presence of the police in settings of victimization influences strategies of resistance. Simply because the police are present does not mean that victims can enlist them as allies for resistance. We instead need to consider what *kind* of police are present.

Following recent work that underscores the role of police capacity and complicity in shaping patterns of lethal violence (Yashar 2018), I distinguish between police who are unable or unwilling to enforce order while adhering to the rule of law. The latter are police that have been captured by criminals and are thus complicit in extortion. This occurs when criminal actors use bribes and/ or coercive force to obtain the complicity of the police in their criminal activities. Criminal capture can manifest in ways that range from passive to active. Police may passively overlook the illicit activities committed by criminal actors or persecute rival criminal actors, thereby building a facade of the rule of law. Police can also participate more actively in crimes, including kidnappings, extortion, and murders. Regardless of the forms of complicity involved, criminal capture means that victims cannot enlist the police as allies in their resistance. Victims who report their victimization risk having the police ignore their grievances or denounce them to the criminal actor who, in turn, will punish victims for violating the informal understanding that the criminal actors operate with impunity. For example, during my field research in Michoacán several interview respondents recalled that as the criminal groups who extorted them became more predatory, some people approached the local police only to be told that "it would be better to keep quiet." Later some of those who reported their victimization to the police were disappeared or killed by criminals.[31] Thus, police who learn of potential organized resistance that threatens to upend criminal rule are also likely to convey this information to criminal actors lest they themselves risk violent punishment for failing to do so. Hence victims will exclude police from their planning and organizing of resistance and may even target police once they enact resistance.

One reason police fall prey to criminal capture is limited institutional capacity. Police forces across Latin America lack basic institutional resources, including adequate salaries for personnel, functional police facilities and

---

[30] See also Soifer and Vom Hau (2008).   [31] Field notes, Michoacán, June 2018.

equipment, and continuous and high-quality professional training (Prado, Trebilcock, and Hartford 2012; Ungar 2002, 2011).[32] Meager salaries combined with limited resources with which to carry out their assigned – and often dangerous – responsibilities can leave police vulnerable to capture by criminal actors who often have greater coercive capacities and exponentially larger budgets (Dal Bó, Dal Bó and Di Tella 2006; Flom 2016). Carrying out police duties while adhering to procedural responsibilities, including proper investigation of crimes, requires institutional capacity. Thus limited institutional capacities inhibit the abilities of police to enforce order while simultaneously adhering to the rule of law (González 2020).

However, from the perspective of victims seeking to engage in forms of resistance that involve extralegal practices, police who are autonomous from criminal actors but who have limited institutional capacities can actually be valuable resources for their resistance. The notion of an autonomous, but institutionally weak, police in the presence of powerful armed criminal actors may at first seem counterintuitive. After all, where powerful criminal actors operate and control territory, we would expect police to be captured as part of criminals' strategy. But there are contexts and periods of time when low capacity and criminal capture do not go hand in hand. In periods of confrontation between governing authorities and criminal actors, the latter may use violence that specifically targets the police in order to reduce damages to criminal markets and prevent their arrest and incarceration.[33] Here even low-capacity police have incentives to maintain autonomy from the criminals carrying out the violence against them.[34] As Magaloni et al. (2020, 559) note: "It stands to reason that when police offers are killed [by criminal actors], they are likely to retaliate out of anger and a desire for retribution, and because they feel vulnerable and need to deter future aggression." In these settings police may perceive that their own survival depends on taking

---

[32] Here I follow Centeno, Kohli, and Yashar (2017, 3) in conceiving of capacity as "the organizational and bureaucratic ability to implement governing projects." Enriquez and Centeno (2012, 134) note that scholars of state capacity rely on varied terminology, including "power" and "strength" and "institutions." So too do scholars of policing when referring to police capacity, including police "efficacy" (Worrall 1999), "strength" (Bayley 2005, Chapter 4), and "effectiveness" (Sung 2006).

[33] Lessing (2017) argues that this is most likely when the state engages in unconditional repression against criminal organizations, thus reducing the incentives for criminal groups to eschew violence against the state.

[34] For example, in Sao Paulo, the Primeiro Comando do Capital (PCC) – one of Brazil's largest criminal organizations – has engaged in several campaigns of targeted assassinations of police and public security agents, at times in retaliation for police killings of PCC members (Bailey and Taylor 2009, 13–18; Willis 2015, 110–27). Between 1958 and the early 1970s, the Italian authorities cracked down on the Sicilian mafia, who retaliated by killing dozens of police officers (McWeeney 1987, 5). In periods of outright confrontation when criminal groups specifically target the police, even a low-capacity police may eschew the overtures for collusion by criminal groups who they view as the "enemy."

measures outside of those proscribed by the rule of law (Willis 2015).[35] Thus settings in which criminals actively target police are fertile terrain for the low-capacity police to be autonomous from criminal actors. As we shall see, this autonomy is likely to be most evident among those street-level police personnel most exposed to violence by criminal actors. The vulnerability to violence by criminals stemming from state-criminal conflict is unevenly distributed within police institutions across ranks. While street level police are physically exposed to criminal actors by virtue of their position in the police hierarchy, personnel at higher ranks spend more time in administrative roles that reduce their everyday contact with and vulnerability to criminal actors. This means that we are most likely to see police autonomy despite limited institutional capacity among lower- ranking personnel in settings of state–criminal conflict.

A second scenario whereby low-capacity police may be autonomous is when police are "purged" by government authorities attempting to root out corruption – a common phenomenon in Latin America (Frühling 2009).[36] Although these wholesale dismissals shift the narrative surrounding police corruption, they rarely lead to a broader and sustained project of reform that increases the institutional capacities of the police.[37] The result is that police become caught up in the wake of institutional change, whereby their linkages of complicity with criminal actors are momentarily severed but their limited capacity (which made them vulnerable to capture in the first place) persists. But I show that purges can also emerge endogenously from the very process of resistance to victimization – what I call "bottom-up" purges. Collective action to resist criminal victimization threatens not only criminal victimizers but also local police who are complicit in their criminal activities. Governments must then put into place police who may be autonomous from criminal actors but who continue to exhibit limited capacity – and are thus again susceptible to criminal capture. In this context, victims face a low-capacity, but autonomous, police that are partially of their own making.

What do victims gain from enlisting autonomous, yet low-capacity, police into their resistance? The gains vary in nature depending on the type of resistance that victims pursue. For victims in atomized political economies who lack organizational structures to support sustained and institutionalized collective action, police participation enables victims to carry out piecemeal vigilantism. Here police provide some coercive force to help victims enact episodic acts of extralegal violence, including physically participating in murders and other crimes. Police also provide victims in these settings with basic but crucial tools of disguise, such as police uniforms and vehicles to cover

---

[35] See Moskos (2008) for a similar argument in the context of policing in Baltimore, Maryland.

[36] Since the start of Mexico's war on drugs, for example, revelations of DTO corruption of police have led to the dismissal of "thousands of officials and police officers . . . and entire departments and agencies have been disbanded" in a "historic pattern [that] is incredibly sticky and seemingly immune from periodic and ritualistic purges" (Morris 2012, 31).

[37] In some instances, a purge is simply followed by another purge, as occurred with municipal police in Ciudad Juárez, Mexico, starting in 2008 (Campbell 2011, 20).

their tracks, and information that helps victims to avoid having other parts of the state (e.g., judicial institutions or other police who don't support the use of extralegal tactics) learn about their extralegal activities. The individual police who participate in piecemeal vigilantism, in turn, obtain assistance in perpetrating extralegal violence against the criminal actors who threaten them. The police can also leverage their participation in piecemeal vigilantism to obtain material benefits, including money.

Victims pursuing coproduction engage the police to build the institutional capacity of government to impose the rule of law while also ensuring victims' influence over how that order is produced. Under coproduction, victims' assistance to the police can take different forms, including not only financial support but also timely and granular information about local criminal dynamics – a resource that is central to the abilities of police to effectively carry out their duties. But crucially, and in contrast to piecemeal vigilantism, victims provide this support to police via official channels that involve political authorities and local governments. This is important because it precludes victims from only using the police for their own particularistic interests; in other words, coproduction generates some positive externalities that benefit broader populations beyond those victims who are providing this support to the police. Yet, as I discuss above and show empirically in Chapter 6's analysis of coproduction in the Mexican cases, victims do leverage their supportive ties to the police – and local government – in order to obtain forbearance as they continue to engage in extralegal practices as part of resisting victimization.

It is important to underscore that the some of the strategies of resistance that I discuss above are not always fixed outcomes. They can shift into other strategies as the catalyzing factors that led to initial responses change either exogenously or, alternatively, endogenously from the very process of resistance to criminal victimization. I unpack an instance of the latter in Chapter 6 where forms of collective vigilantism in Michoacán altered core local dynamics in ways that led victims to subsequently pursue the coproduction of order. Moreover, particular strategies of resistance can also end up becoming ongoing forms of criminal victimization that echo those which sparked them in the first place. Vigilantism, for example, can slide into its own form of extortion as former victims begin demanding remuneration for their services of protection and order – a dynamic I identify in Chapter 4's analysis of piecemeal vigilantism in El Salvador.

2.2.8 Scope Conditions

This argument should apply to cases where the crime is carried out face-to-face and takes place repeatedly over time. The theory's focus on the interactions between victims and criminals would provide limited added value for studying cases involving crimes where the two actors do not interact. Instead, the range of cases to which the theory is applicable are those where victimization is an interactive and dynamic process. The emphasis on sustained interaction means that the theory is most useful for cases where criminal actors seek to both govern some aspects of everyday life and simultaneously engage in criminal offenses against local populations.

My focus on resistance to victimization does not mean that victims cannot engage in other strategies vis-à-vis their victimizers. For example, we could imagine that instead of resistance, some victims could pursue an "exit" (Hirschman 1970) strategy through which they flee from the physical grasp of their victimizers by moving to other neighborhoods, cities, or countries. As I indicate above, formal judicial processes and strategies of resistance are not mutually exclusive. As I discuss in Parts II and III, in some of my cases victims had indeed turned to the police in search of justice, yet, aligning with my argument, this resulted in violence against the victims if the police had been captured by the criminal actors. Hence the empirical focus in this book is on instances whereby victims pursue justice via measures outside of or in tension with the rule of law rather than wholly through formal institutions.

The claims made here apply to cases where victims face powerful armed actors. It is in these contexts that victims face challenges to mobilizing resistance when contrasted with settings in which victimizers are individual or poorly organized armed actors. The theory applies to cases of victimization in which criminal actors aspire to establish territorial control. When criminal actors do not require territorial control, such as "virtual" forms of extortion, victimization looks very different than when victims encounter their victimizers on a regular basis. My focus is instead on forms of victimization when territorial control is necessary – though not sufficient – to carry out victimization.

2.3 BUILDING ON EXISTING RESEARCH

Existing research helps us understand important facets of the politics of crime and violence, but it struggles to account for variation in the strategies of resistance that victims pursue. Studies of the politics of crime focus on relations between states and criminal actors, with particular concern for understanding how different types of relations between the two generate distinct patterns of violence (Bailey and Taylor 2009; Durán-Martínez 2017; Lessing 2017; Magaloni et al. 2020; Snyder and Durán-Martínez 2009). By bringing the dynamic nature of state–criminal relations to the foreground, however, these studies relegate victims to the background, as actors without agency in the dynamics of crime and violence. The result is that our understanding of how victims engage armed criminal actors remains comparatively underdeveloped. This gap is particularly striking when we consider that one of the findings in this book is that some forms of resistance to criminal victimization contribute to dynamics of violence and insecurity. Folding these phenomena under the overarching umbrella of drug-related crime makes it difficult to parse, observe, and theorize distinct forms and logics of violence.

Research on vigilantism provides useful insights for my analysis. Anthropological, sociological, and historical research on vigilantism does bring victims more squarely into the analysis. Scholars have interrogated the determinants of vigilantism in the United States during the nineteenth and early twentieth centuries (Brown 1975; Pfeifer 2004; Tolnay and Beck 1995), while outside of the United States, studies have analyzed vigilantism as a legacy of civil wars (Bateson 2013), a tool that communities use to bridge the disconnect between traditional and contemporary institutions of justice and governance (Smith 2019), and violent performances by the subaltern to protest marginalization by the state (Godoy 2004, 623; Goldstein 2003, 22–43). However, the empirical terrain for these studies rarely ventures into settings where powerful armed criminal actors operate. More broadly, studies of vigilantism do not make the conceptual distinction registered in this book between varieties of vigilantism. Doing so invites us to trace and analyze the contrasting processes and mechanisms that lead to distinct forms of vigilantism. Likewise, by comparing cases in which victims who vary along multiple dimensions nonetheless pursue the same forms of resistance, I show that even those who prefer collective violence may not have the capacity to carry out such preferences, while those with the capacity to do so may nonetheless opt not to given the time horizons of criminal actors.

Scholars identify absent or weak states as key explanatory factors to account for victims taking the law into their own hands (Abrahams 1998; Buur and Jensen 2004; Starn 1999).[38] But this has difficulty explaining strategies of resistance for which victims enlist elements of the state into their extrajudicial actions. This is particularly puzzling when some police who lack institutional capacity form part of victims' resistance. Likewise the conventional focus on the absence or weakness of the state struggles to account for when victims' strategies of resistance include opting to work in close coordination with both police and political authorities to advance practices that simultaneously strengthen and undermine the rule of law. By comparing how strategies of resistance vary with regard to when they occur and the nature of police involvement as well as that of political authorities, this book complicates our understanding of the role of the state in the extralegal measures that victims pursue.

Analyses also examine how preexisting institutional arrangements influence extralethal violence by everyday citizens. Bateson (2013) shows how individuals use the skills they obtained while fighting with paramilitaries during civil wars to violently establish order in contemporary contexts. What we need now is to build on this point to analyze whether and how variation in the nature of preexisting

---

[38] The historian of nineteenth-century vigilantism in the United States Hubert Howe Bancroft (1890, 10) argued that vigilantism is "a priori proof of the absence of good government."

organizations can also have differential consequences on the particular strategies that victims pursue to confront criminal victimization, particularly relating to the structure, practices, and sustainability of those strategies. Studies also examine the socioeconomic determinants of vigilantism. For example, Phillips (2017) argues that settings of socioeconomic inequality are more likely to experience vigilantism, in part because poorer populations tend to live in insecure areas and are thus more likely to take the law into their own hands. Yet, not all populations targeted for extortion in settings of stark socioeconomic inequality turn to vigilantism.[39] We need to consider the nature of the structural arrangements through which inequality is both produced and perpetuated. Phillips also links inequality with extralegal violence by drawing attention to forms of vigilantism sponsored by wealthy patrons who pay workers to defend their narrow interests, essentially generating private militias. I build on this important insight by showing how preexisting organizations within local political economies can negotiate tensions along class lines as part of enabling and sustaining broad and violent collective responses to criminal victimization.

More broadly, a current in the literature on social movements argues that the availability of resources influences collective mobilization. Could this help to explain variation in strategies of resistance? The comparison in this book shows that resources influence resistance to criminal victimization, but they are not fully determinative of its structure, practices, and trajectory across time or space. The atomized political economies in which the Colombian informal vendors and Salvadorean small-scale farmers operated limited the ability of the two populations to collectively pool resources that they could then direct into their resistance. Yet, despite similar resource bases, the nature of resistance between the two cases varied considerably, with informal vendors pursuing non-violent and individual-level everyday resistance, and small-scale farmers engaging in violent practices of piecemeal vigilantism. Similarly the cases in Michoacán, Mexico, resist explanation through attention to resources alone. Both the avocado and berry sectors are globally oriented enclave economies that represent Mexico's second and third largest exports, respectively. Michoacán produces and exports a majority of its agricultural products to domestic and global markets, and accounts for 80 percent of Mexico's avocado production. The United States imports nearly 90 percent of its avocado supply from Mexico (Williams and Hanselka 2018). Today Mexico supplies slightly over half the world's avocado market (*Secretariá de Economía* 2012, 7). But Michoacán also has two-thirds of the total acreage used for berry production in Mexico, and accounts for over 70 percent of the berries – primarily blackberries but also

---

[39] Other studies have also problematized the notion of a direct relationship between inequality and vigilantism, including recent work by Obert and Mattiacci (2018, 611) who find a negative relationship between inequality and the formation of vigilance committees in early twentieth-century United States.

strawberries and raspberries – that Mexico exports abroad.[40] In recent years both sectors have also begun to make inroads into the East Asian markets, including Japan and China. By 2016, Michoacán's avocado sector was worth USD 1.2 billion, which by then had earned it the label of "green gold," which media stories pointed to in discussing why criminal actors were attracted to the sector. Yet, the berry sector in Michoacán is worth USD $820 million.[41] Moreover, when assessed by volume of exports, berries are actually worth more than avocados: in 2015 the nearly one million tons of avocados that Mexico exported abroad was valued at USD 1.8 billion, while the nearly 400 tons of berries exported that same year was valued at USD 1.5 billion.[42] However, despite the sizable amount of money concentrated in both sectors as well as their global linkages, resistance to extortion in the two cases varied considerably, with Tancítaro's avocado sector pursuing centralized forms of collective vigilantism and the coproduction of order, while decentralized variants of the same strategies materialized in La Unión's berry sector. Explaining the sharp difference in the structure, practices, and trajectories of resistance thus requires analyzing how resources are channeled through contrasting political economies that allocate rents in distinct ways among sectoral actors.

2.4 RESEARCH DESIGN, CASE SELECTION, AND METHODS

My goal in this book is to deepen the understanding of the different processes and mechanisms that lead to distinct forms of resistance to criminal extortion. Carrying out the research for this project entailed moving back and forth between induction and deduction to develop and revisit cases, hypotheses, data collection strategies, and other aspects of the research design both within the field and outside of it. This is what Kapiszewski, MacLean, and Read (2018) refer to as "analytic iteration." Using news archives and policy analyses, I first focused on countries where criminal extortion is a systemic feature of the operations of organized criminal groups: Colombia, El Salvador, and Mexico. Because I wanted to trace and analyze the process of resistance, I then looked for cases where there was evidence of the general outcome of interest, that is, resistance by victims to criminal extortion.[43]

[40] University of California, Davis, Migration Dialogue Project. "Major Mexican Fruit and Vegetable Exports." May 9, 2018.

[41] Figures calculated using data from Mexico's Secretariat of Agriculture and Rural Development (SAGARPA). Servicio de Información Agroalimentaria y Pesquera (SIAP), *Anuario Estadístico de la Producción Agrícola* (2016), https://nube.siap.gob.mx/cierreagricola/.

[42] Laura Quintero, "Berries: El Oro Rojo en Michoacán y Jalisco," *El Economista*, March 28, 2016.

[43] This is a standard strategy as part of an inductive theory-building research design (Ragin and Schneider 2011).

The cases here are the dyadic relations between victims and criminals. Identifying cases of resistance required zooming down to the subnational level at which criminal extortion takes place.[44] These spaces are the most relevant for identifying and tracing the choices and behaviors of the key actors in my theoretical framework – what Arjona (2019) calls the "locus of choice." This approach enabled me to isolate the theoretically relevant characteristics of the locus of choice, which then helped me identify analytically comparable units of analysis – what Przeworski and Teune (1970, Chapters 5 and 6) term "cross-system equivalence." Though the units that I analyze are located within different spatial contexts, they are analytically equivalent from the standpoint of the theory that I develop.[45]

During preliminary phases of fieldwork I located cases of resistance by triangulating information from interviews with journalists, community leaders, government officials, and local academics. In the end I focused my fieldwork on five localities across the three countries. I then conducted several periods of field research across Colombia, El Salvador, and Mexico between 2015 and 2019.[46]

The cases in Colombia and El Salvador take place in micro-level localities within subnational units, specifically territorial subdivisions of municipalities. In Colombia I conducted fieldwork in an informal market in the city center of Medellín where several hundred informal vendors were extorted by a criminal actor known as a Convivir that worked for a large criminal organization. There are dozens of similar open-air markets throughout the city of Medellín – which is divided into sixteen districts [*comunas*] – and particularly within the busy city center. The city center forms part of district 10, also known as *La Candelaria*. While I do use the actual name of the city, I do not provide specific geographic details about where the market is located to protect the identity of the vendors given their ongoing extortion at the time of the writing of this book. In El

---

[44] This approach aligns with the broader micro-level shift in research on violence wherein scholars use "disaggregated analysis and data collection [to trace] the behavior and interactions of subnational actors" (Cederman and Gleditsch 2009, 489; see also Kalyvas 2008b).

[45] On the combination of different types of units of analysis as part of theory-building, see Giraudy, Moncada, and Snyder (2019, 359). For examples of studies that combine different units of analysis, see Lessing's (2017) analysis of interactions between governments and criminal actors at the national (Colombia and Mexico) and subnational (Rio de Janeiro, Brazil) levels, Heller's (2012) comparison of sets of relations between political parties, state institutions, and civil society in the Brazilian city of Porto Alegre, the Indian state of Kerala, and the country of South Africa, and Pasotti's (2020) study of resistance to urban development projects in a range of territorial settings across ten cities.

[46] I spent a total of thirteen months in the field spread out over the five-year period: five months in Colombia, four in Mexico, and four in El Salvador. On the role of fieldwork in political science research and different fieldwork strategies, see Kapiszewski, MacLean, and Read (2015). I was going to spend additional time in each research site in 2020, but the Covid-19 pandemic forced me to revise my plans, including switching what would have been some in-person interviews into virtual interviews conducted via telephone, email, and video conferencing platforms.

Salvador I conducted fieldwork in two cantons, which are rural communities located within municipalities.[47] I use pseudonyms for the municipalities given the continued presence of armed gangs and extortion in both localities. One canton is located in the municipality of "Cienfuegos" in the eastern part of the country close to the Pacific coast and the second canton is located in the municipality of "El Pilar" in the western part of the country. I initially began my research focused on the case in El Pilar, but I was able to secure data for the second case in Cienfuegos through a contact in the judiciary who brought it to my attention and offered to help secure access to judicial materials similar to those I had obtained in the case in El Pilar. Given the scarcity of data on the mechanics of vigilantism and the similarities in strategies of resistance across the two cases, I thus included both in my analysis, pooling the data to provide a richer empirical foundation for the project. Both cantons are farming communities where small-scale subsistence farmers grew a range of crops, including beans, maize, and sorghum, as well as vegetables that they both used for both household consumption and sold to intermediaries. The farmers were extorted by local cells of the MS-13 gang.

My analysis of the cases in Medellín and El Salvador focuses on the dynamics of extortion at the micro-level among businesses that operate largely in informality. Both the vendors and small-scale subsistence farmers operate outside of a state-sanctioned regulatory framework: vendors occupy public space to sell goods that are not taxed, while subsistence farmers own small plots of land from which they produce mainly for their own consumption or to sell via informal transactions to informal intermediaries that supply agricultural markets and/or supermarkets. The vendors and the farmers lack permanent social protection, and instead their access to state support is episodic, individual-level and clientelistic in nature. The emphasis on firms that occupy this gray zone of economic activity is important for several reasons. The informal economy in Latin America is among the world's largest, where it accounts for over one-third of the region's gross domestic product (Medina and Schneider 2018). Much of the existing research on criminal extortion, particularly that which focuses on Europe, examines the victimization of firms only in the formal sector (e.g., Lavezzi 2008). I thus broaden the scope of analysis to include firms operating in the gray zone of economic markets in a region where the informal sector accounts for a substantial portion of economic activity. Moreover, the firms that I analyze here operate in political economies with minimal, if any, ties to the state. This enables me to trace how the absence of such linkages influence the dynamics of resistance, and to show how even firms that lack such ties can pursue sharply contrasting strategies of resistance given variation in other variables identified in the argument. As I noted above, the firms in these cases

---

[47] The territorial administrative divisions within El Salvador, from largest to smallest in size, are departments, municipalities, cantons, and *colonias* or *caserios* (neighborhoods).

have limited economic resources, yet pursued distinct strategies of resistance, allowing me to show how resources are not wholly determinative of the specific type of resistance victims may pursue.

The vendors and farmers obviously occupy distinct spatial settings, with the former located inside an urban center and the latter in the countryside. One potential concern with including the vendors in my analysis is that forms of collective extralegal violence as a practice of resistance are not feasible in such a context given the relatively more pronounced state presence. Yet, organized collective extralegal violence in response to crime in Latin America is far from exclusively a rural phenomenon.[48] Organized collective extralegal violence by victims against criminals is evident in dense metropolises in Brazil (De Souza Martins 2015) and Mexico (Binford and Churchhill 2009; Rodríguez Gallen 2011). Survey studies find that urban/rural residence is uncorrelated with support for vigilantism (Zechmeister 2014, 102). Indeed, as I discuss in Chapter 3, extralegal violence against criminals perpetrated by everyday citizens, elements of the state, and sometimes both has a long history in Medellín.[49] Furthermore, Chapter 3 shows that the very population of vendors that I interviewed considered extralegal violence against the criminal gang that was extorting them – only to have those efforts derailed by the absence of a political economy to enact and sustain such high-risk collective action.[50]

In Mexico I analyzed cases of resistance in two municipalities in the southwestern state of Michoacán. In early versions of this manuscript and presentations of the research project, I used pseudonyms for both municipalities. However, in the process of writing this book, one of the cases in Michoacán starting garnering international media coverage and emerging scholarly analysis. Because both media coverage and scholarly analyses made public some of the dynamics particular to this case and which I analyze in this book, I therefore decided to use the name of the municipality – Tancítaro – while keeping my commitment to respondents that participated in interviews and focus groups to not use their names or detailed personal information that could be used to identify them.[51] The absence of criminal territorial control or extortion in the municipality of Tancítaro, where victims in the avocado sector organized centralized collective vigilantism and coproduction of order, at the time of this writing also sets it apart from the other cases in this book. I do use a pseudonym for the second lesser-known case of resistance in Michoacán in the berry sector in the municipality of

[48] Emerging research by Nussio and Clayton (2020) similarly finds that lynching is evident in urban centers throughout much of Latin America.
[49] During my time conducting fieldwork in Medellín, a group of everyday civilians in the city center captured and killed an alleged thief: Santiago Cárdenas, "Comunidad Linchó a Un Supuesto Ladrón en el Centro de Medellín." *El Colombiano,* April 9, 2017.
[50] I discuss this further in Chapter 3.
[51] As part of the research protocol – and as detailed in the Appendix – I relied on oral consent from respondents. In the script that I used to ask for oral consent I explained to respondents that I would not use their names in any publications or presentations that emerged from this study.

La Unión, where a criminal actor maintains territorial control. Across all cases I attempt to balance between drawing attention to aspects of these contexts that are relevant for understanding the cases on the one hand and, on the other hand, zooming out to identify comparable dynamics in order to build a broader argument of resistance to criminal extortion. Several facts unrelated to the outcome of interest – mainly personal details of some of the respondents that participated in interviews and focus groups – have been changed as part of crafting layers of "protective abstraction" (Peritore 1990, 366).

The comparative approach in this book combines the logics of several analytic strategies. Following the logic of a most-different analysis (Przeworski and Teune 1970; see also Gerring 2007, 139), I analyze a period of time in which all cases exhibited the same outcome of everyday resistance, that is, the strategic, but sporadic, use of individual-level rhetorical practices to negotiate criminal victimization. The cases had this outcome despite variation in the nature of the local political economies and the status of the police. This enables me to isolate the influence of the time horizons of criminal actors on the range of strategies of resistance that victims pursue. More specifically, and in line with my argument, because criminal actors in all of the empirical cases at this point in time had long time horizons wherein they did not face challenges from either the state or rival criminal actors and provided some goods and services to victims, the latter preferred to negotiate the terms of their victimization via everyday resistance. Here they tried to secure some material and immaterial benefits while avoiding violent punishment from criminal actors. Chapter 3 presents this analysis and then unpacks the processes and mechanisms associated with everyday resistance through a focus on the case of recyclers in Medellín.

In Chapters 4–6, I analyze cases of resistance once the time horizons of the criminal actors have shortened given state confrontation and/or criminal competition. Here I trace how this shortening prompts victims to shift their preferences from negotiating to seeking to end victimization as criminal actors become more predatory, stop providing goods and services, and have their positions of strength compromised. Despite the shared preference for ending criminal extortion, however, I identify variation in the strategies of resistance that victims ultimately pursue, as shown in Table 2.3.

Contact with many participants in the study began far in advance of my fieldwork to help build trust in contexts of insecurity. At least several months before traveling to each field site, I reached out to people there who I had identified through local newspaper articles and social media posts. I initially contacted these respondents via emails and messaging services, though most then requested that we shift to WhatsApp, a messaging and voice over IP service that uses encryption technology. On two separate occasions people who I reached out to in Mexico and El Salvador asked that I first speak to extended family members living relatively close to my home before they would agree to be interviewed. One of these meetings took place in New York City in 2017, and the second in Elizabeth, New Jersey, in 2018. In both cases

TABLE 2.3 *Case studies: Overview and variation in strategies of resistance*

	Time period	Criminal actor's time horizon	Nature of local political economy	Criminal capture of police	Strategy of resistance by victims	Chapter
Medellín, Colombia	2013–16	Short	Atomized	Yes	Everyday resistance	3
El Pilar, El Salvador	2013–16	Short	Atomized	No	Piecemeal vigilantism	4
Cienfuegos, El Salvador	2013–16	Short	Atomized	No	Piecemeal vigilantism	4
La Unión, Mexico	2011–14	Short	Segmented	Yes	Decentralized collective vigilantism	5
La Unión, Mexico	2014–18	Short	Segmented	No	Decentralized coproduction of order	6
Tancítaro, Mexico	2011–14	Short	Encompassing	Yes	Centralized collective vigilantism	5
Tancítaro, Mexico	2014–18	Short	Encompassing	Yes	Centralized coproduction of order	6

family members wanted to know why I was interested in speaking with their relatives about these issues, but they also used the meetings to make sure that I was who I claimed to be by asking questions about my job and my home institution. When I was not in the field I was also seeking out, requesting, and analyzing archival materials, sometimes through formal requests to different government agencies. I also spent considerable time remotely monitoring news and media in my field sites to keep up to date on relevant local developments. I am aware that I was only able to enter many of the spaces where I carried out field research and access particular types of data because of my gender, ethnicity, class, and affiliation with a US academic institution. In the Appendix I discuss the implications of these traits on the research process, analysis and conclusions.

I used different methodologies to map variation in strategies of resistance to criminal victimization, establish how cases scored on the explanatory factors, and trace the processes and mechanisms that led to different structures, practices, and trajectories of resistance. The Appendix provides a detailed discussion about the methods that I used to collect data, the strengths and limitations of each, and how the different methods complement each other. It also includes anonymized lists of interviewees in each locality, the composition of the focus groups, and the procedures that I used to carry them out. Overall I undertook my research with an "ethnographic sensibility" because it enabled me to generate the data that could help answer the particular types of questions that motivated the research in this book. An ethnographic sensibility can generate data that "take[s] into account individuals' lived experiences and how they perceive" (Schatz 2013, 10) many of the concepts at the center of social science research. In my case, this approach and the data it generated enabled me to learn about – and learn from – the experiences, perspectives, and understandings of varied actors in my field sites in ways that helped me refine both the questions that I asked and the outcomes I sought to explain. It also prompted me to consider additional questions during the research process: How do victims interpret the intent and meaning of the strategies that criminal actors use to establish dominance and extract resources? How do the criminal actors who coordinate extortion view their relations with victims and the state? Using an ethnographic sensibility enabled me to better grasp the fluid nature of the relationships among different actors in the field, how they perceive its different dimensions across space and time, and how actors then reason from their experiences, including how they justify carrying out violence. This meant realizing that victims who encounter criminal actors are not always passive subjects, and that while victims may have strikingly similar understandings of resistance, the latter can vary in its structure, practices, and trajectories in theoretically important ways. Studying and becoming attuned to these issues would have been impossible without having used an ethnographic sensibility.

This book draws on 127 interviews carried out between 2015 and 2019 across my field sites. I conducted one hundred of these by myself and eleven in conjunction with research assistants when we agreed that their presence would facilitate the conversations. The remaining sixteen interviews were carried out by research assistants who I trained to conduct the interviews independently and who followed a pre-established questionnaire developed collaboratively between the two of us. The Covid-19 pandemic in 2020 interrupted plans to collect additional data in the field. Unable to travel, I carried out telephone interviews with some people who I had interviewed during my previous fieldwork or who had been interviewed by my research assistants. Following Fujii (2010, 40), multiple interviews with the same individuals generated new questions, topics of discussion, and layers of knowledge. The interviews for this project were primarily with victims of criminal extortion, former and active members of criminal groups, as well as police, politicians, journalists, religious leaders, social workers, community members, lawyers, judges, and academics.

I also used focus groups as part of my data collection strategy. I organized and participated in nine focus groups with victims in Colombia, one with victims in Mexico, and one with police in El Salvador. The Appendix contains more information on the logistics of organizing focus groups in these settings, including the precautions that I and my research assistants took to minimize the exposure of the participants to undue risks. As part of the focus groups with victims in Medellín, I also conducted participatory drawing exercises in which I asked participants to draw something in response to the following prompt: "Please think about the place where you work every day. Now draw what you feel generates either insecurity, security, or both in this place." I used this methodology to ensure that the voices of individuals who otherwise shied away from the often-lively conversations during the focus groups were included in the study's data and analysis. I asked participants to not include information in their drawings that could be used to identify themselves, other individuals, or the locations of the informal markets, but many did so anyway and, interestingly, often purposefully as a way to further exercise voice as part of the research project. I discuss this further in the Appendix. In those cases that included identifiable information, I either omitted those drawings from this book or, if possible, redacted those parts of the drawings (only after contacting the authors of the drawings to ask if this would be acceptable to them). Some of the authors that I attempted to contact no longer had the same phone numbers or, as I learned through interviews, had simply disappeared. In those cases I also omitted the drawings from the book. I broached the notion of participatory drawing exercises in Mexico, but sensing reticence among the victims in the focus group, I opted not to pursue it further. I detail in the Appendix some of the reasons why participants in the focus group in Mexico may have been reticent to do so. I opted not to suggest participatory drawing exercises in El Salvador given that the focus group was with active duty police agents in a context where fellow agents had been arrested for extralegal violence.

Finally, in the case of El Salvador I was granted access to large judicial files for the trials of the two ad hoc groups of victims and handfuls of police personnel who carried out piecemeal vigilantism against gangs. The trials for these groups, known popularly as "extermination groups," were initiated as part of an exhaustive investigation by a specialized unit that focuses solely on high-profile cases of organized crime and is housed in the main offices of the Attorney General of the Republic of El Salvador (Fiscalía General de la República [FGR]) in San Salvador. The judicial files contain detailed information on the history and practices of the two groups over several years as compiled through multiple sources, including transcripts of cell phone conversations and text message exchanges among participants as they discussed engaging in extralegal violence; interviews conducted by investigators in the FGR with witnesses to the groups' acts of violence; and testimonies by former group participants–turned–state informants. I triangulate this unique data on the mechanics of piecemeal vigilantism with insights secured through fieldwork in the communities where the groups emerged and carried out their violent activities, interviews with judges who oversaw the cases, and with some of the FGR personnel who investigated the groups. As I note in the Appendix, it is nearly certain that my position as a foreign scholar influenced my ability to access this information. Taken together, the data that I collected for this research project thus provides fresh insights into criminal extortion, resistance, and, more broadly, the politics of crime in Latin America.

PART II

EVERYDAY RESISTANCE AND PIECEMEAL VIGILANTISM

3

Everyday Resistance

Under what conditions do victims engage in everyday resistance? According to the argument developed in Chapter 2, there are two pathways to everyday resistance. In the first pathway, victims pursue everyday resistance when they face criminal actors who have long time horizons – regardless of differences in the nature of local political economies or whether or not there is criminal capture of the police. In the first part of this chapter I illustrate this first pathway by examining four empirical cases across El Salvador and Mexico where victims all faced extortion coordinated by criminal actors with long time horizons and all pursued everyday resistance. Victims did so because the criminal actors enjoyed positions of strength in the absence of state crackdowns or criminal competition and they provided victims with some goods and services.

In the second pathway to everyday resistance, criminal actors have short time horizons and victims prefer to end their victimization, but they lack the capacity to do so. To illustrate this second pathway I use a within-case analysis of resistance by informal recyclers in Medellín. Aligning with my argument, the recyclers pursued everyday resistance when they were extorted by a criminal actor with a long time horizon. But when the criminal actor's time horizon shortened amid threats from both the state and rivals, the vendors' preferences also shifted to favor ending extortion. However, the vendors operated in an atomized political economy wherein they lacked both a preexisting organization with which to mobilize collectively and established linkages to the state. Moreover, the vendors also faced local police captured by the criminal actor extorting them. Together these conditions limited vendors to the individual and sporadic practices of everyday resistance that they used to contest the strategies of domination that the criminal actor invoked to enforce extortion, but which did not end victimization.

3.1   EVERYDAY RESISTANCE UNDER CRIMINAL ACTORS WITH LONG TIME HORIZONS

In this section I do not make in-depth comparisons about the practices of everyday resistance that victims used. I leave the task of unpacking the micro-dynamics of everyday resistance to the second part of this chapter where I draw on and triangulate rich data from interviews, focus groups, and victims' drawings in Medellín. The analysis in this first section is meant to show how the time horizons of criminal actors influence different victims' preferences in similar ways. Table 3.1 summarizes these cases.

In 2012 in El Salvador, a truce was negotiated between the MS-13 and the two factions of the Barrio 18 gang, the central government, and the Catholic church.[1] The gangs reduced their use of lethal violence and, in return, the government relaxed restrictions on imprisoned gang leaders' interactions with members, access to amenities, and family visits. The government also committed to providing social and economic assistance for gang members and their communities, though these largely failed to materialize. Levels of lethal violence did decline while the truce was in effect (Katz, Hedberg, and Amaya 2016), but extortion by gangs persisted (InSight Crime and CLALS 2018, 19).[2]

In the two cantons in the municipalities of El Pilar and Cienfuegos, MS-13 cells extorted small-scale farmers who produced grains and vegetables for household consumption as well as for cash crops sold to intermediaries who sourced wholesalers and retailers throughout the country. In the atomized political economy shaped partly by the country's waning agricultural economy, the farmers lacked organizations to coordinate with each other or represent their collective interests. The agricultural sector had over the course of twentieth century been the underpinning of an enduring alliance between the state, the military, and economic elites to sustain an authoritarian regime (Stanley 1996). But starting in the late twentieth and through the early twenty-first centuries, the country's political leaders and economic elites largely abandoned institutionalized ties to the domestic agricultural sector. Organizational structures among small-scale farmers broke down in the wake of state abandonment which, in turn, limited their ability to collectively resist extortion.

During the truce the gangs charged the farmers in El Pilar and Cienfuegos a few dollars on a weekly basis. But in the absence of either state confrontation or competition from rival gangs, the MS-13 cliques in the two cantons refrained

---

[1]   Then Minister of Defense, David Munguía Payés, negotiated on behalf of government authorities, and the Catholic church was represented by Bishop Fabio Colindres. The main conduit between the gangs on the one hand and the state and the Church on the other hand was Raul Mijango, a former rebel insurgent with ties to the gangs. In 2016 El Salvador's Attorney General ordered the arrest of Mijango and several other government officials for their participation in the 2012 negotiations with gangs. General Munguía Payés was arrested in 2020.

[2]   Katz, Hedberg, and Amaya (2016, 662) found that average monthly homicides in El Salvador declined from 354 before the truce to 218 after the truce.

TABLE 3.1 *Cases of everyday resistance under criminal actors with long time horizons*

Localities	Time period	Victims	Criminal actor's time horizon	Level of collective action enabled by local political economy	Nature of local political economy	Criminal capture of police	Victims pursue everyday resistance
El Pilar, El Salvador	2012–13	Small-scale grain and vegetable farmers	Long	Low	Atomized	No	Yes
Cienfuegos, El Salvador	2012–13	Small-scale grain and vegetable farmers	Long	Low	Atomized	No	Yes
La Unión, Mexico	2004–06	Berry farmers and packing houses	Long	High	Segmented	Yes	Yes
Tancítaro, Mexico	2004–06	Avocado farmers and packing houses	Long	High	Encompassing	Yes	Yes

from outright predation. According to one farmer in the canton in Cienfuegos: "The interaction with [the gang] was minimal. They would come by, and I knew what they wanted already. You paid them, exchanged a few words, and that was it."[3] The gangs also provided victims with some basic protection from everyday crime, resolved personal conflicts, and thus maintained order.[4] In the canton in El Pilar, for example, several farmers recalled the story of a man who was caught by his wife sexually abusing their underage daughter. The wife asked the gang to intervene. The gang members dragged the man out of his house one morning and beat him in front of his daughter, wife, and neighbors.[5] Likewise in Cienfuegos, farmers indicated that during this period the gang could be enlisted to help resolve a range of personal conflicts.

Extortion in both localities was underwritten by the gangs' threats of coercion. Interviews and archival records – which I analyze in Chapter 4 – show that though the police in the two localities were autonomous from the gangs, they lacked the institutional capacity to provide order while enforcing the rule of law.[6] Additionally, the truce generated little incentive for the police to confront the gangs as doing so would have sparked unnecessary violence given the relative – albeit ultimately short-lived – peace under the truce.

Thus the gangs provided some degree of order where the state struggled to do so, and largely refrained from violence against their victims beyond the threats needed to sustain extortion. They enjoyed hegemonic positions in the two localities. Together this shaped victim–gang relations and influenced small-scale farmers' preferences for everyday resistance in the two research sites.

This everyday resistance focused on negotiating the amount and frequency of the criminal taxes that victims had to pay. Victims used rhetorical tools to contest extortion without challenging the gangs' authority to tax them. To accomplish this delicate task, one strategy that victims used was to highlight the shared social histories between themselves and the gang members. Many of the gang members were young men who victims had watched grow up in their communities and whose parents or other relatives were often familiar to them. As one farmer in the canton in El Pilar recounted:

I saw him [referring to a member of the MS-13 that was extorting him] grow up . . . right here. I knew his father and his aunt and uncle. They were people who I would greet if I saw them and they would greet me. When he came to charge the rent, I told him that I had seen him . . . from a child to a man. That I knew his family. Sometimes that was enough and he would go [without requiring the rent] or accept that I only give him some [of the rent].[7]

---

[3] Interview with René (ESV1616), farmer, Cienfuegos, July 2017.
[4] Field notes, Cienfuegos, October 2018.   [5] Field notes, El Pilar, July 2017.
[6] Field notes, El Pilar, July 2017 and Cienfuegos; October 2018.
[7] Telephone interview with Ricardo (ESV12), farmer, El Pilar, May 2020.

By reminding the gang members of shared social histories, victims strategically tried to elicit some forbearance from the criminal actor with regard to material taxation. Farmers in the canton in Cienfuegos also recounted evoking shared social histories during interactions with gang members, which echoes findings in studies of social relations in other violent contexts.[8] For example, Zubillaga, Llorens, and Souto (2019) find that mothers of gang members in Venezuela strategically use their familial ties to negotiate for periods of relative peace. My analysis shows that the instrumental use of social linkages is not limited to the relatives of gang members but can instead include other individuals who have social knowledge of members of armed criminal groups.

Despite differing from the cases in El Salvador in several ways, victims in the cases that I analyzed in Mexico also initially pursued everyday resistance to criminal extortion. Starting in late 2004, the berry and avocado sectors in La Unión and Tancítaro, respectively, were extorted by the Familia Michoacana DTO. The Familia Michoacana emerged to combat violence in Michoacán perpetrated by the Zetas, a fearsome DTO led by former specialized Mexican military personnel (Correa-Cabrera 2017). Having forced the Zetas from much of Michoacán, and with the federal government's crackdown on the drug trade under President Felipe Calderón (2006–12) still two years away, the Familia Michoacana operated on a long time horizon.

The DTO provided protection and order in the territories where it operated, particularly for agricultural sectors long frustrated with the state's failure to do so. Berry producers in La Unión welcomed the Familia Michoacana's use of violence to stop theft on their farms. Farmers suffered from ant theft [*robo hormiga*] whereby small groups of thieves would arrive at farms under cover of darkness, pick berries, and bring them to drivers in tractor trailer trucks waiting on the sides of nearby roads to be transported and sold to supermarkets. The Familia Michoacana made clear that it would not tolerate this form of theft when it apprehended several thieves and strung their dead bodies to the fences of berry farms for all to see. The DTO used similar tactics to dissuade avocado thieves in Tancítaro, leaving the tortured bodies of several thieves on roads throughout the municipality with handwritten signs warning that anyone caught stealing avocados would meet a similar fate. The DTO also resolved personal conflicts, including collecting personal and business debts. It initially provided this protection and order without charge, but soon demanded regular "contributions" in the form of criminal taxes.[9]

Unlike the small-scale farmers in El Salvador, the avocado and berry sectors operated in political economies that enabled a relatively high level of collective action to coordinate sectoral activities – though the nature of the political economies differed sharply. Tancítaro's avocado sector had an encompassing political economy in which a core organization oversaw all sectoral activities

---

[8] Field notes, Cienfuegos, July 2017; October 2018.
[9] Field notes, La Unión and Tancítaro, August 2018.

from planting crops to packaging them for export. The organization included all local sectoral actors, featured a strong decision-making structure, provided members with selective benefits, and coordinated with local government authorities. By contrast, La Unión's berry sector had a segmented political economy with multiple organizations that provided few selective benefits, had cleavages between and within them, and lacked sustained communication with local government authorities. Unlike in El Salvador, police in La Unión and Tancítaro were captured by the criminal actor that used police to facilitate drug operations and carry out extortion, including "arresting" victims who failed to pay and delivering them to the DTO for punishment.[10] Yet, despite these differences between the cases in Mexico and El Salvador, as well as between the two Mexican cases, victims in La Unión and Tancítaro also pursued everyday resistance. The shared condition among the two cases, as shown in Table 3.1, was the long time horizon of the Familia Michoacana.

Like victims in El Salvador, those in La Unión and Tancítaro opted for everyday resistance to extortion given the DTO's provision of protection and order and the bleak prospect of challenging a hegemonic armed criminal actor. These tactics were noncontentious, individual-level, and sporadic. In Tancítaro, victims harnessed the powerful local norm of respect for the entrepreneurial spirit of the avocado producers and exporters to negotiate criminal taxation. As I discuss in Chapter 5, avocado producers and exporters were protagonists in securing access for their products to the lucrative US consumer market in the late twentieth century.[11] Stories of their ingenuity and risk-taking as they experimented with different grafting and growing techniques were commonly brought up during informal conversations in Tancítaro.[12] But victims also used these narratives to remind members of the DTO that the sector needed to be sustained for the good of everyone, including the criminal actor itself. As Juan, an avocado grower, explained:

I tried telling them that if things go well for [the avocado sector], then things go well for everybody. For that reason it was good that they were helping to stop thieves. But they also needed to respect the sector in order for it to produce for them.[13]

A member of one of the first families in Tancítaro to grow avocados laughed as he explained his use of the norm that held the sector's pioneers in reverence to negotiate with the DTO on material taxation:

I would tell them stories about how hard my father worked to build the avocado [sector]. How he did this for himself and his family but also for the community and for Tancítaro.

---

[10] Field notes, La Unión and Tancítaro, August 2018.
[11] See Stanford (1998) on the construction of entrepreneurship as a fundamental component of the emergence of the avocado industry in Michoacán.
[12] Grafting refers to manually joining two distinct avocado trees to produce new varieties that combine elements of each individual type.
[13] Telephone interview with Juan (MCN90), avocado grower, Tancítaro, May 2020.

I would talk and talk until they got so tired of listening that they accepted my excuses [for not paying the full amount of criminal tax expected of him]. That's how I handled that and it worked until it didn't work.[14]

Victims in La Unión's berry sector also used rhetorical practices to evade and shirk criminal taxation by the Familia Michoacana. But as I discuss in Chapter 5, the origins of the local political economy in La Unión meant that victims in the berry sector lacked the narrative available to victims in Tancítaro of local entrepreneurs who collectively built a successful economic sector. Victims in La Unión nonetheless used other individual-level and noncoercive practices to contest material domination. Here victims appropriated the very narrative that the Familia Michoacana used to justify its emergence in the first place: to provide people with protection and order, particularly after the extreme violence by the Zetas. Victims appropriated this narrative and used it against the DTO. As one berry producer explained:

[La Familia] said that they came here to put an end to the barbarism [produced by the Zetas]. And they did. But the challenge for them was now avoiding the same fate of eating itself. When they started demanding the contributions [referring to the criminal taxes], I told them to be careful, because if they went too far, they could lose the support of the community. I would tell them: "Do your business [referring to the illicit drug trade] and keep us safe, but don't get greedy and take more than you need from us, too."[15]

Several points from this statement are worth unpacking. First, the berry producer underscores the importance of organized criminal groups having social bases in the territories in which they operate. From their perspective, there is a fine line between extortion being an acceptable (though contestable) tax on the one hand and a corrosive element of the social base of organized crime on the other hand. Second, the producer expresses a sentiment I came across repeatedly in Michoacán, but also in my field research sites in El Salvador and Colombia: acceptance of criminal groups operating illicit markets as long as they do not harm communities by extorting them beyond an "acceptable" level. This shows how victims in these contexts – where the state is unable or unwilling to impose order while adhering to the rule of law – are accepting of non-state actors filling this gap so long as they limit their predation. By reminding the criminal actor of these points, victims tried to negotiate material taxation.

Thus across distinct empirical cases at particular points in time, victims pursued everyday resistance regardless of whether they operated in a political economy that limited (atomized in Medellín and El Salvador) or facilitated (segmented in La Unión and encompassing in Tancítaro) collective mobilization, or faced police that were captured by or autonomous from criminal actors. Victims pursued everyday resistance given the shared condition

---

[14] Telephone interview with Cristobal (MCN1938), avocado grower, Tancítaro, May 2020.
[15] Telephone interview with Germán (MCN002), berry producer, La Unión, May 2020.

of being victimized by criminal actors with long time horizons. The next section delves deeper into the process and mechanisms of everyday resistance as a strategy against criminal extortion and illustrates how even when criminal actors have short time horizons, the preference among victims to end criminal victimization must contend with whether they have the capacity to do so.

Analyzing everyday resistance in the case of the recyclers in Medellín, I first show how the long time horizon of the criminal group that extorted the recyclers shaped victim-criminal relations in a way that led victims to pursue negotiating extortion. I then trace how criminal competition and state confrontation shortened the time horizon of the criminal actor and reshaped relations between the recyclers and the criminal actor. Despite wanting to end their victimization once the criminal actor's time horizon had shortened, the vendors' lack of strong ties among themselves and between them and governing authorities inhibited collective mobilization, while they also faced a police captured by the criminal actor. Taken together, these factors limited them to continuing with everyday resistance. But here the analysis also shows that under a short time horizon the criminal actor invoked strategies of social and political domination to facilitate criminal taxation. In turn, victims amplified their repertoire of practices of everyday resistance to contest these added dimensions of victimization.

3.2 CRIMINAL EXTORTION IN AN INFORMAL MARKET IN MEDELLÍN

The municipal government of Medellín and the city's police force estimate that approximately two-thirds of the city's neighborhoods are controlled by criminal organizations (Collazos et al. 2020, 6). I conducted fieldwork in one such locality: an informal market in the city center. Medellín is divided into sixteen districts called *comunas,* and the city center is located in Comuna 10, as shown in Map 3.1.

The city center is Medellín's economic engine with nearly twenty thousand formal firms – approximately one-fifth of the total number of formal firms in the entire city – but almost the same number of informal firms (RAED 2019, 18–25). The district is a mix of commercial and service retailers, residential housing, and industrial warehouses and factories. Interspersed throughout are informal markets of varying kinds occupying public spaces. The area has also historically been an epicenter of crime and violence. In the late twentieth century the national government responded to insecurity in the city by establishing and arming small groups of citizens to provide order but which ended up becoming part of the criminal structures that today coordinate extortion in the Comuna 10, including in the informal market where I conducted research.

In 1994 the national government created the *Cooperativas Comunitarias de Vigilancia Rural* (Community Cooperatives for Rural Vigilance, or

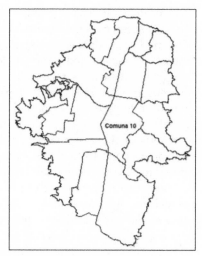

MAP 3.1 Medellín, Colombia

Convivir) – civilian self-defense groups trained and armed by the military to help combat insurgent forces in the country's decades-old civil war. By the end of 1997 there were over five hundred government-approved Convivir operating throughout the country.[16] Politicians and economic leaders, however, often established and used these groups to advance their political and economic interests. Álvaro Uribe Vélez, then governor (1995–97) of the department of Antioquia (of which Medellín is the capital), enthusiastically supported the Convivir and helped to establish them in nearly all of Antioquia's municipalities, including in Medellín.[17] In 1997 growing reports of abuse of power by the Convivir and ties between the groups and paramilitaries led Colombia's Constitutional Court to severely limit the activities that the Convivir could undertake, barring them from using the military-grade weapons that they had received from the armed forces, and nullifying the ability of their members to remain legally anonymous. But by then Convivir were entrenched in the micro-territories they controlled, from which they extracted protection fees, commonly referred to as *vacunas* (vaccinations), from businesses and residents.[18] Moreover, the Convivir soon developed ties with a range of criminal organizations, including DTOs. At the time of my fieldwork, city officials estimated that approximately twenty Convivir (with between 750 and 1,200 members) were extorting in the Comuna 10, though civil society leaders placed the figure closer to forty.[19] This was not the first time that armed non-state actors extorted in the city. In the 1980s urban militias linked to leftist insurgents made inroads into Medellín's peripheral districts where they also forcibly charged residents in return for providing security and informal justice.[20] But today in the city center the Convivir are the main criminal groups engaged in extortion.

One such Convivir controlled the informal market where the recyclers worked. The market emerged shortly after about six hundred vendors were displaced from a building that the municipal government had ceded to them in another part of the city center in the 1990s. In the building the vendors had small stalls where they could store and sell their merchandise. But in the 2000s municipal authorities displaced the vendors, ostensibly out of concern that criminals were selling marijuana and cocaine in the building. The recyclers

---

[16] I should note that the term *Convivir* is sometimes used in reference to both the practices of extortion and the criminal groups who coordinate and enforce them. I use it here to refer to the latter.

[17] Uribe was subsequently president (2002–10) and then senator (2014–20). Throughout much of his political career Uribe has been alleged to have links with right-wing paramilitary groups. See Rodrigo Hurtado, "2011: Las Guerras de Uribe," *Razón Publica*, December 19, 2011.

[18] On the history of the Convivir and paramilitary groups in Medellín more broadly, see Rozema (2007).

[19] James Bargent, "Las Convivir: El Legado de la Criminalidad Ciudadana como Modelo de Seguridad," *InSight Crime*, May 26, 2015.

[20] Militias held popular councils [*cabildos populares*] in which they convened residents of communities to ask for them to denounce criminals and corruption among local leaders (Medina Franco 2006, 118).

admitted that criminals had indeed used the building to sell illicit narcotics. But they also indicated that municipal authorities, including local police assigned to the building, had been aware of this criminal activity taking place for some time, and it was only when the land where the building was located was selected as a suitable site for expanding the city's public transport infrastructure that authorities shut down the building and kicked out the recyclers.[21]

Following their displacement, nearly two hundred of the recyclers scattered across the city, abandoned the informal economy, or simply disappeared. The remaining vendors eventually settled on the concrete island where I conducted fieldwork. Members of the criminal group who controlled the area told the vendors that the market was under their protection: "They introduced themselves as the Convivir that controlled the plaza. They came by on a Thursday. And they said they would be coming by every Saturday to collect COP 1,000 from each vendor in return for providing security."[22] Soon after the Convivir began collecting the tribute: "It's like the sun rising. You can count on them showing up and opening their hand to get paid."[23] Members of the Convivir warned vendors that failure to pay the criminal tax would be punished with violence.

This particular Convivir had linkages to organized criminal groups with long histories in the city dating back to the era of Pablo Escobar, the leader of the Medellín DTO, who founded a group of assassins known as the *Oficina de Envigado* to collect debts from other drug traffickers. After Escobar was killed in 1993 by Colombian security forces aided by the US Drug Enforcement Administration (DEA), the Oficina de Envigado split into two warring factions: one involved in the international drug trade and another that controlled the majority of the city's street-level criminal groups, including the Convivir operating in the Comuna 10.[24] The latter emerged the victor and became the *Oficina del Valle de Aburrá* (Office of the Aburrá Valley, or OVA). To organize criminal markets across the city, the OVA functioned as a federation that included what Colombian authorities refer to as Criminal Organizations Integrated with Drug Trafficking (ODINs). Each ODIN is based in one of Medellín's peripheral districts. The ODINs oversee the Convivir and other street-level criminal groups and their illicit activities, including extortion but also the micro-trafficking of drugs, prostitution, the sex trafficking of minors, and loan sharking. The Convivir provide the ODINs with a percentage of their profits, a portion of which then goes to the OVA's federated leadership. The Convivir that controlled the market worked for the

---

[21] Field notes, Medellín, July 2016.

[22] Armando (MDE_FG1_921), informal vendor, focus group, Medellín, July 2016. Based on the 2016 exchange rate, COP 1,000 are approximately USD 0.34. With approximately 400 vendors, this translated into nearly USD 136 weekly or USD 544 monthly from this single market.

[23] Interview with Douglas (IV_MDE_1010), informal vendor, Medellín, July 2016.

[24] For an overview of the emergence and evolution of the Oficina de Envigado, see Serrano (2013).

ODIN *Picacho*, which was based in the 12th of October district in the northwestern part of the city. Picacho controlled approximately a dozen Convivir in the Comuna 10 alone.

Recyclers opted only to negotiate rather than end extortion. I find that the long time horizon of the Convivir shaped relations between it and the vendors in a way that fostered this preference for everyday resistance. At the time that the recyclers were establishing the informal market, the Convivir that controlled the area was operating on a long time horizon facilitated by a truce reached between the OVA and its main criminal rival, the *Urabeños*. The Urabeños was a criminal group that emerged as a breakaway faction of the country's right-wing paramilitaries, the United Self-Defense Forces of Colombia (AUC). The Urabeños had refused to participate in the AUC's national demobilization in 2006, and instead set about establishing territorial control in part by founding, co-opting, or eliminating street-level criminal groups to capture illicit revenues, including from extortion. To avoid costly conflict in Medellín, the OVA and the Urabeños established a truce called the Pact of the Rifle [*Pacto del Fusil*]. Both organizations and the street-level criminal groups working under each, including the Convivir, refrained from fighting each other, which produced a decline in levels of lethal violence in the city center and other localities throughout Medellín.[25]

Under the long time horizon, the Convivir in the informal market provided the vendors with high-interest loans known as drop by drop [*gota a gota*]. The name refers to the way in which the loans bleed dry those who seek them out given that they normally end in vicious cycles where people have to take out additional loans just to pay off the interest charges from their original loans (Moncada 2019). The Convivir did not provide the funds directly to vendors, but instead offered protection to individual loan sharks that administered the high-interest loans with the backing and protection of the Convivir – which required providing the Convivir with a cut of the profits from the financial scheme. But the vendors also received protection and order as part of the arrangement with the Convivir. This was particularly useful in the setting in which the market operated. As shown in Figure 3.1, patterns of violence vary significantly across both time and space in Medellín. But remarkably, violence in the city center has long eclipsed that of the city's other districts.

In return for paying criminal taxes the Convivir physically beat thieves who tried to steal from the vendors: "Thief they caught, thief they beat."[26] The Convivir also regulated the behavior of the homeless people in the area who often harassed the vendors for money, food, or merchandise. But the Convivir also enlisted the homeless into selling cocaine and marijuana on their behalf to consumers who came to the market specifically to buy drugs. As one vendor explained during a focus group, "[The Convivir] would beat people. I would

---

[25] There have been several pacts between criminal rivals in Medellín throughout the second half of the twentieth century. For a detailed history of these pacts, see Ramírez (2013).

[26] Armando (MDE_FG1_921), informal vendor, focus group, Medellín, July 2016.

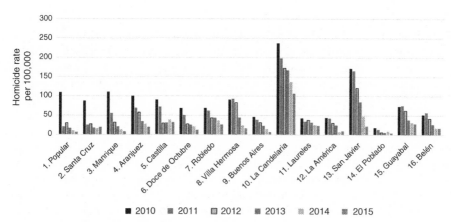

FIGURE 3.1 Medellín: Homicide rates by district (2010–15)
Sources: Homicide data is from the Observatorio de Políticas Publicas de la Alcaldía de Medellín. Population data is from the Alcaldía de Medellín and the National Administrative Department of Statistics (DANE). "Proyecciones de Población Municipio de Medellín por Comunas y Corregimientos, Años, 2005–2015."

feel bad when they'd beat the crazies [referring to homeless people]. But then they would put them to work selling drugs. And they would still beat them [if they didn't sell enough drugs by the end of the day]."[27]

The Convivir also shaped order in the market by regulating behaviors by the homeless that could negatively affect foot traffic. For example, prior to the arrival of the recyclers the homeless had used the area where the market was established as their bathroom. Once the vendors complained about the smells, the Convivir required that any of the homeless individuals who sold drugs for them also use the bathroom in a nearby house that the Convivir used to store drugs. Those who failed to obey were banned from the market: "It was good because it meant that the homeless would no longer go to the bathroom on the street right where we worked."[28]

The Convivir also resolved conflicts among recyclers as part of bringing order to the market. Individual vendors would lay out worn tarps or bedsheets on the ground to mark the boundaries on which they could set up and sell their merchandise. But fierce competition was a constant source of tension among vendors – particularly when they lacked an organization that could resolve conflicts. Sometimes a vendor would use multiple tarps or bedsheets in an attempt to increase the size of their space. Other times a vendor's merchandise would spill over into the spaces belonging to their neighbors. When these conflicts could not be resolved amicably, they would

---

[27] Eliseo (MDE_FG1_922), informal vendor, focus group, Medellín, July 2016.
[28] Augusto (MDE_FG1_899), informal vendor, focus group, Medellín, July 2016.

devolve into yelling and physical fights – phenomenon that foreshadows the atomized nature of the local political economy as discussed below. It was at those moments that the Convivir would intervene. Members of the group would pull the conflicting parties apart, listen to each side of the story, and declare a decision that would be enforced with violence if the parties did not adhere to it.[29]

The Convivir's hegemonic position in the market and its provision of protection and order fostered a preference among vendors for everyday resistance in order to reduce and evade taxation without challenging the authority of the criminal actor to engage in illicit activities, including victimization. As one vendor reasoned, "It should not have happened [referring to extortion]. Because one supposes that the state is the one that should do these things [referring to providing order]. But in that moment, [the Convivir] were the authority here."[30] To resist material domination, vendors appealed to the very asymmetry in power between themselves and their victimizers. This echoes James Scott's (1990, 18) point that the "safest and most public form of political discourse is that which takes as its basis the flattering self-image of elites." As in the case of berry farmers confronting the Familia Michoacana in Mexico, recyclers strategically used the original reasons for the Convivir's emergence to indirectly negotiate the criminal tax. As one vendor, David, explained, "When it comes time to pay them the vaccination, we have to become movie actors because it is better to have them [referring to the criminals] as friends than as enemies."[31] This "acting" as resistance took multiple forms.

A common strategy was to exaggerate the criminals' dominance and vendors' subordination. Several vendors recited some of the "lines" they used to this end:

ALFREDO: You as the ones who see and know everything here must know that I haven't sold a thing in so long. So how could I have money to pay when no one is buying?[32]

CRISTIAN: Oh brother, you know better than I do that things have been tough this week. What can I do? What can I say?[33]

MAURICIO: Well, nothing moves [in the market] without you saying it's okay. So can't you make people move their pockets and let loose some money here?[34]

Focus group participants made it clear that these lines were said using tones meant to signal submission, as two vendors noted during an exchange:

MANUEL: There is a saying that you shouldn't make deals with the devil. But we have to do that every day. And the first thing you have to do is make him think he is an angel.[35]

---

[29] Practices of conflict resolution by the Convivir confirmed by discussions in multiple focus groups with informal vendors.

[30] Telephone interview with Henry (MDE09), informal vendor, Medellín, May 2020.

[31] David (MDE_FG8_1112), informal vendor, focus group, Medellín, March 2017.

[32] Alfredo (MDE_FG7_101), informal vendor, focus group, Medellín, March 2017.

[33] Cristian (MDE_FG7_1212), informal vendor, focus group, Medellín, March 2017.

[34] Mauricio (MDE_FG3_735), informal vendor, focus group, Medellín, March 2017.

[35] Manuel (MDE_FG7_929), informal vendor, focus group, Medellín, March 2017.

LAURA: And what does that mean? Look, it's something strange. We have to negotiate, sometimes without them even knowing that we are doing that. It's exhausting, it really is.[36]

Vendors strategically used the existing power imbalance as a way to mitigate rather than accept the Convivir's domination by appealing to and exaggerating their authority:

So two or three of these little boys [referring to the members of the Convivir] will arrive with their chests puffed out and tell us that it's time for our 'collaboration.' But whether and how much you pay depends on the attitude one assumes with them. Without being rude . . . if you make them feel like men, then they might even let you go that day without paying.[37]

Though vendors used these discourses to try and reduce material taxation, the reductions were not always granted, and when they were, they were marginal. Sometimes criminals would either only charge individual vendors half the normal tax or allow them to skip a payment during a week. This underscores that everyday resistance can only mitigate, but not end, criminal victimization.

Vendors also contested the material dimension of criminal taxation by leveraging norms regarding gender and age. Younger vendors indicated that the Convivir showed a comparatively greater degree of respect for elderly vendors. Federnel, who sold used shoes in the market, noted, "So if you go to Don Pepito [made up name] or Doña Maria [made up name], they [the criminals] respect their gray hairs. Why mess with that little old man or old woman?"[38] But older focus group participants indicated that they secured this preferential treatment only by indirectly reminding the members of the Convivir of social norms regarding the treatment of elders:

MARTA: With me, they [members of the Convivir] are respectful: 'Mother, will you help us with the tax?'[39]

The entire group, a mix of young and old, erupts into laughter.

MAGDA: They respect the gray hairs![40]
MARTA: No, you have to make them respect the gray hairs. And once they do, then they don't demand the money, they *ask* for it, and if they have to ask for it, then you can tell them 'no.' I tell them: 'It's too hard right now for this little old woman [*viejita*]. I don't have anything to give.'[41]

Vendors also harnessed gender identities to mitigate material domination. Several female vendors invoked social norms as to how men should treat women in order to reduce the amount of financial tribute demanded of them:

[36] Laura (MDE_FG7_103), informal vendor, focus group, Medellín, March 2017.
[37] Federnel (MDE_FG6_45), informal vendor, focus group, Medellín, March 2017.
[38] Federnel (MDE_FG6_45), informal vendor, focus group, Medellín, March 2017.
[39] Marta (MDE_FG5_30), informal vendor, focus group, Medellín, March 2017.
[40] Magda (MDE_FG5_1511), informal vendor, focus group, Medellín, March 2017.
[41] Marta (MDE_FG5_30), informal vendor, focus group, Medellín, March 2017.

MAGDA: We are all humble and poor. That doesn't mean that we are bad people, just that this is what we were given in life—not much. But we have to use what we do have to defend ourselves. And for me and other women, that means that sometimes we have to use what else *we* have … [At this point, the female vendor stands up and motions at her body with her hands. The other females in the group nod their heads in agreement.] I don't mean anything physical. What I am saying is that I make it clear to them that you have to respect women, especially when you have power over them.[42]

MARTA: Sometimes I have to talk to them when there's six or seven of them because they decided to come in a group that day. Can you imagine that? Me, a woman, with six or seven men, all armed, charging me money! But that's when I tell them, 'Come on boys, you know I can't [pay] today.' And I look at them so that they have to look at me and imagine that they're talking to their mothers. And so they say, 'Ok, ma.' And they leave me alone or I just give them a coin … that day.[43]

Though these practices only marginally reduced taxation under extortion, several vendors indicated that given their economic circumstances, it still represented a gain: *algo es algo* [it's better than nothing].[44] But the victims perceived that being able to deny the criminal actors exactly what they demanded was more powerful than the marginal financial gains.

In sum, recyclers in my field site in Medellín faced a criminal actor who threatened violence against them if they failed to pay regular criminal tributes. But victims opted to negotiate criminal taxation via practices of everyday resistance. Aligning with my argument, vendors did so because of how the long time horizon of the Convivir shaped relations between the victims and the criminal actor. Under the long time horizon made possible by a criminal truce, the Convivir provided vendors with protection and order in the market while enjoying a position of strength given their unchallenged status. The next section considers how despite wanting to end criminal extortion when the Convivir's time horizon shortened, vendors' lack of capacity coupled with a police captured by the Convivir restricted them to the continued use of everyday resistance. However, I show that as the Convivir expanded its practices of domination under their short time horizon, so too did the victims expand their practices of resistance.

3.2.1   A Short Criminal Time Horizon and Everyday Resistance

The peace between the OVA and the Urabeños fell apart about a year and a half after the Pact of the Rifle. The reasons behind the truce's collapse are unclear, but the general consensus pointed to personal differences between the leadership of the two criminal organizations. Regardless, the rupture

---

[42] Magda (MDE_FG5_1511), informal vendor, focus group, Medellín, March 2017.
[43] Marta (MDE_FG5_30), informal vendor, focus group, Medellín, March 2017.
[44] Eva (MDE_FG4_51), informal vendor, focus group, Medellín, July 2016.

unleashed dynamics that shortened the time horizon of the Convivir, altered the dynamics of extortion and, in turn, the preferences of the vendors.

A violent criminal war ensued in Medellín in the wake of the truce's end.[45] But it primarily unfolded in the Comuna 10 given the fierce contest between the OVA and the Urabeños over the lucrative illicit economies in the city center.[46] The two criminal organizations ordered the ODINs and Convivir to target each other's members, but they also engaged in acts of indiscriminate violence. In one notorious case a grenade was detonated in the city center, only a few blocks from the municipal government offices.[47] Such public displays of violence as part of criminal competition, in turn, forced the local government to crack down on the criminal groups. The *Policía Metropolitana del Valle de Aburrá* (Metropolitan Police of the Valley of Aburrá, or MEVAL) arrested several leaders of the ODINs who oversaw the Convivir in 2014 and 2015, including some of those in the ODIN Picacho that controlled the Convivir in the informal market.[48] The combination of criminal competition and state crackdown reconfigured the process of extortion.

Several leaders of the Convivir who extorted the vendors were either killed by rivals or arrested by local authorities. Members stopped providing protection and order in the market, but continued to extract criminal rents. Given continued threats of state confrontation and criminal competition, the OVA ordered increased levels of criminal taxation across the city to finance their fight against the Urabeños. Weekly tributes that the Convivir charged the recyclers doubled from COP 1,000 to 2,000.[49] As one recycler noted, "That thing of coming by the market, to ask us if we needed help, watching ... and beating the fucking shit out of the thieves—all of that stopped. But they did keep asking for money. *That* they didn't stop doing."[50]

But extortion by a criminal actor operating on a short time horizon is about more than increased material taxation. Given they provide fewer services but still act in a predatory fashion, criminal actors add practices of social and political domination to facilitate a continued influx of tributes and to squelch victims' reticence to make such payments. The Convivir appropriated the broader negative social perceptions of the recyclers as fodder for practicing social domination. As in other parts of the developing world, informal vendors in Medellín are criticized as both manifestations and

---

[45] Federico Gutiérrez, "El Centro Pide Ayuda," Minuto 30, July 24, 2014.
[46] Ruben Darío Zapata, "Guerra de las Convivir en el Corazón de Medellín," *Periferia*, August 1, 2014.
[47] Reinaldo Spitaletta, "¡Peligro! Granadas en el Centro," *El Espectador*, August 4, 2014.
[48] "A la Cárcel 14 Integrantes de las 'Convivir,'" *Vanguardia*, December 11, 2014; "En Gigantesco Operativo Cayeron Veinte Miembros de 'las Convivir,'" Minuto 30, December 2, 2014; Policía Nacional de Colombia, "Operación contra la 'ODIN Picacho,'" August 29, 2015.
[49] Field notes, July 2016, and interviews with former Convivir members Mateo (IV_MDE_141) and Gabriel (IV_MDE_142), Medellín, July 2017.
[50] Interview with Douglas (IV_MDE_1010), informal vendor, Medellín, July 2016.

sources of urban disorder.[51] But recyclers that scour garbage cans and landfills to obtain merchandise are seen as occupying the bottom of the socioeconomic ladder within the informal sector and thus disposable [*desechable*].[52] Members of the Convivir used this perception to publicly humiliate the vendors as part of extortion. Members stepped or stomped on vendors' merchandise, or publicly shoved and pushed vendors to the ground. Several vendors described how members of the Convivir would often stare at vendors whose merchandise they had damaged or who they had just toppled, as if daring the vendors to challenge not only the criminals' coercive capacities but also their perceived higher social authority to govern the informal market and its population.[53] Other practices that the members of the Convivir used to encourage vendors to pay criminal taxes included slapping them on the backs of their heads or immobilizing them with Tasers before urinating on them in public. But the most common social tax that criminal actors used to impose social domination were verbal insults that reaffirmed the notion of vendors as disposable.

Members of the Convivir insulted the vendors' dirty clothes, how they smelled, and their livelihoods selling *checheres* [slang word for assorted trash items]. As one vendor noted, "Some Saturdays they just stick out their hands. Other Saturdays they wake up on the wrong side of the bed, because they come with their foul words to make one feel insignificant. As if taking our money wasn't enough!"[54] Another reflected on how these insults reaffirmed broader social norms regarding the recyclers: "They just say what everyone in society already thinks about us."[55]

Criminals intertwined practices of social and material domination by forcing vendors to witness the physical humiliation of their own. For example, three participants in a focus group reflected on one Convivir member's favorite punishment for failing to pay the increased criminal tax:

SEBASTIAN: We call him [the member of the Convivir] the Enforcer. He likes to take people into his truck that he keeps parked right next to the market, where he has a motorcycle helmet for those moments. He hits us in the face with it and if you try to get in the back seat away from where everyone can see what is being done to you, he gets angry and hits you harder. He makes sure everyone can see what is happening to you, he *wants* us to see each other getting a beating.[56]

MAURICIO: Hitting a man in the face. Seeing that. [Mauricio grimaces and shakes his head.] They make us lose respect for ourselves and for each other. You have to keep your mouth shut while they do these things to you and your friends. You have to be . . .

---

[51] Informality has nonetheless been useful for advancing political objectives under both non-democratic (Collier 1976; Cross 1998) and democratic (Holland 2017) political regimes.

[52] On the recycler population in Colombia, see Rosaldo (2016).

[53] Field notes, Medellín, July 2016.

[54] David (MDE_FG8_1112), informal vendor, focus group, Medellín, March 2017.

[55] Evelyn (MDE_FG2_720), informal vendor, focus group, Medellín, July 2016.

[56] Sebastian (MDE_FG3_406), informal vendor, focus group, Medellín, March 2017.

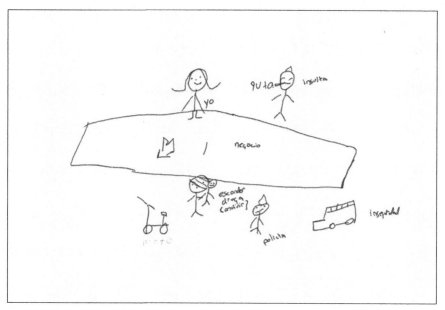

FIGURE 3.2 Beatriz's drawing
Note: Drawing by Beatriz (MDE_FG3_550), informal vendor, focus group, Medellín, March 2017.

[Mauricio covers his mouth with his hand, indicating the need to be silent]. That stays with you a long time.[57]
BEATRIZ: That's hard for all of us, to see that and know that we cannot move or say anything. But it's harder for them, the men. To have to watch each other being humiliated. It demoralizes the men ... all of us.[58]

While the Convivir had sold drugs in the market using the homeless population, the pressure to generate more revenue under a short time horizon led it to forcibly incorporate the vendors into its illicit drug sales. To do so the Convivir required that vendors allow the criminal actor to hide drugs and weapons in their piles of merchandise, as shown in Figures 3.2 and 3.3.

A first step in forcing recyclers to hide drugs entailed publicly insulting them in front of the other vendors. As Beatriz discussed while sharing her drawing (Figure 3.2) with the other participants in the focus group:

This is me [*yo*] and my business [*negocio*]. What generates insecurity [*inseguridad*] for me? Lots of things. The police [*policía*], the cars and motorcycles [*moto*] that speed by so fast. But the worst is when they [Convivir] make me hide their drugs [*esconder droga*].

---

[57] Mauricio (MDE_FG3_735), informal vendor, focus group, Medellín, March 2017.
[58] Beatriz (MDE_FG3_550), informal vendor, focus group, Medellín, March 2017.

FIGURE 3.3 Dolores's drawing
Note: Dolores (MDE_FG3_818), informal vendor, focus group, Medellín, March 2017.

And when they do it they insult [*insulta*] me, say ugly things to me [*puta*, Spanish slang for "whore"].

While sharing her drawing (Figure 3.3), Dolores explained to the group how social domination by the Convivir entailed choosing between storing drugs and weapons for the criminal group and protecting her daughter:

Here I drew myself and my daughter [*yo + hija*]. This is our spot in the market. I sell pants —all kinds, I have them. But here there are also the people from the Convivir. And although it doesn't look like it (referring to the drawing), here they are, let's say early in the morning, hiding drugs and a gun in my merchandise. I don't want that. But I can't say anything to them—because we know what they will do to me. My daughter is young, she is five years old. But although she's young, she knows when something is wrong. Children can sense when a parent is upset or scared. Sometimes she asks, "Why don't you tell them to stop [hiding the drugs and the gun in the merchandise]?" Because she sees how nervous it makes me when they do this to me [Dolores taps her finger angrily at the two figures in the drawing representing the members of the Convivir]. She's a little girl, she doesn't know. But what can I do? I put our lives at risk if I say something. I worry that this will affect her in her future.

Hiding doses of cocaine and marijuana joints and blunts among the vendors' wares allowed the criminals to roam the market enticing potential clients without having to always carry drug-filled baggies. As the danger of incursions by rival criminal actors increased, criminals also forced vendors to hide weapons for them in the market. Vendors interpreted their forced complicity as a form of social domination because it insulted their efforts to make an honest living:

SEBASTIAN: How are you going to justify taking a man's work—the place where he earns the food for his family—and use it to sell drugs? You can't. No one that respects you could justify it. We are disposable to everyone.[59]

DAVID: This is our work. Hiding the drugs in our merchandise, selling the drugs next to us—all of that is not only bad for us, because we are the ones that would suffer the consequences, it is also disrespectful to us as workers.[60]

The Convivir also engaged in political domination to carry out extortion. To do so, the criminal group flaunted its capture of the local police assigned to the informal market. The National Police of Colombia reports to the national Ministry of Defense. But political authorities at different levels of government oversee various police divisions distributed across the national territory. The country's major urban centers, including Medellín, have dedicated police forces who are in part overseen and funded by municipal authorities. The MEVAL is responsible for public safety in ten municipalities in Antioquia, including Medellín, where it oversees the city's sixteen districts and 249 neighborhoods. Starting in 2010 the National Police of Colombia adopted the *Plan Nacional de Vigilancia Comunitaria por Cuadrantes* (National Plan for Community Vigilance by Quadrants, or the PNVCC), under which policing in the country's eight largest cities, including Medellín, was decentralized to foster collaboration between police and populations within neighborhoods. Under the PNVCC, districts normally assigned to a single police station were subdivided into zones based on georeferenced crime data to identify crime hotspots, each of which was then assigned a *Centro de Atención Inmediata* (Immediate Attention Center, or CAI). The police assigned to the CAI then divided their assigned zones into quadrants that a handful of police would patrol in order to strengthen police-community relations. In the informal market, however, vendors soon understood that the police assigned to the quadrant in which the market was located were captured by the criminals.

During the pact between the OVA and the Urabeños, criminal capture of the police had manifested in *passive* practices by the police that enabled extortion to take place without them interfering. Vendors consistently described the passive nature of criminal capture during this period as an exchange between the criminals and the police: "[P]art of the issue is that there is solidarity between the police and the Convivir. The police say [to the criminals]: 'I will let you

---

[59] Sebastian (MDE_FG3_406), informal vendor, focus group, Medellín, March 2017.
[60] David (MDE_FG8_1112), informal vendor, focus group, Medellín, March 2017.

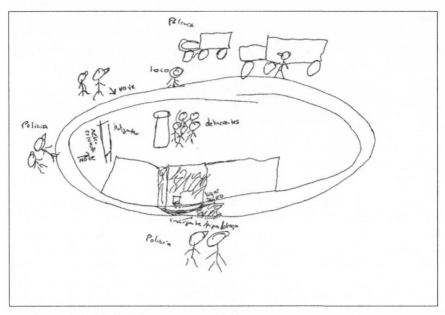

FIGURE 3.4 Mario's drawing
Note: Mario (MDE_FG1_911), informal vendor, focus group, Medellín, July 2016.

work, give me my cut, and we'll proceed that way.' "[61] Criminal capture had allowed for extortion and accompanying illicit activities to proceed unimpeded. As one vendor noted, "The police are there [referring to the market] ... but not watching out for us."[62] Police in the market strategically chose not to see these illicit activities. Vendors expressed frustration that police consistently opted to turn a blind eye [*hacerse de la vista gorda*] to the criminal activities in the market. At times this literally entailed the police positioning themselves in places where they could not see extortion or drug sales taking place. Mario explained this aspect of the criminal capture of police while using his drawing shown in Figure 3.4:

Here are the police patrols [*policía*], sometimes two or three guys that should be walking are just standing, talking, texting on their phones. Here's a crazy person [*loco*]. There's lots of them. And so the crazies and the homeless, they buy drugs from the delinquents [*delincuentes*], start hitting the pipes [using drugs] right there, maybe they fall asleep all high there. Now no one wants to go near me, so I don't sell anything. But the delinquents are also bothering me, demanding money or insulting me or whatever. And the police just keep standing where they know that they cannot see anything [*no ve*] or only where they see the crazies and the homeless, but never the delinquents. Why? Because they are corrupt police.

<hr />

[61] Simon (MDE_FG2_230), informal vendor, focus group, Medellín, July 2016.
[62] Evelyn (MDE_FG2_720), informal vendor, focus group, Medellín, July 2016.

Police would arrest individual members of the Convivir or the homeless selling drugs in the market only when people shopping in the market would point out illicit activities to them. But even then, criminal capture of the police did little to stop illicit activities:

LEO: How is it possible that they can capture a big guy with 500 blunts [*basucos*] of marijuana, they take him away, and then two hours later he's back? We know how. It isn't that hard to figure out.[63]

BLANCA: When [the police] do take them [someone from the Convivir] away, then a few minutes later both of them are back.[64]

However, once the Convivir's time horizon shifted, so too did the way in which victims experienced criminal capture of the police. While the Convivir had initially only required the police to ignore its illicit activities, they subsequently required them both to report on potential threats to the Convivir's control over the market and to participate in crimes to preserve the criminal actor's power. Thus the police transitioned from passively to actively participating in criminal activities, which affected how victims could pursue other forms of resistance. As one informal vendor summarized the relationship between the police and the vendors, "We're more afraid of the police than we are of thieves."[65] Paula explained this dynamic to the group using her drawing shown in Figure 3.5:

If I see a thief [*delincuente*] and tell the police [*polícia*], then the police should take him away [*se debe llevar*] to jail [*CAI*]. But instead they will go around the corner and make a deal [*se arreglan*] where the police take off the handcuffs [*esposas*] in exchange for some money. And if the thief offers enough money, the police will tell him who reported him [*sapo*], and they will come to where I am working [*trabajando*] and kill me [*me matan*].

Vendors repeatedly told me that the inability to turn to the police reaffirmed one of the key informal rules that governed their relations with the criminals: "the snitch has to die" [*el sapo tiene que morir*].

Damary communicated the recyclers' inability to turn to the police given criminal capture using her drawing shown in Figure 3.6:

For me it is difficult to say that there is security. So instead I wrote that there is fear and that silence prevails [*abunda el temor y prevalece el silencio*]. The police [*polícia*] are with the criminals, they sell themselves [to the criminals]. And we are the ones that suffer because we see illicit businesses but we can't say anything about it to the police [*ver negocios ilicitos y no poder hablar*]. The minute we do that, then the Convivir can go after us or our families [*... por que pueden atentar contra la vida nuestra o de nuestra familia*].

---

[63] Leo (MDE_FG2_1630), informal vendor, focus group, Medellín, July 2016.
[64] Blanca (MDE_FG7_328), informal vendor, focus group, Medellín, March 2017.
[65] Simon (MDE_FG2_230), informal vendor, focus group, Medellín, July 2016.

FIGURE 3.5 Paula's drawing
Note: Paula (MDE_FG2_01), informal vendor, focus group, Medellín, July 2016.

Using the drawing shown in Figure 3.7, Elena explained regret that the capture of the police and the engagement in widespread illicit activities that it facilitated were negatively affecting her business:

You asked what generates security and insecurity. But I don't see security, so I drew what generates insecurity for me. And that's being cornered between the police and the Convivir. The police are indifferent because they are paid by the Convivir to ignore everything they do, the drugs, the [crack] pipes, the charging of vaccination [*vacunas*, the criminal taxes] . . . everything that the criminals do is paid for. And so, you can see, that the people with the drugs [*jíbaros*] sell their products on my street where I work in the market [*venta de vicio en mi cuadra*]. And over here the Convivir are paying the police to be quiet so they can keep hurting us [*pago a polícia*]. Meantime, the clients see all of this, and don't want to be there anymore.

But the Convivir used its capture of the police to both ensure vendors' obedience and reinforce how this rendered their citizenship hollow. Douglas recounted during an interview how one day he had not sold enough to even "pay for my bus ride home." Instead of threatening or using coercive force, the member of the Convivir simply reminded him that he could not turn to the police for help:

FIGURE 3.6 Damary's drawing
Note: Damary (MDE_FG8_16), informal vendor, focus group, Medellín, March 2017.

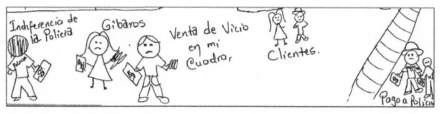

FIGURE 3.7 Elena's drawing
Note: Elena (MDE_FG4_900), informal vendor, focus group, March 2017. The top-half of this drawing was redacted because the author wrote her name and the names of other vendors at the top.

He smiled at me because they are all shameless [*descarados*]. And he said to me, "Of course, you could call the police, but even if they show up, it's more likely that they work for us than that they'll work for you."[66]

---

[66] Interview with Douglas (IV_MDE_1010), informal vendor, Medellín, July 2016.

When physically assaulting vendors who had fallen behind on their weekly tributes, members of the Convivir taunted, "Call the police! Call the police!" – a reminder that the criminal actor thwarted their access to this basic institutional resource to which they were theoretically entitled as citizens.[67] Focusing only on the material aspect of extortion overlooks the social and political taxes that victims incurred as part of criminal extortion, which victims also pursued as important targets of a more expansive form of everyday resistance.

3.3   EVERYDAY RESISTANCE

Despite the shift in the vendors' preferences regarding how to resist criminal extortion, they did not mobilize beyond the individual and sporadic practices of everyday resistance. We might expect that victims would consider seeking help from police officials situated at senior levels above that of the informal market. But during focus groups, vendors expressed fear that if they reported capture of the police in the market to higher-ups in the police chain of command, it would get back to the local police, who would in turn report them to the Convivir. One vendor explained: "We *should* be able to stop [criminal capture of the police in the market]. But who is going to risk talking to some [police] official when the surest thing is that they will tell the police in the market and then it won't be long before the Convivir come to see you?"[68] Vendors were likewise hesitant to report their victimization to local political authorities. One vendor, Jerónimo, used the drawing shown in Figure 3.8 to explain the danger associated with enlisting help from other parts of the government when its most tangible manifestation for the recyclers – the police in the market – was complicit in their victimization:

In the market the situation is this. The police are part of the state [*estado*], right? I would say the most important part because they're supposed to protect us. Isn't that true? But they don't. In reality they repress [*represión*] us. They are the servants of the criminals, in the market, they serve the criminals—that's repression. So the state ... here [in the drawing], I drew it thinking now of everything that goes inside it, like the rights that we are supposed to have and the support that it should provide us with ... those are opportunities [*oportunidades*]. But that [the opportunities] are something up there, and how can we get them if the state is repressing us down here? The way the police acts, how it ... that it sells itself to the criminals instead of doing the job for which it exists, that makes the opportunities seem high above us. Instead I am repressed at the hands of the state and the armed actors that control the place where I work.

Recyclers reasoned that this acquiescence was driven, in part, by the inability of political authorities to challenge the powerful criminal groups in the city center. One story that circulated widely among vendors and which was retold to me several times in interviews and focus groups illustrates this perception of the

---

[67] Field notes, Medellín, Colombia, July 2016.

[68] David (MDE_FG8_1112), informal vendor, focus group, Medellín, March 2017.

FIGURE 3.8 Jerónimo's drawing
Note: Jerónimo (MDE_FG6_538), informal vendor, focus group, Medellín, March 2017.

government's perceived impotence. The story was about a prominent human rights defender in Medellín who had spoken out against extortion in the city center. Ramon Eduardo Acevedo was a municipal police officer before joining the Municipal Committee for Human Rights in the Comuna 10. The committee advocates for the human rights of the different populations who live and work in the city center, including the homeless, sex workers, street children, and informal vendors. Acevedo was one of the committee's founding members and among its most outspoken figures. Acevedo had begun to publicly denounce extortion by the Convivir operating in the Comuna 10 during public meetings of the human rights committee. People advised Acevedo to stop, but he refused, even when he began receiving death threats via emails, text messages, and anonymous phone calls. He was sitting outside his house located in the Comuna 10 drinking his morning coffee when a man pulled up in a car and shot Acevedo multiple times in the neck. The assassin fled on foot, and Acevedo died shortly after arriving at a local hospital.[69] From the perspective of

---

[69] "Ramón Acevedo Rojas, Defensor de Derechos Humanos, Fue Asesinado en Medellín," *El Espectador,* June 7, 2016; "Convivir Tendrían Responsabilidad en el Asesinato del Defensor Ramón Eduardo Acevedo," *Contagio Radio,* June 8, 2016.

the vendors, this showed the vulnerability of elements of the state – in this case, a leader in a quasi-state committee dedicated to advocating on behalf of marginalized populations in the city – to violence by the armed actors that exerted territorial control within the city center. But as I discuss below, the lack of robust ties between victims and political authorities as a feature of the atomized political economy in which vendors operated also meant that they viewed the local state as complicit in their victimization.

3.3.1 The Structure of Everyday Resistance

The informal vendors were limited to individual-level sporadic acts of everyday resistance given an atomized political economy consisting of a lack of an organizational structure to sustain ties among them and between them and local government authorities. The absence of this organizational structure can be traced back in part to the antagonistic relationship between local government and the vendors. The local government had previously assigned six hundred vendors to work in a municipal building, at which time they had established an organization called the *Unión de Venteros* (Union of Vendors) that was led by a committee of six elected vendors. The union collected monthly dues from every vendor to purchase communal supplies for the building, including toilet paper, hand soap, and brooms. The organization drafted and enforced schedules so that every vendor contributed to cleaning passageways and communal spaces. The organization resolved conflicts between vendors within the market regarding issues related to space (e.g., how vendors put their merchandise in communal hallways) and sanitation (e.g., the cleanliness of individual stalls). The organization also served as the vendors' representatives in dealings with the municipal authorities who threatened to displace the vendors when they tried to set up their wares outside of their building during the hot summer months or the holidays when foot traffic was particularly heavy. But aligning with research which shows that forced displacement not only negatively affects productivity and income (Guggenheim 1994) but also fragments social networks and reduces social capital (Cernea 1997), the vendors union did not survive displacement from the building.

Nearly two hundred vendors – or one-third of the entire group – scattered across the city to other informal markets, abandoned the informal economy, or simply disappeared after they were displaced. Three of the six committee members joined other markets in different parts of the city. A fourth committee member died from "stress" shortly after the vendors arrived in the market.[70] The two remaining committee members stayed with the group, but no

---

[70] Marta (MDE_FG5_30), Magda (MDE_FG5_1511), Laura (MDE_FG7_103), and Manuel (MDE_FG7_929), informal vendors, focus groups, Medellín, March 2017.

longer saw themselves as organizational leaders. Most of the vendors stopped paying dues as "people were focused on surviving, not on organizing."[71]

Toward the end of each focus group with the informal vendors, I asked why they did not organize among themselves to stop paying the criminal taxes. Vendors repeatedly countered that they feared denunciation, indicating that despite their daily proximity to each other in the informal market, there was never enough certainty as to whether fellow vendors would be forced to denounce potential collective mobilization to resist victimization:

ALEJANDRO: Let's see, what's the problem with that? Well, the problem is that one is never one hundred percent sure that another [vendor] won't go and tell the Convivir. Let me tell you why. Not because [the criminal group] has corrupted us. But because if people start joining together to stop this [referring to extortion], then if you know about it and don't tell the criminals, what happens? They'll come after you because you didn't do your job as a snitch [*sapo*].[72]

Another vendor specifically indicated that the absence of an organization increased the risk of collective resistance being denounced:

VALERIA: Before we were displaced, at least we worked with each other. Now it's everyone doing for themselves. [Before] we would meet with each other, there were leaders in the Unión [referring to the Union of Recyclers] that kept us informed and helped us to be involved for the good of everyone. That ended when the state displaced us. I trust people to watch over my things if I have to go to the bathroom, or to hold on to money for me if a client buys something when I'm not there. Even to listen to me complain about the *vacuna* and the Convivir. But there's a difference between complaining about it and telling people to join a revolution! Talking about organizing into some sort of group to confront the Convivir … [shakes his head.] There are sometimes people that talk about doing something … that we should all stand up together against them. But how do I know that people won't tell them about me if we actually start to do it?[73]

Several stories circulated among the vendors that they would recount as part of discussing their inability to engage in high-risk collective action against the criminals that were extorting them. The first entailed the danger of simply speaking out against the extortion perpetrated by the criminal group: Don Alfonso was an informal vendor that sold old tools in the market. One day he began to publicly complain about the security tax. Another vendor lamented: "We told him it was better to be quiet. But he didn't listen. He was old and tired of this shit. Soon the media arrived. That was the beginning of the end."[74] Weeks after stories about criminal extortion appeared in local papers, Don Alfonso was shot in the head in the middle of the market – allegedly by one of the members of the Convivir that controlled the market. The killer was never

---

[71] Paula (MDE_FG2_01), informal vendor, focus group, Medellín, July 2016.
[72] Interview with Alejandro (IV_MDE_6010), informal vendor, Medellín, June 2016.
[73] Interview with Valeria (IV_MDE_423), informal vendor, Medellín, July 2016.
[74] Interview with Leo (IV_MDE_1630), informal vendor, Medellín, July 2016.

apprehended. The next Saturday the extortion collectors were back in the market collecting the criminal tax from the vendors. The second commonly told story involved a specific effort to organize collective resistance in the market that also ended with lethal punishment by the criminal group. In this case, a vendor named Ronaldo tried to convince fellow vendors to support him in trying to entice a rival Convivir in the city center to take over the market. Ronaldo told the vendors that they could negotiate with the rival Convivir to charge a lower criminal tax and treat them better than the criminal group that was extorting them. But some of the vendors that Ronaldo confided in about this denounced him to the criminal group in the market, because he was killed by the criminal group shortly afterward while he assembled his wares to sell that day in the market. Thus the absence of a preexisting organization that could support robust social ties and trust among the vendors undercut their ability to mobilize collective resistance.[75]

The atomized political economy in which the vendors operated also meant they lacked a clear channel of communication and ties with local government officials. In turn, vendors dismissed local government as complicit in their victimization by virtue of not intervening to bring an end to extortion – what they widely described as an open secret in the city. Here vendors alleged that the mayor at the time had essentially opted to live with organized crime's operations in the city center instead of challenging it. The mayor, Federico Gutiérrez (2016–19), had actually proposed during his campaign to confront extortion and the Convivir in the Comuna 10 as part of a plan to "recuperate" the city center.[76] But shortly after assuming office, local authorities intercepted telephone exchanges between members of the criminal groups running extortion in the Comuna 10 during which they discussed plans to assassinate Gutiérrez in retaliation for threats against their criminal enterprises in the Comuna 10.[77] The assassination never materialized, but several similar threats of violence against the mayor by the same set of actors surfaced periodically throughout his first year in office. The recyclers as well as civil society leaders noted that measures by municipal authorities to confront the Convivir and criminal extortion were quietly dropped from the mayor's public pronouncements in the wake of these revelations. In turn, and lacking ties through which to communicate with local government, vendors interpreted the seeming silence from the mayor and local government as evidence of complicity.

---

[75] Interview with Marta (IV_FG5_30), informal vendor, Medellín, March 2017.

[76] "Primer Acto de Federico Gutiérrez como Alcalde Será Liderar un Consejo de Seguridad," *El Colombiano*, December 23, 2015. Gutiérrez had a long history of support from both the city's elite political establishment and conservative national political circles, including from former President Alvaro Uribe's Partido de la U (Social Party of National Unity—Party of the U), during a successful 2007 bid for a seat on Medellín's municipal council. Gutiérrez's victory in the 2015 mayoral elections came as a surprise given that he ran against former President Uribe's chosen candidate.

[77] "Como se Reacomoda el Crimen en Medellín y Amenaza al Alcalde," *Semana*, February 19, 2016.

3.3.2 The Practices of Everyday Resistance

Vendors thus continued to use everyday resistance to contest the material dimension of criminal taxation. They specifically appealed to the purported reason for taxing them: the provision of protection and order. The vendors would "remind" the criminal actors when they demanded criminal tax payments that they used to provide order as part of their extortion.[78] This practice harnessed the very rationale that the criminal group initially used to justify the illicit tax to instead negotiate the arrangement's contemporary predatory nature under the Convivir's short time horizon:

MARIO: I tell them [members of the Convivir] when they come by. I tell them: 'I waited for you but you didn't come. So I hit them [the thief] myself. If you don't collaborate and help, if you only come on Saturdays, then you're just coming to charge the money.'[79]

But as the criminal actors expanded their repertoire of practices to maintain extortion, so too did vendors broaden their practices of everyday resistance. Vendors also used rhetorical practices to resist social domination by framing themselves *and* the Convivir as businesses – countering criminals' efforts to denigrate their positions in the social hierarchy:

I tell them that 'no' [when the criminals verbally insult the vendors]. We are in the same situation. Working on the streets, out here where *nobody* cares about *either* of us. Both of us work hard to make a living, to feed our families and to survive. We are not that different.[80]

When criminals attempted to hide illicit drugs and weapons in the vendors' merchandise, they demanded to be treated with dignity as respectable business owners.

FEDERNEL: Yes, they try to extend the *plaza* [name given to micro-territory used for the sale of illicit drugs] into our businesses. So we sometimes find a little "package" that doesn't belong in our things, and so with a lot of respect, we say: 'boss [*jefe*], the thing is, my food is at play here. Please help me and don't hide this here.' Or if they take a chair and start selling [drugs] from right next to where I'm working, we say, 'Oh, I'm so sorry, but I need the chair back for my customers.' And then you take it and they don't have anywhere to sit. You have to make them feel uncomfortable. But also, in a respectful manner, we make our businesses get respected too.[81]

MARTA: They screw us by hiding drugs in our merchandise. They begin to sit around, and we see them ... [crack] pipes, [crack] rocks ... all mixed in our merchandise. And inside [of ourselves] we say, 'Oh god, not again! People using us, disrecting us

---

[78] This echoes similar practices that civilians use in other high-risk wartime settings. Kaplan (2017b) analyzes the use of "rhetorical traps" by civilians in wartime settings to reduce their vulnerability in order to protect themselves from armed groups.

[79] Mario (MDE_FG1_911), informal vendor, focus group, Medellín, July 2016.

[80] Interview with Antonella (IV_MDE_899), informal vendor, Medellín, July 2016.

[81] Federnel (MDE_FG6_45), informal vendor, focus group, Medellín, March 2017.

because we're disposable.' But on the outside, we have to walk carefully and do the dance. So we say, 'Look, boys [*muchachos*], the thing is that everyone here, you and me, we're all working. And *this* is my business. And if I get caught with your product, then it's *my* business that suffers.'[82]

Finally, though criminal capture prevented enlisting the police in their resistance, vendors rhetorically invoked their relationship with other parts of the state to resist political domination. Here it is important to underscore that they did not affirm their relationship to specific state institutions or actors, but instead to the abstract notion of rights accorded to them by the state. Vendors specifically invoked the frames and rhetoric of the ideal-type of citizenship found in the Colombian Constitution. This exemplifies what Scheingold (1974) calls the "myth of rights," wherein believing in the rights that the state formally grants, but denies in practice, can still provide a powerful catalyst for mobilization.[83] Vendors invoked this belief to show criminals that they rejected being seen as second-class citizens:

They [the members of the Convivir] tell us that we are trash, like what we sell. But we show them. We mobilize, we talk about rights, about the Constitution—our bible. We celebrate it while we work, talk about it, laugh about it, so that they hear us when they're coming to collect their money.[84]

On several occasions I observed a few vendors enact their resistance to political domination by strategically discussing their constitutionally guaranteed right to work. One morning three neighboring vendors at the market were discussing whether the city's Public Space office would take their merchandise to the "North Pole" – the far-off warehouse where vendors must pay large fines to retrieve their wares. The vendors complained that the legal code that gave Public Space agents this power was essentially a "law that allows the state to steal."[85] The three vendors then noticed one of the members of the Convivir crossing the street and approaching. "Here comes the tough one [*aquí viene el duro*]," one of the vendors whispered. At that point I expected the conversation to end, but instead the vendors began talking more loudly about how the trip to the North Pole was another example of how Public Space did not respect their "constitutional rights as citizens of this county." A second stated loudly: "We all have rights, no matter how we earn [money] for our bread [*pansito*], fuck [*carajo*]!" The third vendor replied: "Even though we may not look like it, we are also citizens!"[86] I later asked one of these vendors why they carried on this way in

---

[82] Marta (MDE_FG5_30), informal vendor, focus group, Medellín, March 2017.

[83] Scheingold (1974, chapter 2); see also McAdam (1982) on how African Americans asserted formally accorded rights to mobilize against structural racism; and Ewick and Silbey (1998) on everyday interpretations of laws as political acts.

[84] Interview with Alicia (IV_MDE_911), informal vendor, Medellín, July 2016.

[85] Several vendors across multiple focus groups used variants of this phrasing.

[86] Field notes, Medellín, July 2016.

front of a member of the Convivir. He answered: "So that they remember that they are not the only authorities here."[87] Far from being organic conversations, such dialogues are strategic, but indirect declarations, meant to remind the victimizer that the vendors reject political domination as part of their victimization.

Less common forms of resistance to political domination included small-scale events, such as rallies that handfuls of vendors coordinated within the market to highlight their vulnerability to displacement by local authorities. Lampposts and cement walls in parts of the market became canvases for politically infused images reaffirming the vendors' citizenship, from tattered Colombian flags to laminated news clippings discussing previous rallies. What is analytically notable is that these rallies took place on Saturdays – the very day the Convivir collected taxes from the vendors. When I asked one of the rally's coordinators why they would do so, they replied: "We don't have guns. We don't have politicians. But we do have dignity and rights and this [pointing to her head], and so you need to use it to make them [the criminal extortionists] realize that they haven't cornered us—that we are citizens."[88]

3.3.3 The Trajectory of Everyday Resistance

Everyday resistance does not imperil continued extortion. As my interviews with two former members of the Convivir who coordinated extortion in the market revealed, they did not view marginal reductions in material taxation as challenges to their power or the continuation of victimization:[89]

MATEO: Of course they [the vendors] tried to pay less or not pay sometimes. Most times I had to stand firm. But yes, every once in a while you let it alone [allowing the vendors to pay less or skip a payment of the tribute]. There were lots of people to charge, you couldn't just spend all day arguing with one fool who didn't have all the money that they had to give or that wanted to fuck with you that day. The next time you had to collect, you made sure they paid.

GABRIEL: Not paying one day didn't mean that I wouldn't be back the next week to collect the *vacuna*. So let them only give me 500 [pesos], it's okay. Because I wasn't going to stop making them pay. They weren't telling me "no," just not today.

The practices that vendors used to contest social and political domination, while delivering important emotional benefits to the vendors, also did not endanger continued criminal taxation:

---

[87] Interview with Tomas (IV_MDE_551), informal vendor, Medellín, July 2016.

[88] Interview with Douglas (IV_MDE_1010), informal vendor, Medellín, July 2016.

[89] The first member left the Convivir after he was permanently injured during a shootout with rivals, and the second was pushed out of the Convivir because his drug addiction began to interfere with his responsibilities to the criminal group, particularly ensuring the timely collection of the criminal tax. Interviews with former Convivir members Mateo (IV_MDE_141) and Gabriel (IV_MDE_142), Medellín, July 2017.

GABRIEL: Sometimes [the vendors] talked too much.

ME: What do you mean? Like about what?

GABRIEL: I don't know. They would talk about how we should not be fighting with each other. That we were in the same situation so we needed to help each other. But it was just them talking. I only did my job and took their money. If I had listened too much to each one of them I probably would have never finished with the collection.

EM: What did you think when they said these things to you?

GABRIEL: That I would also probably say things like that. To try to not let people step on me and disrespect me. But that's the situation, the reality, and nothing's going to change that.

The second former Convivir member specifically referred to the conversations that handfuls of vendors would hold about their political rights when he was in the market:

MATEO: That shit [referring to the political conversations] would get me angry. That they were "citizens" and that they had "rights." Okay, okay, it's good, it's good. Now go talk to mayor and see if he thinks you have rights. No. So? Shut up and pay.[90]

In brief, though the practices associated with everyday resistance yielded some material (but mainly nonmaterial) gains for vendors, it did not threaten the continuation of criminal extortion.

3.4 CONCLUSION

This chapter uses the argument developed in Chapter 2 to analyze everyday resistance to criminal extortion. In the first part of the chapter I use the logic of a most-different comparison to analyze cases of resistance in El Salvador and Mexico. The analysis shows that despite variation in political economies and status of the police, victims in these cases all pursued everyday resistance given the shared condition of facing a criminal actor with a long time horizon. Both of the criminal actors who were perpetrating extortion – the MS-13 in El Salvador and the Familia Michoacana in Mexico – provided victims with degrees of protection and order in settings where both were scarce given limited security provision by the state. Access to these resources coupled with the unchallenged status of both criminal actors led victims to prefer to negotiate their victimization via everyday resistance rather than risk punishment in seeking to end it.

In the second part of this chapter I analyzed the second pathway to everyday resistance, whereby despite facing criminal actors with short time horizons, victims were unable to move beyond noncontentious, individual-level, and sporadic practices given important structural constraints. Using the case of recyclers in Medellín, I show how criminal competition and then state confrontation shortened the time horizon of the Convivir. The analysis also provides empirical substantiation for my claim that criminals rely on combinations of material, social,

---

[90] Interview with Mateo (IV_MDE_141), former Convivir member, July 2017.

and political strategies to sustain victimization. This finding highlights the need to broaden our analytic lens beyond lethal violence to incorporate the other tactics that criminal actors use. Doing so not only provides a more complete descriptive understanding of criminal victimization but also signals where we might expect victims to engage in corresponding forms of resistance. I show that vendors contest not only the use of coercive force by criminals but also their social offenses and the ways in which they denigrate the political status of vendors. Studying criminal victimization and victims' resistance requires that we fuse the conventional emphasis on coercive force with attention to the less visible aspects of victimization. Focusing solely on the surrendering of cash under threat or use of violence obscures the other dimensions of criminal extortion analyzed here and in the empirical chapters that follow.

My analysis reveals that recyclers opted to continue with everyday resistance even when the Convivir increased physical coercion and introduced strategies of social and political domination. The atomized political economy inhibited collective action and fostered a perception of governing authorities as complicit with criminal extortion, leaving recyclers to continue with everyday resistance. The recyclers' practices of everyday resistance, however, did expand to counteract the social and political strategies that the Convivir deployed to maintain the heightened extraction of rents under a short time horizon. Though the material gains that the recyclers secured through everyday resistance were marginal, the immaterial dividends from retaining some sense of dignity as entrepreneurs and citizens enabled the vendors to see themselves as exercising agency. The empirical analysis thus affirms that studying victimization as a dynamic process can yield analytic benefits unattainable using a conventional view of victimization as a static, one-time act.

Chapter 4 builds on the findings presented here to analyze piecemeal vigilantism in El Salvador. Like the recyclers in Medellín, small-scale farmers in my field sites in El Salvador functioned in an atomized political economy and with scant links to governing authorities. But unlike the recyclers, farmers did have access to police who were autonomous from the criminal gangs perpetrating extortion, although with limited institutional capacity. The analysis shows how these conditions yielded ad hoc groups of victims engaging in sporadic acts of extralegal violence as part of piecemeal vigilantism.

4

Piecemeal Vigilantism

In 2015 in a canton in the municipality of Cienfuegos in eastern El Salvador, a farmer named Rafael called a man on his cell phone and asked if he wanted to join a few other farmers who were going to kill a member of the MS-13 responsible for holding on to the criminal taxes, or "the rent" [*la renta*], that the gang collected from extortion in the canton. That night a police agent from the PNC provided Rafael and the other farmers with dark blue police uniforms to wear as they dragged the gang member out of the house. A different police agent stood guard nearby ready to alert the farmers if a police patrol happened to come by. The next day the gang member's lifeless body was found nearly fully buried in a field a few miles away from his house. In 2015 several such instances of what I call *piecemeal vigilantism* carried out by small groups of victims and individual members of the police were investigated by the *Unidad Especializada Contra el Crimen Organizado* (Specialized Unit against Organized Crime), which is part of El Salvador's FGR. This particular group of victims and police killed at least ten people between 2014 and 2016.[1]

In this chapter I analyze why victims resist extortion through ad hoc and sporadic acts of extralegal violence against criminals in coordination with individual police. I draw on interview data, field observations, and judicial files from two cases of piecemeal vigilantism: one that began in a canton in the municipality of Cienfuegos in the department of San Miguel and another that originated in a canton in the municipality of El Pilar in the department of La Libertad (see Map 4.1).

---

[1] Investigators in the FGR who researched these cases indicated that it was likely that members of this group carried out additional killings, but that there was insufficient evidence to attribute these additional cases to them (field notes, San Salvador, June 2017). Interviews with community members in the canton in Cienfuegos indicate that the group began killing gang members in 2013 (field notes, Cienfuegos, June 2017). Brief descriptions of the individual judicial cases can be found in the Appendix.

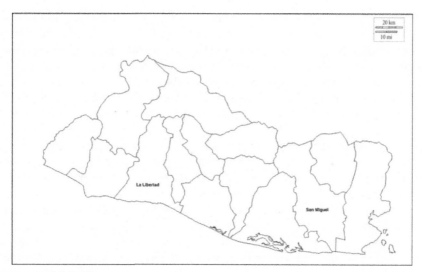

MAP 4.1 El Salvador

The next section situates criminal extortion within the broader politics of criminal gangs in El Salvador. In Section 4.2 I detail and analyze the conditions that led to piecemeal vigilantism as well as its structure, practices, and trajectory. Like Medellín's recyclers in Chapter 3, small-scale farmers in both cantons in El Salvador lacked preexisting organizations to advance collective resistance and had negligible ties to local governing authorities – in other words, farmers operated in atomized political economies. But in contrast to the police in Medellín's informal market, police in the two localities where I conducted research in El Salvador were autonomous from the criminal gangs coordinating extortion because gangs had adopted an explicit strategy of targeting police as part of the broader state–criminal conflict. Yet, the police lacked the institutional capacity to provide order while adhering to the formal rule of law. Victims in the two cases thus enlisted individual police as collaborators in occasional acts of piecemeal vigilantism. Over time victims faced pressure to scale up their coercive capacities, territorial reach, and extralegal violence because of their inability to end victimization outright. However, efforts by both groups to do so ultimately distorted their objectives and contributed to their dismantling by another part of the state: national-level judicial authorities.

4.1 GANGS, EXTORTION, AND POLITICS IN EL SALVADOR

Gangs operate in almost all of El Salvador's 262 municipalities (International Crisis Group 2018). There are an estimated 60,000 gang members in the country.[2] Though the term *mara* is applied to the two main gangs, the MS-13 and the Barrio 18, it was used during the 1970s and 1980s to describe groups of friends who gathered to socialize in public spaces and who lived in the same neighborhood or belonged to the same church (Smutt and Miranda 1998, 25).[3] Contrary to the popular narrative that traces the origins of gangs to the 1980s wave of migration from the United States (Arana 2005; Manwaring 2006), gangs were active in El Salvador as early as the 1960s (Cruz 2010; Van de Borgh and Savenije 2019).

Gang violence increased in El Salvador after the 1992 Chapultepec Peace Accords were signed between the national government and the Farabundo Martí National Liberation Front (FMLN) insurgency.[4] This ended a twelve-year civil conflict that claimed approximately 75,000 lives. But between the end of the civil war and the mid-1990s, over half a million Salvadorans also returned to their home country. Under the Illegal Immigration Reform and Immigrant Responsibility Act, the United States deported nearly 122,000 convicted criminals to Central America between 2001 and 2010 (Thale and Falkenburger 2006). Over 40,000 were sent to El Salvador (InSight Crime and CLALS 2018, 15), including Salvadorans who had migrated to Los Angeles and either joined the gangs of Mexican immigrants and Chicanos, including the Barrio 18, or established and joined the MS-13 (Cruz 2010; Hayden 2004; Zilberg 2011). The MS-13 and Barrio 18 were not enemies until relations between them soured in the late 1980s for reasons that remain unclear (Ward 2013). But the resulting rivalry became a defining feature of life in gang-controlled territories.

Gang members deported to El Salvador had tenuous familial linkages, rough Spanish language skills, and limited job opportunities (Smutt and Miranda 1998, 36). Preexisting gangs thus become their interlocutors and, as a result, these gang members adopted new cultural traits, including forms of dress, slang, and tattoos (Cruz 2010, 384; Hume 2007).[5] During this time gangs structured themselves into cliques (*clikas*) affiliated with the MS-13 or the Barrio 18 through loose neighborhood-level federations that operated largely autonomously and lacked internal governing bureaucracies, but which provided some degree of order in territories where the state lacked the capacity to do so (Cruz 2010; Smutt and Miranda 1998).

[2] A 1996 survey of active gang members in the metropolitan area of San Salvador found that 85 percent belonged to either the MS-13 or the Barrio 18 (Cruz 2010, 387, citing Cruz and Portillo Peña 1998).

[3] The MS-13 and Barrio 18 together accounted for nearly 90 percent of gang membership in El Salvador by 2002 (Aguilar and Miranda 2006).

[4] On how the end of El Salvador's civil war is a case of democratization "from below," see Wood (2000).

[5] While deportation spurred important organizational and cultural changes in the nature of gangs in El Salvador, it is not the case that the deportees were the primary source of growing gang membership. By 2001 only approximately 12 percent of gang members in El Salvador had ever been in the United States (Santacruz and Concha-Eastman 2001).

The nature of state–gang relations changed dramatically in the mid-2000s when El Salvador targeted gangs with hardline security measures.[6] In 2003 then-president Francisco Flores (1999–2004) of the conservative Nationalist Republican Alliance (*Alianza Republicana Nacionalista*, ARENA) implemented the Iron Fist (*Mano Dura*) policy that criminalized gang membership and imprisoned youth for publicly displaying gang tattoos and gang hand signs. One year later nearly twenty thousand alleged gang members were arrested, though 95 percent were ultimately released after judicial authorities again dismissed core elements of the policy.[7] ARENA nonetheless hardened its anti-gang position to maintain party cohesion and stave off the FMLN in the 2004 national elections (González 2004; Holland 2013). The political imperative to focus public attention on crime and gangs as the country's primary challenges enabled politicians to sidestep thornier issues like corruption and socioeconomic inequality.[8] President Antonio Saca (2004–09), also of the ARENA party, developed the *Super Mano Dura* policy that allowed the PNC to detain suspected gang members or anyone having any association with gangs. Imprisonment, however, did not reduce levels of crime. It instead prompted street-level members to obey the orders of imprisoned leaders who had the capacity to decide who would or would not receive protection behind prison walls, transforming gangs into hierarchically organized structures with organizational bases inside the country's prisons (Cruz 2010).[9]

The restructuring grouped street-level cliques into "programs" concentrated by geographic areas in order to facilitate communication with imprisoned gang leaders. The latter is known as the *ranfla* and its members are *ranfleros*. Individual cliques are led by *palabreros* [those who have the word] who manage their everyday operations. The programs are led by *corredores* [runners] who have demonstrated loyalty to the gang through violence and length of time as members. This structural transformation in response to state crackdowns altered gang operations and coercive capacity, as one journalist who had long covered the gangs explained to me: "Originally these gangs were highly visible, sitting on street corners in their territories, throwing gang signs [*rifando*]. Today they are highly structured organizations that operate, partly,

---

[6] In 1996 El Salvador had adopted an emergency law [*ley de emergencia*] that expedited trials against criminals, increased prison sentences, and allowed the state to jail youth in adult prisons. Several of these measures were repealed in 1997 after being challenged in the country's Supreme Court. But the 1996 law was neither explicitly focused on gangs nor was it as punitively severe as the measures that followed (Smutt and Miranda 1998, 13).

[7] The Salvadoran Supreme Court declared that the Mano Dura policy violated the United Nations Convention on the Rights of the Child.

[8] In 2018 President Saca was sentenced to a decade in prison for embezzlement of public funds and money laundering. His predecessor, President Flores, was arrested for embezzling international aid provided to El Salvador in the wake of the 2001 earthquakes. Flores died in 2016 awaiting trial. President Funes (2009–14) fled to Nicaragua to escape charges of bribing judicial authorities to avoid investigations into the 2012 truce that was established between the government and gangs.

[9] See Skarbek (2011; 2014) on how mass imprisonment prompts organizational change in gangs.

in the clandestine."[10] Bureaucratization gave the gangs' imprisoned leaders power over street-level operations and increased their leverage vis-à-vis the government. This was evident during the 2012 truce negotiations between the MS-13, the two factions of the Barrio 18, and the Salvadoran government when gang leaders could credibly commit to reducing street violence in return for government concessions (Cruz and Durán-Martínez 2016). But under the truce gangs increased extortion to generate revenue and solidify territorial control (Van der Borgh and Savenije 2019).

The breakdown of the truce, however, also prompted a shift in how small-scale farmers in the cantons in Cienfuegos and El Pilar experienced criminal extortion amid state–criminal conflict. The gangs began threatening and using violence more readily to extract more resources from farmers. Instead of occasional "contributions," criminal taxation became a regular, costly, and humiliating facet of everyday life. Whereas the gangs had limited extortion to a few dollars every week under the long time horizons afforded by the truce, the pattern of extortion became more unpredictable and costlier when they operated under the short time horizons. As Pablo, a grain farmer in Cienfuegos, recounted:

When they asked someone for money and [the victim] didn't give it to them, they would throw anonymous threats their way by telephone. And if that didn't work, they would threaten their families, they would threaten them saying that they were going to take their kids. They would ask them if their kids' lives were worth five thousand dollars. I know people who gave from several years of their own work five thousand dollars so that the gangs would let them live in peace, but that was a lie, because later the gangs took more and more money from them until they had nothing left to give.[11]

Farmers in both cantons confirmed that state crackdowns and competition for territory between Barrio 18 and the MS-13 radically changed the nature of extortion. As the amount and frequency of extortion escalated, some farmers had to ask family members living abroad to help pay the criminal taxes.[12] The departments of La Libertad and San Miguel have among El Salvador's highest levels of receipt of foreign remittances.[13]

But extortion also became more humiliating for victims as gangs used practices of social domination to sustain increased extraction. As a researcher in El Salvador's Procuraduría para la Defensa de Los Derechos Humanos (Attorney General for the Defense of Human Rights, or PDDH) explained, "The vertical structure of the gang enables it to carry out its main activity: extortion. But at the end of the day ... the logic for paying [the criminal tax] is intimately tied to fear and humiliation. The person being extorted must think: 'I am nothing. And if

---

[10] Interview with Joaquín (ESV100), journalist, El Salvador, June 2017.
[11] Telephone interview with Pablo (ESV16161), farmer, Cienfuegos, February 2020.
[12] Field notes, El Pilar and Cienfuegos, June 2017 and October 2018.
[13] On the remittance economy in El Salvador, see Gammage (2006).

I don't pay, they can kill me.'"[14] Gustavo, a farmer in Cienfuegos, described how extortion affected the way he viewed his own self-worth:

Before it was boys asking for help. And they helped . . . keeping things calm around here, so you would give them something. But that changed. [They] showed up with tattoos on their hands and necks and they *demanded* the rent. Every week they insult us with what they say and do. What can I do? Nothing. I have to keep paying . . . paying for the privilege of being robbed and humiliated.[15]

And echoing the practices of political domination related by informal vendors in Medellín, gangs also disparaged farmers' status as citizens:

They tell me that no one can protect me, not even the government. If the government was able to keep me and my family safe, then I could tell them to go to hell. But in some ways, they are the ones with the authority . . . because they decide who lives and who dies. So what good is it to be a citizen then?[16]

Interviews with former MS-13 gang members from each locality further illustrate the logics of social and political domination when criminals operate on short time horizons.

Through conversations with pastors of evangelical churches in Cienfuegos and El Pilar, I learned of two young men – one from each municipality – who the pastors had helped negotiate their way out of the gangs by joining the church.[17] From El Pilar I interviewed Samuel, and from Cienfuegos I interviewed Will. Samuel described the shift in the nature of extortion as the gang's time horizon shortened amid state–criminal conflict:

I think it is important to say something, which is to know that the maras were not always bad things. Before the maras were part of the community, something that people wanted because they could ask the mara for help. Now the mara operates very differently, because it has to survive. Now [the maras] have to extort, force people to pay, threaten people if they don't pay. They are more involved in other illicit things. But they do all of this to survive.[18]

Samuel's interpretation of gang–community relations should be evaluated critically given his previous participation in the gang and its extortive practices. But notable here is that he traces the general evolution of extortion from beneficent to predatory. Will delves into how this evolution affected the nature of extortion:

WILL: When I was part of [extorting], I had to do many things, ugly things. God is capable of miracles, and I believe that one of those miracles was helping me to leave that part of my life behind.

[14] Interview with Luis (ESV1713), researcher, PDDH, San Salvador, June 2017.
[15] Interview with Gustavo (ESV414563), farmer, Cienfuegos, October 2018.
[16] Interview with Emiliano (ESV112577), farmer, El Pilar, June 2017.
[17] On religion as an exit point for gang members in Central America, see Cruz and Rosen (2020) and Brenneman (2011).
[18] Interview with Samuel (ESV2020), former gang member, El Pilar, October 2018.

EM: What types of things did you do back then?

WILL: Threaten people—that I would kill them or their family if they didn't do what we told them to do. Sometimes, well, one had to hurt people ... What did they have to do? To pay the rent, to not talk to the police or our enemies ... to keep silent.

EM: But didn't the mara provide people with security or protection?

WILL: That was before. Not anymore. That's why people don't like the maras, why they fear them. Because the maras talk about keeping people safe, but it's not like that in reality. Before, yes, but today ... it's only about the rent.

EM: What happened if someone didn't or couldn't pay the rent?

WILL: You did everything. You insulted them and their families ... followed their kids to school and took pictures to show them that you knew who lived in their house, what they did or where they went and when. Threaten to rape their daughters, their wives.

EM: Was this something that only needed to happen once? Or did the mara have to do it repeatedly?

WILL: You had to make people feel that no one was coming to help them, not the police, not the government. It's like here, in the church, we read and listen to the word of God over and over until it is in the heart. We had to tell people things over and over, too ... ugly things. It was a way to make them feel like the mara was the only authority.[19]

Samuel further explained the logics of social and political domination for extortion:

They are many bad things ... what we had to do. But it was to make people believe that there was no other way. If they were doing well or not [in their businesses] at that moment, it didn't matter, because they had to pay. If I didn't bring the amount of money back to the mara, it was my problem. So people could not see any other way. For them, to get me to stop insulting and scaring them and their families, they had to pay.[20]

In sum, both victims and criminals concurred that criminal extortion was a dynamic process that was sensitive to the shifting time horizons of the criminal actors amid state crackdowns and criminal competition.

4.2 PIECEMEAL VIGILANTISM

In this section I trace the process and mechanisms that led farmers to resist criminal extortion via piecemeal vigilantism. In both field sites the political economy was partly shaped by broader national trends starting in the late twentieth century with a shift away from agriculture and toward secondary and tertiary markets. The retreat of state support for small-scale agricultural production led to an atomized political economy with farmers operating independently from each other while highly dependent on informal transactions with individual intermediaries in the agricultural markets who occupy a gray zone between the licit and illicit, as well as the occasional clientelist strategies of political parties and politicians. Farmers lacked preexisting organizations to

---

[19] Interview with Will (ESV3223), former gang member, Cienfuegos, June 2017.

[20] Interview with Samuel (ESV2020), former gang member, El Pilar, October 2018.

mobilize collectively or substantive institutionalized ties to governing authorities. At the same time, farmers faced police who lacked the capacity to enforce the rule of law but who, crucially, were autonomous from gangs given state–criminal conflict. Together these factors led farmers to opt for the ad hoc structure and sporadic acts of piecemeal vigilantism that set this strategy of resistance apart from both the individual-level and nonviolent practices of everyday resistance and the institutionalized and sustained nature of collective forms of vigilantism.

4.2.1 The Decline of the Agricultural Economy and the Rise of Atomized Political Economies

The majority of firms in the municipalities of El Pilar and Cienfuegos are small-scale farms headed by one or two family members who work alongside other household members and extended relatives to produce basic grains (e.g., beans and sorghum) and vegetables (e.g., maize, peppers, and cucumbers). There are over three thousand small-scale farmers in El Pilar and slightly less than that in Cienfuegos (Ministerio de Economía 2009). Most of this farming takes place in the cantons outside of the urban center of the municipalities, including the two cantons where I conducted fieldwork. There farmers engage primarily in subsistence and cash crop farming,[21] with most of the cash crops being used for domestic consumption. Yet, despite agriculture's historical centrality to the country's economy, these small-scale farmers lack preexisting organizations to represent their interests and to coordinate with governing authorities.

The agricultural sector was the foundation for oligarchic rule in El Salvador throughout the nineteenth and twentieth centuries and the main source of foreign exchange earnings and employment (Bulmer Thomas 1987, 33). Landowners and investors controlled much of the agricultural economy with the support of members of the armed forces who held political office and repressed rural labor in exchange for elites' support (Almeida 2008; Stanley 1996; Williams 1994). The country's civil war prompted the decline of the agricultural economy as insurgent extortion of export-oriented agricultural firms coupled with state-led expropriation of land in the 1980s reduced the agro-export sector's productivity (Wood 2000).[22] But after the peace accords political and economic elites prioritized the service and industrial sectors over the agricultural sector amid rapidly changing global economic dynamics.

After the war, economic elites shifted their investments to industry, real estate, and the service sector. The state reduced or eliminated structural aid for small-scale

---

[21] Farmers in the departments of San Miguel and La Libertad divide their yields nearly evenly between household consumption and cash crops (Ministerio de Economía 2009).

[22] Between 1932 and 1980, El Salvador undertook four different land reform projects, with some – such as the 1932 land reform – designed to further and sustain the concentration of land ownership, whereas others – such as that in 1980, during the civil war – proposed measures to redistribute land to peasants, tenants, and sharecroppers.

farmers, including technical assistance, guaranteed prices, storage systems, state marketing, and institutionalized mechanisms for obtaining information and bringing products to market (Almeida 2008, chapter 5; Superintendencia de Competencia 2013, 6). Under market liberalization, the Salvadoran government lowered barriers to entry for the import of foreign agricultural goods using revised tariff structures that stipulated minimal import requirements for basic grains (Acevedo, Barry, and Rosa 1995, 2156). After having nearly half of the country's population employed in the agricultural sector in 1971, this figure had dropped to 17 percent by 2017 (Baumeister 2018, 73–74). In 2018 El Salvador actually imported the majority of its vegetables and basic grains (USDA Foreign Agricultural Service 2018, 2).

Political authorities thus have little incentive to organize small-scale producers, in part because of the shift in economic priorities, but also for political reasons. Today relations between governing authorities and the small-scale agricultural sectors in the cantons are individualized and clientelistic. The exchange of political support for material favors in small-scale farming communities takes place through particularistic aid programs. An example is the Programa de Paquetes Agrícolas (Agricultural Packages Program), through which individual farmers register with the Ministry of Agriculture and Livestock to receive free bags of maize and bean seeds as well as fertilizer on an annual basis. However, the program largely serves as a tool for clientelist exchange for whichever party is in power in order to generate political support in the countryside leading up to electoral cycles. The state thus has little incentive to organize producers given that clientelist relations both sustain and rely on the "atomization" of the small-scale producer sector.[23]

Economic reconfiguration and state retreat in El Salvador's agricultural markets also led to the growing influence of informal actors who straddle the boundaries between licit and illicit (Baumeister 2018). By virtue of their small scale and lack of state support, farmers are highly dependent on these intermediaries to sell their produce to wholesalers (*mayoristas*) that stock retailers (*minoristas*) throughout the country. The intermediaries, popularly known as "transporters" or "coyotes," physically transport grains and vegetables to central distribution points throughout the country. All transactions between transporters and farmers are informal and individualized, taking place in the fields immediately after harvests throughout the year.[24] The intermediaries appear in the cantons only to engage in individual deals before loading up and departing with farmers' crops. Limited

---

[23] Telephone interview, Maria (ESV16162), government official, San Salvador, August 2020. On the atomizing effects of clientelism, see Rock (1975).

[24] One study estimates that 85 percent of corn sales by El Salvadoran farmers are informal transactions (García-Jiménez and Gandlgruber 2014, 14). Coyotes purchase basic grains and vegetables primarily in November and December, when prices were nearly at their lowest levels each year (Superintendencia de Competencia 2013).

access to information on market pricing further disadvantages farmers vis-à-vis the transporters.[25] This enables transporters to pay farmers below market prices with none of the stability associated with guaranteed contracts and relationships (Angel 2008), and which are crucial to fostering collective organization in agricultural markets.[26] The transporters, however, are also reportedly involved in the contraband and smuggling economies that run through rural El Salvador and much of Central America. Transporters are rumored to sometimes work for larger criminal groups who are, somewhat confusingly, also known as "transporters."[27] The latter, however, have long histories of transporting contraband goods, from electronics to foodstuffs, as well as human smuggling and, most recently, illicit drugs brought in from South America to be delivered in Mexico (Dudley 2010). Given the threat of clientelism and the withholding of material goods, farmers consequently fear how not only the state but also intermediaries who occupy a "gray zone" between the licit and illicit would react to their organizing collectively.[28] Thus small-scale producers in El Salvador are also seen as the "victims of intermediary structures" (Tolentino, Elí Martínez, and Stanley 2006, 21).

Sectoral organizations among small-scale agricultural producers in rural cantons and municipalities are largely nonexistent. Over 95 percent of the small-scale farmers in both El Pilar and Cienfuegos – including those in the cantons – do not belong to any type of sectoral organization (Ministerio de Economía 2009). This lack of organization is a primary barrier to the economic betterment of the small-scale farmers.[29] More broadly, these dramatic economic transformations transpired in rural settings that bore the brunt of elite-sponsored violence throughout much of the twentieth century (Martín-Baró 1989; see also Portes and Landolt 2000, 543).[30] But while farmers extorted by gangs are limited in their collective capacity given atomized political economies, they do count on autonomous – though low-capacity – police.

[25] These market prices normally reflect the buying price for specific grains and vegetables in the country's main market, the Gerardo Barrios Central Market located in San Salvador.
[26] The resulting price discrepancies along the commodity chain can be quite substantial. For example, in 2005 while the price per ton of maize for producers was USD $679.57, for the wholesalers who purchase the product from coyotes, the price per ton was USD #861.74 (Tolentino, Elí Martínez, and Stanley 2006, 22).
[27] Field notes, El Pilar and Cienfuegos, June 2017 and October 2018.
[28] See Auyero (2007) on the concept of the gray zone between criminality and the state.
[29] The lack of state investment in organizing the sector is further compounded by the pressure that producers face from transporters against organizing. Informal conversations with farmers indicated that transporters openly oppose any organizing efforts, no matter how small, so as to preserve their power over the farmers. Field notes, Cienfuegos, October 2018 and El Pilar, July 2017.
[30] See Bauer et al. (2016) for an overview of the findings from the literature that examines the effects of wartime violence on social capital.

4.2.2 Autonomous but Low-Capacity Police and Political Support for Extrajudicial Violence

The PNC was established as part of the peace negotiations that ended the civil war. Previously the Ministry of Defense had overseen a National Police for urban settings, a National Guard for rural settings, and a Treasury Police for border patrols and customs duties (Call 2003, 831; Holiday and Stanley 1993). The FMLN prioritized security sector–reform during the peace negotiations given the central roles that the security apparatus had played in sustaining exclusionary regimes (Stanley 1996; 1999; Popkin 2010, chapter 4). Under the peace accords the three police institutions were eliminated and internal security was handed to the PNC.

However, from the outset national political authorities failed to set up the PNC to become a high-capacity police institution. They did not provide the PNC with either physical facilities and equipment to train recruits or adequate financial support (Cruz 2006, 154–55; Stanley 1999, 114, 116–17). Internal and external accountability and disciplinary mechanisms for the PNC were not established until several years after it began operating (Cruz 2006, 158).[31] Police personnel received little training on how to conduct criminal investigations (Popkin 2010, 178). Together, these conditions stunted the PNC's capacity to enforce the rule of law (Stanley 1999).

Yet, low institutional capacity does not impact all ranks within a police organization the same way. The negative effects disproportionately impact the lower ranks that are direct responsibility for enforcing the rule of law on an everyday basis. These individuals are more directly exposed to the daily conflicts, tensions, and risks that are staple parts of everyday policing – and particularly so in settings of state–criminal conflict where street-level police are the most physically exposed to opportunities for criminal actors to target them. The uneven effects of the PNC's limited institutional capacity are evident in multiple ways.

One such manifestation of the uneven capacity within the PNC is salary differences among ranks and their effects on personnel. The PNC's organizational structure is divided into three levels: basic, executive, and superior. Each level, in turn, consists of three ranks, from lowest to highest. The basic level consists of agents, corporals, and sergeants. The executive level consists of sub-inspectors, inspectors, and chief inspectors. The superior level is made up of sub-commissioners, commissioners, and commissioner generals. Depending on seniority, police agents – who represent over 80 percent of all PNC personnel – can earn between USD four hundred and six hundred

---

[31] International actors also played a role in the early stages of the PNC. The United Nations verification mission in El Salvador monitored the transition from the previous security apparatus to the establishment and initial operation of the PNC, and also provided the PNC with some training (Stanley 1999, 113–14).

a month.[32] And although the minimum salary in El Salvador is a little over USD three hundred (Ministerio de Trabajo y Provisión Social 2018), this is insufficient to cover even half of the basic monthly cost of living (Centro para la Defensa del Consumidor 2019). Basic-level personnel repeatedly demand higher salaries, particularly given their role on the frontlines of the state's fight against gangs.[33] Under the Ley de Carrera Policial (Police Career Law), police personnel in El Salvador should receive salary increases for every four years of active service. Yet, a recent survey of PNC personnel conducted by the Instituto de Derechos Humanos de la UCA (Institute for Human Rights, Iduhca) at the Central American University in San Salvador indicates that many police fail to receive regular salary increases.[34] A clear path for career advancement is fundamental for a professional and capable police organization (Bayley 2005). But a majority of surveyed police personnel believe that there are no opportunities for career advancement within the PNC (Iduhca 2019, 58). Police organizations are expected to provide all personnel with similar working conditions, from weapons and ammunition to areas for resting in police stations. But here, too, there are marked differences in the quality and access to such provisions across ranks, with agents largely left to their own devices.[35]

Evidence of the uneven effects of the PNC's low institutional capacity can also be found in analyses that the institution itself carries out. In 2015 the PNC organized eighty focus groups among twelve hundred police personnel across ranks and administrative positions as part a rare multiyear planning process. The results were sobering. Nearly 70 percent of focus groups identified the organization's failure to improve the well-being of police personnel as its key shortcoming (PNC 2015, 9–10). It is therefore not surprising that the survey by Iduhca found significant dissatisfaction among police personnel: nearly 47 percent of survey respondents indicated that they had little or no motivation to carry out their jobs.[36]

Another challenge for the PNC's capacity to impose order via the rule of law is the violence carried out by gangs targeting police agents. The 2012 truce collapsed amid public criticism over continued criminal extortion by gangs. In 2013 the country's Supreme Court concluded that President Funes's administration had

---

[32] In 2019 the PNC had 21,727 personnel, of which 17,953 were agents, 1,773 were corporals, and 1,089 were sergeants.

[33] Beatriz Calderón, "Policías Piden Mejor Salario, Seguridad y Buen Uso de Contribución Especial," *La Prensa Grafica*, October 27, 2017.

[34] The survey included over one thousand police personnel from across multiple ranks. It revealed that though 90 percent of respondents should have been earning more than the minimum agent's salary given their years of service, nearly 50 percent were still receiving the minimum salary (Iduhca 2019).

[35] Nearly 9 percent of the police personnel surveyed by the Iduhca acknowledge that there are differences in working conditions, specifically access to amenities within police stations, based on rank (Iduhca 2019, 59).

[36] In response to the survey question "How motivated are you by the police institution to carry out your job?" 54 percent of respondents answered that they were somewhat or very motivated. (Iduhca 2019).

broken the law by placing a military officer, David Munguía Payés, in charge of civilian policing. Munguía's replacement, Ricardo Perdomo, denied the existence of any truce, at which point both ARENA and the FMLN distanced themselves from the arrangement.[37] In the truce's aftermath, gangs targeted members of the PNC in retaliation for the ironfisted policies of former leftist-rebel-turned-president Salvador Sanchez Cerén (2014–18) of the FMLN (UNHRC 2018).

Gangs attacked police stations using machine guns and grenades (McNamara 2017, 11). While in 2013 a total of fourteen members of the PNC were killed in the entire country, in 2015 sixty-three members were killed. In 2019 an unspecified number of PNC agents and their families threatened by gangs actually fled the country and attempted to secure asylum in the United States.[38]

By 2016 the Office of the Attorney General for the Defense of Human Rights – the same government agency that collects and makes public allegations of human rights abuses by the police and other state agencies – called on the Ministry of Justice and Public Security to provide the PNC's agents with better protection in the face of selective targeting by gangs (PDDH 2019, 13, fn. 5). The Iduhca survey found that over 50 percent of the surveyed police personnel had received threats for doing their jobs.[39] These conditions have fueled a wave of resignations since 2010 – primarily among police agents on the frontlines of the government's hardline policies against gangs. Between 2010 and 2017, 1,641 PNC agents resigned.[40]

The victims of extortion in my field sites recognized the dual challenge the police faced of being responsible for maintaining order and the rule of law while lacking the capacity to do so. As Ricardo, a farmer in the canton in El Pilar, complained:

What good does it do for me to call the police and have a degenerate [*lacra*] arrested if they even have the balls to arrest him. He'll be out of jail in a week, and then what? Is the police going to stop him from killing me for reporting him? They can't just arrest him for threatening me.[41]

Another farmer in the canton in Cienfuegos tellingly referenced the lack of state support for the police and contrasted it with state's declarations about the need to uphold human rights and due process:

---

[37] "Perdomo se Desmarca de la Tregua de Pandillas," *Elsalvador.com*, May 29, 2013.

[38] Kevin Sieff, "It's So Dangerous to Police MS-13 in El Salvador that Officers are Fleeing the Country," *Washington Post*, March 4, 2019.

[39] It is unclear, based on the survey data, what percentage of the threats came from gangs. The survey question was, "Have you been the target of attempts or threats for doing your job in the police either while on or off duty?" (Iduhca 2019).

[40] As a point of comparison, sixty-one corporals, thirty-four sergeants, twelve sub-inspectors, ten inspectors, and two commissioners resigned during the same period of time. No sub-commissioners or chief Inspectors resigned during the same window. Data is from response to a freedom of information request that I submitted to the Unidad de Accesso a la Información Pública (Access to Public Information Unit) of the PNC.

[41] Interview with Ricardo (ESV12), farmer, El Pilar, June 2017.

The police are in a very difficult situation. They don't have the support to do their job. The state doesn't provide it. Why are they going to fight the criminals, arrest them and then become the targets of violence, if all they get is a miserable salary? Meanwhile people say that the state needs to respect the human rights of the gang members! What? What about *our* human rights?[42]

Interviews and a focus group that I conducted with PNC agents shed light on how they themselves experienced and understood their limited institutional capacity.

In El Pilar, one police agent that I interviewed became visibly upset when I asked whether they had the resources to do their job:

Look, the last time we got something from the government ... do you know what it was? They gave us two motorcycles—because up until then we only had one to share among all of us—and a microwave. Today if I were to take you to the [police] station you would see the motorcycles in pieces! Why? Because it doesn't help us if we get the motorcycles and don't have the resources to buy gas or replacement parts or tires. But the microwave ... that's still going strong, at least [agent laughs].[43]

Another agent lamented what their police station's state of disrepair communicated to citizens:

You go there and you see that the [police] station is dark and ugly ... for one who is a police officer, one doesn't even want to enter it, much less a common citizen who has a problem or was just robbed. Last year when I went to turn on the lights [in the police station] ... nothing. I tried a few times ... it wouldn't come on. What happened? The government hadn't been able to pay the electricity bill. It's very discouraging.[44]

In 2017 in the department of La Libertad, where El Pilar is located, twenty-one police stations were in danger of having their electricity shut off because the PNC could not pay its bills. Seven PNC stations were also scheduled to have their water shut off by the state-owned water and sewer agency for failure of payment.[45]

Four police agents from municipalities in the department of San Miguel, including Cienfuegos, expressed similar concerns during a focus group. The lack of material support from the government negatively impacted the agents' perceptions of themselves as a core part of the state:

---

[42] Interview with Marcos (ESV9092), farmer, Cienfuegos, October 2018.

[43] Interview with Police agent #1 (ESV001), El Pilar, June 2017. Indeed, nearly 50 percent of police personnel surveyed in the Iduhca study indicated that police transportation in their stations, from patrol cars to pickup trucks to small buses, is inoperable (Iduhca 2019, 73). The figures are similar for motorcycles.

[44] Interview with Police agent #2 (ESV303), El Pilar, June 2017.

[45] "21 Puestos Policiales de la Libertad no Tienen para Pagar Recibos de Agua y Luz," *El Salvador Times*, April 10, 2017.

Police agent #4: There are days when we get a call to go investigate something and we get on the motorcycle and see that it doesn't have any gas. Someone maybe took [the gas] or took the money to pay for gas and didn't do it. So what do you do? Because your superior isn't going to accept that you didn't do your job because the gas tank was empty. So maybe borrow your friend's car to either go investigate and then pay them back, or maybe go get gas that you pay for with your own money.[46]

Police agent #3: Our [station] is the worst, I tell you this in total honesty. It's a square building made with bricks that are falling apart. You've seen it, right? Who would want to work there . . . in a place that shows a lack of self-respect for the institution and for our jobs? No.[47]

The limited institutional capacity of the PNC and its disproportionate impact on the street-level agents most directly exposed to gangs, however, sit within a broader political context in which elements of the state encourage extrajudicial violence. National government officials do so when they loosen constraints on police actions vis-à-vis gangs in ways that blur the boundary between legal and extralegal. With the exception of the truce, national government administrations have adopted largely hardline policies toward gangs that increase police discretion in the arrest and use of violence (Bergmann 2019; Hume 2007; Savenije 2014). Policing has been oriented away from everyday problem-solving to instead carrying out the state's "war" against gangs. Such militarization of policing is associated with greater frequency of human rights abuses (Flores-Macías 2018; Flores-Macías and Zarkin 2019), particularly when the mechanisms to hold police accountable are already weak. For example, 2013 reforms to El Salvador's Code of Criminal Procedure allowed judicial authorities greater discretion to dismiss charges of excessive or extralegal use of force by state security personnel. In 2015 gangs were classified as "terrorist organizations" and "enemies of the state" under the Special Law Against Acts of Terrorism, which the attorney general justified in part because of gang attacks against the police in the wake of the truce's collapse (García-Pinzón and Rojas Espina 2020).[48] Between 2014 and 2019 the Attorney General's Office moved to dismiss over half of all cases of alleged excessive use of force or extrajudicial violence by security personnel (UN 2018, 7).

But as Daniel Brinks (2007) has shown, informal institutions also enable extrajudicial state violence.[49] Norms that reflect and sustain social inequalities perpetuate state violence when political and judicial authorities fail to punish extrajudicial actions. In El Salvador, governing authorities consider gangs to be existential threats to the state; this social construct, in turn, paves the way for

---

[46] Police agent #4 (SS_FG_02), focus group, San Miguel, June 2017.

[47] Police agent #3 (SS_FG_01), focus group, San Miguel, June 2017.

[48] The law significantly increased the potential jail time that convicted gang members could face for being part of a gang and/or committing a crime as a gang member.

[49] On informal institutions, see Helmke and Levitsky (2006) and Brinks, Levitsky, and Murillo (2019).

security sector actors to pursue measures that push against and exceed the rule of law. In 2019 a national legislator and leader in the Grand Alliance for National Unity (GANA) party was asked whether hardline tactics against gangs would lead to extralegal violence. The legislator responded by saying: "I care more about the life of a police agent than of a gang member [*marero*] . . . And if at a certain point in time a police agent has to defend themselves and kill a gang member, then it is not the first time that we are going to work to defend them so they can get out clean."[50] The director of the Academia Nacional de Seguridad Publica (National Academy for Public Security, ANSP), which is responsible for training all police personnel, declared during a speech for a graduating class of police agents in 2017 that police could use violence to take over the territories that gangs controlled because the:

full legitimacy of the state to preserve the police is in your hands. Do not led your hands tremble. There is no need to think that there are human rights involved, that there will be criticism from the press or international organizations: when the legitimacy of the State is disrespected, you have to make use of all tactics and everything you have learned.[51]

Jeanette Aguilar (2019, 70–71) argues that the common practice among politicians of calling gang members *ratas* (rats) and *lacras* (degenerates) on social media platforms when proposing hardline policy measures or celebrating the capture of alleged gang members fosters acceptance of extrajudicial violence. For example, politicians in both the legislative and executive branches have proposed removing the deaths of gang members from official homicide statistics. But even when police in El Salvador are arrested for extralegal violence the risk that they will be punished is low. Even in those cases that do go to trial, there are also informal practices that further favor the police such as the tendency of judges to allow police defendants to be free while on trial and to hold the trials in secret. By contrast, police often intimidate or violently punish witnesses and relatives of victims of extralegal violence, at times prompting them to migrate and thus bringing the trials to inconclusive ends (PDDH 2019, 85).

There are a number of different state security actors that combat gangs in El Salvador, including specialized squadrons within the PNC, such as anti-gang units (Escuadrones Anti-Pandilla) and police reaction groups (Grupos de Reacción Policial, or GRP), as well as joint forces between the PNC and the military, such as the special reaction forces (Fuerzas Especiales de Reacción, or FES).[52] Yet, in the majority of publicly known cases of extrajudicial violence by state actors against gangs, the perpetrators have been from the PNC, and most

---

[50] Walter Sibrián and Gabriel Campos Madrid, "Me Importa Mas la Vida de Un Policía Que la de Un Marero: Gallegos Pide Declarar Guerra a las Pandillas," *La Prensa Grafica*, July 15, 2019.

[51] "'Que no les tiemble la mano': Director de ANSP a Policías," *La Prensa Grafica*, May 6, 2017.

[52] The GRP was dissolved in 2018 after several of its members were found to have participated in the extralegal killing of several gang members and the sexual assaults and disappearance of a female police agent.

have been agents from the bottom of the basic-level ranks (PDDH 2019). Between 2014 and 2016 the number of alleged gang members killed by state security forces increased more than fourfold from 103 to 591 (UN 2018, 8).

This combination of atomized political economies characterized by no organizations to structure relations among farmers and between them and governing authorities coupled with autonomous yet low-capacity police living under constant threat of gang violence led farmers in my field sites to pursue piecemeal vigilantism to resist extortion and associated violence by gangs.

4.2.3   The Structure of Piecemeal Vigilantism

In 2011 or 2012 – different people who I interviewed provided different dates – a handful of small-scale farmers in the canton in Cienfuegos where I conducted research tried to mobilize collectively against criminal extortion. A family of local farmers consisting of a father and several relatives began openly encouraging other farmers to collectively stop paying the criminal taxes and confront the local members of MS-13. But the lack of a preexisting organization made it difficult to overcome denunciation in trying to mobilize collective resistance. One farmer who was approached to join the mobilization explained how the high potential for denunciation persuaded him to not support collective resistance:

They talked to me and tried to convince me and [family member] too. I thought about it. But my [family member] told me not to join them. [The family member] said, 'This is never going to work. We have to take care of ourselves and our families. Anything more than that and you are putting your life at risk . . . ' Because here you don't know who can be trusted, and who cannot. The silence is the law and the best protection. So I told them no . . . and it was the right decision.[53]

The family fled the municipality when the gang threatened to kill them. People in the canton believed that the family was denounced by someone they tried to enlist as part of their attempt at broad-based collective resistance.[54]

Interviews with farmers in the canton in El Pilar revealed that they also understood the lack of a preexisting organization as a barrier to mobilizing collective resistance to extortion:

Some [farmers] have been killed or forced to leave [the municipality] for not paying . . . or because they talked to someone about how we should all stop paying. Those are moments of carelessness. We are many, and they [the gang members] are few. But there is a lot of distrust among us . . . no one wants to work together because we have to work against each other. If not, you don't sell what your produce. People wake up, work their land, and go to bed—sometimes without saying anything to anyone else other than their family. That's why you never know who you're talking to.[55]

---

[53] Interview with Iván (ESV9213), farmer, Cienfuegos, October 2018.
[54] Field notes, Cienfuegos, October 2018.
[55] Interview with Felipe (ESV07851), farmer, El Pilar, June 2017.

The lack of preexisting organizations among farmers in the two cantons thus denied them the structured bonds of trust and familiarity needed to overcome fear of denunciation and pursue high-risk collective mobilization. This was particularly challenging given the widespread presence of gang *postes* (lookouts) in the cantons that monitored the local population and that kept the gangs informed of any incursions by outsiders. In that context farmers distrusted each other for fear that anyone could be an informant for the gang.

Thus instead of widespread collective mobilization given shared grievances, it was individuals from families living in the same part of the canton and even same households that instead began targeting the gang members who were extorting them. In the canton in El Pilar the "extermination group" was founded by two brothers, Antonio and Alfonso, who were farmers that grew grains, vegetables, and owned some livestock. The brothers enlisted two male relatives who tended their crops alongside them to join in violence against the gang. In the canton in Cienfuegos, two brothers who were bean and maize farmers, Rafael and Kevin, began an extermination group with three nearby male family members. In the absence of preexisting organizations, piecemeal vigilantism was initially a family affair consisting of sporadic acts of violence. This departs from the historical origins of death squads in El Salvador that drew on the existing military and police organizational structures working at the behest of government interests and which functioned more like pro-government militias.

But in both cases, the handfuls of farmers also incorporated individual police agents assigned to patrols in their canton and other parts of the municipalities.[56] The farmers followed a similar pattern in that they approached individual police agents with whom they had interacted in the past. In the canton in El Pilar, the wife of one of the farmers sold snacks on a road near their farm where police agents would sometimes stop during patrols.[57] Similarly in the canton in Cienfuegos, Rafael and Kevin enlisted police agents who carried out patrols in the area and who often tried to get local farmers to point out the gang members in the community.[58] Thus in both cases the initial connection between victims and police emerged from the efforts of police agents who lacked institutional capacity but nonetheless were attempting to gather information from populations that could help them enforce the rule of law.[59] Yet, as my interviews with police agents in these field sites and surrounding localities indicate, police were aware of both their lack of capacity and the low

---

[56] Field notes, El Pilar and Cienfuegos, June 2017.

[57] The operational territorial divisions of the PNC are: police headquarters (*delegaciones*), sub-departments (*sub-delegaciones*), and police stations (*puestos de policía*).

[58] Field notes, Cienfuegos, June 2017.

[59] This aligns with the argument by Smith (2019), who finds that extralegal responses to crime in South Africa can result from the state attempting to provide order while adhering to the rule of law, either by seeking to ensure due process or by extending the actual physical presence of the police across its territory.

likelihood that communities and victims would speak out publicly against the gangs given the threat of violent punishment. As one police agent noted during the focus group:

The problem today is that the police officer is operating like a fireman. We go once someone has been robbed, killed, assaulted. And we deal with the situation at that point. But we need to be there before that—to prevent the fire. And once we leave, the fire just starts again. Why do we operate this way? Because the people can't talk to us. They are afraid.[60]

Despite being limited to the individual level, farmers in the two cases recognized the benefit of having the police help them carry out extralegal violence against the gangs. As one farmer in the group in Cienfuegos noted to another in explaining why there was little chance that the killing of a gang member would be traced back to them: "we have the law [*nosotros tenemos la ley*]" – referring to the participation of the individual police agents.[61]

Over time the groups would extend beyond kin and individual police participants to include an assortment of individuals from both within the cantons where they first emerged and beyond, including in parts of neighboring municipalities. But without preexisting organizations to help recruit new members into the groups and manage their behaviors, new participants were instead incorporated through haphazard and unplanned processes. I detail these below as part of analyzing the trajectories of the two groups. I further show that this ad hoc expansion of the two groups was a response to the inherent inability of piecemeal vigilantism to satisfy the societal demand for order and to end criminal victimization.

4.2.4   The Practices of Piecemeal Vigilantism

Farmers and police shared resources to carry out piecemeal vigilantism. Victims provided police with information – a key tool for effective policing under "normal" settings (Bayley 2005). But here information was used to facilitate carrying out extralegal violence. For example, victims told police where gang members lived and hung out, provided cell phone pictures of them, and conveyed real-time data via text messages that enabled the police and victims to catch the gang members off guard and by themselves. The last action was particularly critical because in both localities the gangs had lookouts who monitored the cantons and broader municipalities for suspicious people or activities. Hence detailed information on where a gang member could be located at a given point in time reduced the potential for them to become aware that the groups of victims and police were descending upon them.

Victims also received information from the police as part of piecemeal vigilantism. This information was intended to help them avoid detection by

---

[60] Police agent #5 (SS_FG_01), focus group, San Miguel, June 2017.   [61] Case F, Cienfuegos.

other parts of the state. For example, police participants provided victims with information on whether and when other police from neighboring sub-headquarters or stations would be patrolling the areas where gang members were going to be killed. Sometimes victims in the groups reached out to police shortly before carrying out these violent acts to check whether and when police who were not part of the groups would be patrolling in the area. Highlighting the police's institutional fragmentation, individual police also provided information on the status of investigations by other police divisions into the murders that the groups had carried out in order to make them aware of potential state actions against them.[62] Taken together, the available evidence again indicates that police participation in piecemeal vigilantism was an individual-level, rather than an institutional, phenomenon.

Victims and police shared equipment to carry out piecemeal vigilantism, including weapons. This facilitated victims' participation even if they lacked their own firearms. Other times police or victims paid civilian participants to use their personal firearms to carry out targeted violence. For example, in one case a farmer in the group in El Pilar left the municipality on a trip for several weeks, but before doing so he authorized others in the group to use his vehicle and weapon to carry out a targeted killing if they needed it. Members of the group used both to kill a gang member who had murdered a local farmer for failing to pay the criminal tax. The participants in the killing, including one police agent, each gave a small amount of money to the owner of the vehicle and gun upon his return.[63]

Sometimes police agents would use farmers' personal weapons to minimize the likelihood that other state institutions would detect their activities. In Cienfuegos, for example, a police participant asked a farmer in the group to borrow their gun because he only had his service revolver. If he discharged his weapon he would theoretically be required to file a report with the PNC. And when the PNC fail to provide police agents with ammunition – an omission that police agents indicated to me was more common than not – they sometimes purchase it themselves.[64] Hence using a civilian firearm enabled police to avoid having to account for spent ammunition from their service revolvers.

Police also provided farmers with equipment, including PNC uniforms, boots, and masks. This clothing enabled farmers to travel freely and avoid questions when going to kill a gang member. Wearing uniforms also helped

---

[62] For example, in Cienfuegos, hours after members of the group killed a gang member in his house, one victim received a phone call from a police agent asking for confirmation of the type of vehicle they had used to travel to the gang member's house. It turned out that other police investigating the murder had been given some information about the vehicle by a witness. The police agent called back later, however, to inform the group that the license plates did not match and so the group was in the clear (Case P, Cienfuegos).

[63] Case Q, El Pilar.

[64] See "Policías Compran Munición de Salarios," *La Prensa Grafica*, September 5, 2017.

farmers gain access to their victims: they would wear the uniforms, knock on the doors of targeted gang members, and announce themselves as members of the PNC. Once the doors opened, the uniformed farmers would then assassinate the gang members. At times, police participants also helped farmers get rid of equipment used to murder gang members before they could be traced back to them. Police agents would take personal weapons that civilian members of the groups used to kill gang members and plant them on the bodies of other gang members killed during formal police operations. This initially led police investigators to assume that the murders carried out under piecemeal vigilantism were actually part of gang rivalries.[65]

Using these practices, both groups initially targeted gang members who were extorting them or their family members. The group in the canton in El Pilar attempted fifteen killings and "successfully" carried out twelve, while the group in the canton in Cienfuegos killed nine of its ten intended targets. In some instances the targets were relatives or intimate partners of gang members who were responsible for holding on to the criminal taxes before they were sent to higher-ups in the gang.[66] For example, participants in the group from the canton in Cienfuegos killed a person who had been in charge of holding the criminal taxes that their relative collected on behalf of the gang.[67] Yet, over time the groups expanded the targets of extralegal violence beyond the gang members extorting them. Nine out of the fifteen attempted killings by the group in El Pilar were for reasons other than extortion, while three of the ten people who the group in Cienfuegos attempted to kill were also for reasons other than extortion.

The targets of the groups' violent practices expanded to include gang members who they suspected were monitoring them in order to retaliate against piecemeal vigilantism.[68] That gang members were monitoring the victims illustrates one of the limitations of piecemeal vigilantism: its inability to end criminal rule given its ad hoc structure and sporadic nature. Under piecemeal vigilantism not all criminals are targeted at once to decisively end victimization. In turn, the groups become vulnerable to criminal retaliation. As I detail below, the result was a low-intensity conflict between victims and criminals that over time further contributed to localized dynamics of insecurity. The efforts of the two groups to end victimization via extralegal means transformed into preying on those they professed to defend. But the groups also began targeting civilians with no apparent ties to extortion or gangs. Below I explain why the trajectories of piecemeal vigilantism began to include the targeting of individuals other than criminals for extralegal violence.

---

[65] Cases M and E, El Pilar.

[66] The use of close family members as part of extortion became an increasingly common practice under their short time horizons as gangs were forced to evade state offensives and roundups.

[67] Case H, Cienfuegos.   [68] Case M, El Pilar and Case Q, Cienfuegos.

4.2.5 The Trajectory of Piecemeal Vigilantism

Over time, the inability of piecemeal vigilantism to end victimization can pressure its protagonists to scale up their coercive capacity and extralegal activities. This is evident in the cases of piecemeal vigilantism that I studied in El Salvador. In Cienfuegos, a few months after the group of farmers and police began engaging in the occasional acts of violence, gang members identified the local farmers that were participating in the acts of violence and retaliated. Community members indicated that these confrontations took place seemingly sporadically every few months with injuries and fatalities suffered on both sides.[69] Notes from interviews with residents in El Pilar that FGR personnel carried out and shared with me indicate that several unresolved murders in the municipality were believed to have been retaliation by the MS-13 against the group.[70]

In addition to the threat of criminal retaliation, another factor that influenced the trajectory of piecemeal vigilantism was the demand for order among other victims of extortion who did not participate directly in the group's extralegal practices. As word spread of the groups' activities against the gangs, other victims seeking to end their own extortion offered not to participate in the groups' activities, but instead to pay the groups in exchange for killing their criminal victimizers – sometimes for just a few hundred dollars. Judicial records indicate that in some instances the money to pay for these killings was knowingly provided via remittances from family members of victims who were living abroad.[71]

Despite this dual challenge, the groups' lack of preexisting organizations stymied their efforts to coordinate the level and structure of extralegal violence needed to satisfy the broader demand for ending victimization. Transcripts of wiretaps ordered by the FGR of cell phone conversations among both groups' members reveal that there were repeated last-minute phone calls during which farmers and police struggled to bring together enough people to carry out the targeted killing of gang members.[72] And the ability of the gangs to inflict severe costs on the groups by killing several of their members further escalated the need to scale coercive capacity by involving more individuals in the groups' activities. But without preexisting organizations, the recruitment of new participants was ad hoc.

By the time the attorney general's office announced the arrests of the groups' members, it identified nearly two dozen individuals as having participated at some point in each one's activities in different ways. Table 4.1 shows the participants in the groups based on judicial files and records at the time of their arrests.

As Table 4.1 shows, civilians made up the majority of participants from each of the two groups that emerged in cantons in El Pilar and Cienfuegos – 76 and

---

[69] Field notes, Cienfuegos, October 2018.   [70] Judicial files, El Pilar and FGR interview notes.
[71] Judicial files, El Pilar and Cienfuegos.   [72] Judicial files, El Pilar and Cienfuegos.

TABLE 4.1 *El Salvador: Participants in groups carrying out piecemeal vigilantism*

	Group in El Pilar	Group in Cienfuegos
Total participants (percentage of total number of participants)	25 (100%)	23 (100%)
Civilians	19 (76%)	15 (65%)
Police	6 (24%)	8 (35%)
Basic-level ranks (% of police participants)	6 (100%)	7 (88%)
Civilian participants' backgrounds (percentage of civilian participants)		
Small-scale farmer	11 (58%)	9 (60%)
Commerce	2 (11%)	4 (26%)
Transportation	1 (5%)	0 (0%)
Education	1 (5%)	1 (7%)
Manufacturing	1 (5%)	0 (0%)
Farm labor	1 (5%)	0 (0%)
Construction	2 (11%)	0 (0)%
Private security	0 (0%)	1 (7%)

Sources: Judicial files, El Pilar and Cienfuegos.

65 percent, respectively. In each group small-scale farmers made up approximately 60 percent of the civilian participants. All or the majority of police participants in the two groups were drawn from the basic ranks of the police, with agents making up 50 percent of police participants in each group. Only in the case of the group that operated in Cienfuegos was there a single participant beyond the basic level: a sub-inspector, which is the lowest rank within the executive level.

But without a preexisting organization to recruit trusted individuals, the farmers who founded the groups were forced to shift the burden of finding additional participants to whoever they could get a hold of at a moment's notice. In some cases participants simply brought along whoever happened to be with them at the moment they learned about a killing that the group was going to undertake.[73] Thus several months after emerging in the canton in Cienfuegos, people linked to the group were engaged in extralegal violence across several other parts of eastern El Salvador. Similarly, the group that

[73] Case J, Cienfuegos, and Case D, El Pilar.

began in the canton in El Pilar began carrying out extralegal violence in other parts of La Libertad and surrounding departments. But the groups achieved this increased territorial scope by recruiting individuals largely unfamiliar with the groups' original members.

This expansion had several implications for the trajectory of piecemeal vigilantism. It attracted individuals who wanted to leverage the group for personal gains rather than to end criminal victimization. In both groups individuals who joined them later in their existence coordinated with handfuls of other newly recruited members to carry out strings of house break-ins and robberies.[74] These individuals were known locally for having become part of the groups, and hence their activities became associated with the groups of victims and police who had emerged to resist gang extortion and violence.

Additionally, the FGR leveraged the tenuous ties between the groups' original founders and recent recruits by strategically targeting the latter to become informants on the groups' members and activities.[75] In the case in El Pilar this led to the group targeting one of its own participants: a police agent who participated in the group learned that another group participant – a farmer – was informing other police about the group's activities. The police agent told several participants in the group, who subsequently killed the farmer-turned-informant.[76] Indeed, the ad hoc growth of the groups fueled intra-group conflicts and power struggles as new participants with tenuous, if any, preexisting links to the groups' original founders sought to wrest control of the groups for their own purposes. For example, one transcript of a telephone conversation between Rafael, one of the two founders of the group that emerged in the canton in Cienfuegos, and a relative who was one of the group's first participants, reveals that several individuals from other municipalities in the department San Miguel who had joined the group later on were vying to take over the group. The judicial files for the group in El Pilar identify the emergence of similar internal rifts as the group grew beyond its handful of founders. These cleavages may have contributed to more violence: the transcripts of Rafael's conversation suggest that he planned to kill those individuals who were challenging his leadership of the group.[77]

More broadly, the availability of the groups as sources of coercive power in localities where the state did not enforce the rule of law made them attractive resources for those willing to pay to resolve conflicts unrelated to gangs and crime.[78] Community members in the municipalities turned to the groups to help resolve personal conflicts, such as between neighbors and even family members. As the judge who oversaw the trial of the group in Cienfuegos commented, "It's incredible. How this went from using violence to punish criminals—still

---

[74] Judicial files, El Pilar and Cienfuegos.   [75] Field notes, San Salvador, June 2017.
[76] Case L, El Pilar.   [77] Judicial files, El Pilar and Cienfuegos.
[78] Idler (2019) identifies similar dynamics in Colombia's borderlands.

a serious violation of the law—to using violence to deal with personal problems and family affairs."[79] Thus the groups' expanded use of extralegal violence to target non-gang members in return for financial remuneration marks a dramatic departure from the groups' beginnings, when their self-financed extralegal acts focused on the criminals who had victimized their members. But over time as the groups sought to expand their coercive capacity, they became known in their respective municipalities for having changed from groups who emerged to end extortion to ones that engaged in killings for hire. This change is evident in the interviews that FGR investigators conducted with community members, mainly other small-scale farmers, in both municipalities. As per one witness who lived in the canton where the group in Cienfuegos emerged: "This group emerged to kill gang members extorting in the area, but now they also kill people who are not gang members for money."[80]

Judicial records indicate that as word spread about both groups they also drew the attention of criminal actors other than gangs. These included criminal groups who smuggle people through Central America and Mexico into the United States as well as cattle thieves. These criminal actors also began offering the extermination groups in El Pilar and Cienfuegos money to eliminate their rivals and have police participants help provide protection for their illicit activities. Analysis of the judicial files show that the groups' founders considered working for criminal actors as a way to build up the groups' financial bases shortly before they were dismantled by judicial authorities.

4.3   CONCLUSION

Victims of criminal extortion in the cases that I analyzed in localities in parts of El Salvador and in Medellín in Colombia used different strategies of resistance. Consistent with the argument developed in Chapter 2, the atomized political economies in both cases meant that the nature of resistance was ad hoc and the practices were sporadic given the absence of organizations on which to build sustained and institutionalized resistance. But differences in how resistance unfolded across these cases also align with the logic of my argument.

In Medellín, informal vendors were restricted to individual-level practices given the collapse of their organization in the wake of state-led displacement. Criminal capture of the police further constrained vendors' mobilization because the police served as an extension of the criminal surveillance network in the informal market. An attempt to mobilize collectively under these conditioned ended with harsh and lethal punishment for one vendor as described in Section 3.3. Vendors thus pursued everyday resistance that contested individual dimensions of extortion, but did not end their victimization. By contrast, in El Salvador victims pursued piecemeal vigilantism that initially took the form of handfuls of victims and individual

---

[79] Interview with Judge #2 (ESV009), San Miguel, July 2019.   [80] Judicial files, Cienfuegos.

police agents jointly killing criminal victimizers. Individual-level police participation provided victims with information and equipment to carry out extralegal acts of violence. Police participants secured information and assistance from locals to target and eliminate members of the criminal structure that were targeting police for violence in the wake of the failed gang truce. Farmers obtained protection from individual police for their extralegal acts of piecemeal vigilantism. However, haphazard efforts by the groups' founders to scale up their coercive capacities – born out of their low capacity for sustained collective mobilization – led to their derailment.

The analysis in Part I of the book thus provides several core takeaways. First, whether the police are autonomous from or captured by criminal actors has dramatically distinct consequences for the nature of resistance that victims pursue. The capture of the police in the informal market meant that vendors essentially viewed the police as an extension of the criminal actor. This turns the very essence of public policing on its head: where instead of enforcing the rule of law for the public good, the police are beholden to criminal actors and facilitate criminal victimization. By contrast, in the cases in El Salvador, farmers being extorted were disillusioned by the failure of the police to enforce the rule of law not because of complicity with criminals but because they lacked the institutional capacity to do so. While this perception aligns with the broader literature on the importance of police in shaping the political beliefs of citizens, the fact that victims then turned to police for help in resisting extortion highlights new ways in which limited police institutional capacity can distort citizen–police relations in settings where police are being actively targeted by criminals as part of broader state–criminal conflict. Second, the analysis of the trajectory of piecemeal vigilantism underscores the need to disaggregate the state in theorizing responses to criminal victimization. This is evident first in the specific nature of police participation in piecemeal vigilantism at the level of individuals and not entire institutions. As described in this chapter, one of the most important resources that individual police who worked with victims to target gang members offered was protection from other parts of the state. The need to disaggregate the state is also evident in the analysis of the trajectory of piecemeal vigilantism in El Salvador (see Section 4.2). Here we saw how even in a context where political leaders relaxed formal constraints on police and invoked inflammatory political rhetoric that demonized and "othered" gang members, the office of the Attorney General nonetheless mobilized to punish those who engaged in acts of resistance that violated the rule of law, including police. It is telling that the Attorney General at the time, Douglas Meléndez, was also widely critiqued for launching several investigations into alleged acts of corruption by the country's political elites. The existence of this "pocket of efficiency" (Evans 1989, 577) in the constellation of El Salvador's criminal justice institutions coupled with the haphazard project of scaling-up that farmers undertook in response to the societal demand for order and growing punishment by gangs ultimately derailed piecemeal vigilantism.

While in the case of Medellín I was able to gather granular data on the histories of the case through interviews and focus groups with the victims, in El Salvador I had to rely more on judicial records. I combined this unique archival data with interviews in both localities in El Salvador, as well as with key actors in the judicial proceedings. Although the evidence in the cases of El Salvador shows that there were important changes in the nature of the groups themselves over time, it would be helpful if I had more evidence from the people who participated in the extermination groups. At the start of my fieldwork the groups' participants were not accessible for interviews given that they were in the sentencing phases of their trials. Shortly after they were convicted and jailed, President Nayib Bukele took office and instituted a lockdown on the country's prisons as part of a new crackdown on gangs. During my visits to several government buildings I found lawyers, prosecutors, and judges who thus expressed frustration that the lockdown prevented them, much less foreign researchers, from meeting with their clients. Nonetheless as part of my field observations I was able to discuss extortion in general terms with some local community members that helped me to develop a more textured understanding of the dynamics of extortion in these field sites.

Part III of the book continues with the task of theory-building by examining the processes that led victims of criminal extortion in Michoacán to pursue variants of collective vigilantism and the coproduction of order. Examining these cases is important because it demonstrates how contrasting political economies with differing types of relations among victims and between them and governing authorities can set victims on very different paths to resistance. As we shall see in Chapter 5, the pathway to and nature of piecemeal vigilantism contrasts sharply with that of collective vigilantism in the cases in Michoacán. Unlike in the cases in El Salvador, the victims of extortion in Michoacán counted on political economies that facilitated institutionalized collective resistance and also faced police captured by their criminal victimizers. These contrasting conditions led victims in Michoacán to pursue institutionalized and sustained extralegal violence as well as practices of informal justice, though variation in the nature of the political economies would translate into distinct variants of collective vigilantism across the cases in Mexico.

PART III

COLLECTIVE VIGILANTISM
AND THE COPRODUCTION OF ORDER

5

Collective Vigilantism

When I arrived at the place that Oswaldo had texted to me, I thought I was mistaken: it was a small house with a large sign advertising snacks and soft drinks for sale.[1] Oswaldo, however, was an avocado farmer and member of Tancítaro's self-defense group. But when I got out of my car, a woman wearing blue plastic gloves stepped out and asked, "You must be the researcher?" She invited me to wait inside until Oswaldo returned from his avocado fields. I sat in a red plastic chair and she went back to scraping frost out of a freezer. The temperature in the freezer had been set too low overnight. "But one has to learn from the challenges that one encounters in life," she said more to herself than to me. Once Oswaldo arrived, we sat in the courtyard of an abandoned house across the street to talk. The woman was his sister-in-law. Her husband, also an avocado producer, had been *levantado* [forcibly taken] by the Knights Templar and his dismembered body was left on their doorstep several weeks later. Why had the criminals done this? Oswaldo sighed: "He wasn't able to pay the criminal tax for several months . . . they warned him, but he drank a lot. They hit him a few times, but nothing. And then the criminals decided to make an example out of him."

The Knights Templar were renowned for extortion in the territories that they controlled. In La Unión, the DTO extorted the berry sector using similar practices, including threats, kidnappings for ransom, disappearances, and sexual violence. Ramon was a berry producer in La Unión who fell behind on his payment of the criminal tax because he used the money to buy expensive medications that his daughter required for a medical condition:

[The criminals] told me it was okay. That I could make it up the next time. I believed them because what else could I do? But the next day they took her [referring to his daughter]. They returned her a week later. There are things she

[1] Interview with Oswaldo (MCN5813), avocado producer, Tancítaro, July 2018.

doesn't tell me about—she only tells her mother, not me. I paid them after that. Paying the same trash that did that to my daughter ... I don't know how I did it.[2]

Victims in both Tancítaro and La Unión ultimately resisted extortion through sustained extralegal violence and the related collective practices that constitute *collective vigilantism*. But the processes and mechanisms through which collective vigilantism emerged and, in turn, its structure, practices, and sustainability varied across the cases.

Tancítaro's avocado sector pursued centralized collective vigilantism. A single organization coordinated victims' extralegal violent activities, kept intra-group cleavages from undermining collective mobilization, and used the group's pooled financial assets to sustain their efforts against the DTO. The avocado sector and local political authorities cooperated as part of this mobilization. Victims took steps to protect the mayor from both violent reprisals by criminals and punishment by higher levels of government for the extralegal violence. In return, the mayor deflected demands by federal and state authorities that victims disarm and disband. Centralized collective vigilantism in Tancítaro ended criminal extortion.

By contrast, collective vigilantism in La Unión was decentralized. Berry producers divided into several armed groups that varied in size, coercive capacity, and leadership structure. These groups did not coordinate with each other; instead, they violently competed against each other for money and control of territory and authority. In contrast to collective vigilantism in Tancítaro, relations between victims and local governing authorities were conflictive. Though collective mobilization in La Unión ousted the Knights Templar, its decentralized nature made victims vulnerable to the interventions of both state and rival criminal actors, which ultimately led to the imposition of informal rule by another criminal organization.

How can we explain this variation? In this chapter, I use the framework developed in Chapter 2 to trace the contrasting processes and mechanisms that led to different types of collective vigilantism in these cases. Centralized collective vigilantism in Tancítaro resulted from the avocado sector's encompassing political economy that entailed strong links among victims on the one hand and between them and local governing authorities on the other hand. By contrast, decentralized collective vigilantism in La Unión can be traced back to the berry sector's segmented political economy characterized by cleavages among victims and weak ties between them and local governing authorities.

5.1 CRIMINAL ORGANIZATIONS, DRUG WARS, AND EXTORTION IN MICHOACÁN

Illicit drugs markets are not new to Michoacán. During the nineteenth century, local elites and family clans grew marijuana and smuggled it using the state's

---

[2] Interview with Ramon (MCN959), berry producer, La Unión, July 2018.

MAP 5.1 Michoacán, Mexico

remote rural roads and trails as well as its Pacific coastline as shown in Map 5.1 (Maldonado 2013, 49). In the twentieth century, state efforts to foster economic development inadvertently drew the region more firmly into the global drug trade when it developed Michoacán's agricultural sector as part of a broader agrarian reform project. The state subsidized road and highway construction, redistributed land, offered credit to farmers, expanded irrigation, and built the Lázaro Cárdenas Pacific seaport (Maldonado 2012, 11; Malkin 2001, 104–06). Statism catalyzed agricultural economies that would later become the targets of criminal extortion, but also provided transport infrastructure that traffickers would use to move illicit drugs abroad. The 1982 Mexican debt crisis led to a decline in state support for the agricultural sector. Agricultural producers began growing marijuana as well as poppy alongside licit crops (Barragán 1997, 186–87). Yet, agricultural producers characterized the criminal intermediaries who bought their illicit crops during this time as relatively benign compared to their more organized and violent successors.

In the late 1980s and into the 1990s, the Milenio DTO run by the Valencia family controlled the drug trade in Michoacán and neighboring Jalisco. The Valencias mainly sold marijuana and poppy to traffickers. In the 1990s, however, the crackdown on Caribbean trafficking routes from Colombia to the United States displaced cocaine flows into Mexico (Bagley 2012). The Milenio DTO started transporting cocaine through Michoacán and later aligned with the larger Sinaloa DTO. Drug markets soon included methamphetamines produced using precursor chemicals that arrived in Michoacán's Pacific seaport (Grayson

2011, 66–67).[3] The arrest and death of several of the Milenio DTO's leaders in the early 2000s weakened the organization and sparked a turf war with the Gulf Cartel and its fearsome private militia, the Zetas, which was made up of former Mexican military personnel and special forces (Correa-Cabrera 2017; Trejo and Ley 2020, 125–26).

The Zetas ultimately displaced the Milenio DTO, but its reliance on extreme forms of violence to maintain control prompted the emergence of La Familia Michoacana, which, in 2006, threw several severed heads onto a nightclub dance floor in the municipality of Uruapan along with a sign that read: "The Familia does not kill for money. It does not kill women. It does not kill innocents. Only those who deserve it will die. Everyone will know this: justice is divine."[4] The Familia Michoacana was also involved in the production and trafficking of illicit drugs, though, as noted in Chapter 3, it initially provided protection for producers and exporters in agricultural sectors who had long complained about the state's failure to do so.

While Mexico's war on drugs is often ascribed to President Felipe Calderón (2006–12) of the National Action Party, or PAN, the Mexican federal government had carried out counter-narcotics operations since the mid-1980s. In 1985, for example, President Miguel de la Madrid (1982–88, Institutional Revolutionary Party, or PRI) ordered the arrest of the leaders of the Guadalajara DTO after it killed a US DEA agent. President Vicente Fox (2000–06, PAN) deployed the military to eradicate drug crops and pursue drug traffickers (Astorga and Shirk 2010, 2–3, 17). But President Calderón escalated Mexico's drug wars after winning the presidency with a razor-thin margin against Andrés Manuel López Obrador, who campaigned for the Partido de la Revolución Democrática (Party of the Democratic Revolution, or PRD).[5] Shortly after the elections, Calderón declared organized crime and the drug trade as the principal threats facing the country. He launched "Operation Michoacán" that sent seven thousand federal police and military forces to Michoacán to intercept drug shipments, destroy drug crops, and arrest narcotraffickers.[6] This was the first of several military operations to take place in Michoacán as well as other parts of the country over the next several years.

---

[3] Michoacán has among the highest crystal meth production levels in the world. See "Mexican Meth Production Concentrated in 3 Western States," *InSight Crime*, November 6, 2012.

[4] Leovigildo González, "Sol y Sombra, Ahí Apareció por Primera Vez La Familia Michoacana," *Quadratín Agency*, August 2, 2014. See Ríos and Phillips (2017) on the logic behind DTOs' use of banners. Note that for a brief period in 2005, the La Familia and the Zetas actually collaborated before relations broke down.

[5] Calderón's margin of victory over Andrés Manuel López Obrador was 0.58 percent of the total 41.5 million votes cast, or 233,831 votes.

[6] Presidencia de la República de México, "Anuncio sobre la Operación Conjunta Michoacán," press release, December 11, 2006.

State confrontation fueled DTO fragmentation.[7] In 2010 reports of the death of the leader of the Familia Michoacana, Nazario Morena González ("El Chayo"), unleashed an internal power struggle, out of which emerged the Knights Templar. The Knights Templar, however, soon faced two pressures: state confrontation under the administration of President Enrique Peña Nieto (2012–18, PRI) who launched the first large-scale military operations of his administration against the DTO, and criminal competition from the Jalisco Cartel New Generation (CJNG), whose leaders were former members of the Milenio DTO (Beittel 2015, 26–28).[8] In response to state confrontation and criminal competition, the dynamics of local extortion in my field sites became more predatory.

5.1.1   Shifting Dynamics of Extortion

To understand how extortion of the avocado and berry sectors worked on an everyday basis, we first need to understand who are the key actors in the commodity chains and how they connect to each other. The commodity chain begins with growers, commonly called *productores* (producers). Producers plant, maintain, and harvest crops. Next are the *empacadoras* (packing houses). The packing houses sort and clean the produce before storing them in climate-controlled facilities. Avocados are stored in cardboard boxes and berries in plastic containers called clamshells. From here, both products are transported abroad. The majority of avocados and berries from Michoacán that are consumed in the United States are transported by land via trucks to US-Mexico border cities, mainly in Texas. Exports to Europe and Asia are sent via both ships and cargo planes. The packing houses either work with international brokers and traders or, alternatively, some have in-house sales and distribution capacities. The latter is standard in the berry sector, in which the packing houses are responsible for transporting and selling the product abroad and hence are also referred to as *comercializadoras* (marketers). Where the two are separate actors, as is more common in the avocado sector, the brokers are often based in the same countries as the wholesalers that then sell the produce to retailers and supermarkets.

Other actors that keep the commodity chain moving along include nurseries that provide producers with plants, vendors who sell fertilizer and farming equipment, the *jornaleros* (laborers) who either pick and prepare the produce in the fields or work in the packing houses, and the drivers of the trucks that transport produce within and out of the municipalities. But the producers and packing houses are the main actors in both sectors in the localities where I conducted field work.

---

[7] On how the breakdown of the PRI's decades-long grip on power starting with the gubernatorial elections of Baja California in 1989 prompted organizational change in DTOs and criminal turf wars, see Trejo and Ley (2020, chapter 2).

[8] "Jalisco Cartel New Generation (CJNG)," *InSight Crime*, March 30, 2018.

Aligning with my argument, the Knights Templar initially taxed the two sectors in different ways due to the sectors' contrasting political economies. As I discuss below, Tancítaro's avocado sector counted on a single core organization that kept detailed records of the sector's activities, including information on the assets and productivity of the individual producers and packing houses, necessary to satisfy export requirements established by the US government. But it was precisely this critical feature of the avocado sector's encompassing political economy that led the Knights Templar to force individuals within the core organization to hand over this information so that the DTO could more precisely collect criminal taxes in the orchards, factory floors, and checkpoints on roads leading in and out of the municipality. Avocado producers in Tancítaro initially paid MXN 1,000 annually for every hectare of land they owned, and packing houses paid a tax for every carton of avocados that left their facilities.[9]

By contrast, the segmented nature of the berry sector's political economy in La Unión meant that the DTO lacked a single source for disaggregated data to refine its initial approach to criminal taxation. Criminals thus initially taxed the largest and most visible actor: the berry packing houses. Criminals charged MXN 1 for every box of berries processed for export – a significant sum considering that Michoacán sends several million boxes of berries abroad each year. But the DTO's approach to taxation in La Unión had downstream effects for actors further down the commodity chain. Packing houses deducted the informal taxes that they paid to criminals from their payments to the berry producers who contracted with them as well as the transport companies, both of whom then passed on the additional costs to their respective labor forces.[10]

Under long time horizons, criminals thus customized extortion given contrasting political economies. When state crackdowns and criminal competition shortened those time horizons, the DTOs then harmonized their taxing strategies across the two sectors. In La Unión, the DTO expanded the population it directly targeted to include individual berry producers, laborers, and truck drivers. Likewise in both localities, the levels and frequency of criminal taxation increased. In Tancítaro, the criminal tax that avocado producers paid increased from MXN 1,000 to 2,000 per hectare. Nurseries that prepared avocado plants were charged for every plant they sold, but individual producers also had to start paying MXN 1– 3 for every plant they bought from the nurseries.[11] Likewise the DTO interfered in harvesting and sales processes by forcing producers to sign over their lands to members of the criminal group, who then threatened other producers to delay or completely abandon harvesting so as to both

---

[9] Field notes, Tancítaro, July 2018.   [10] Field notes, La Unión, August 2018.
[11] Based on the 2013 exchange rate, MXN 1 equaled USD .07.

generate upward pressure on prices and secure optimal windfalls for the harvests on the lands that they now owned.[12]

But the shortened time horizon of the Knights Templar also changed the social and political dynamics of extortion, as two berry producers explained:

Edson: The first time [the criminals] came for the *cuota*, they asked me in a nice way. They said it was to provide protection, and told me that if I needed anything I could count on them. Those fuckers even shook my hand and wished me luck! They told this to everyone. But later, they became ugly. Very rude. They would insult and threaten me if I didn't move fast enough to give them their money, insult my wife, my mother ... whatever they had to do to get the *cuota* in their hands— do you understand me?[13]

Uriel: It's because they were getting desperate. That's why. They saw that the situation was getting really fucked, now that they had more enemies than friends and their time was ending.[14]

Under their short time horizons, criminals also began violating social norms regarding the treatment of women, including threats and use of sexual violence:

The first time they asked for the new *cuota* [referring to the increased tax], they told me: 'If at some point you don't pay what you're supposed to, it's ok. Don't worry, because we can collect it from your wife.'[15]

Criminals also strategically flaunted the capture of the municipal police in both localities by forcing them to help carry out extortion in ways that fused criminal and state authorities and distorted both in the process. Municipal police "arrested" citizens for failing to pay the criminal tax, placed them in the back of police cars, and drove them to the outskirts of the municipalities where they were handed over to the DTO for punishment. One community member in La Unión described how seeing this affected his perception of the police:

Before this, you could almost forgive the police—they were scared, threatened by people who obviously had power over them [referring to the criminal groups]. But then when you saw these things, when they began to be the ones collecting people to charge them the *cuota*, it was that the police were part of the *maña* [criminal group] and things had gotten to a point where they didn't care who knew because they no longer hid it.[16]

Others indicated that seeing the police carry out the tasks normally undertaken by the criminal groups made them question the value of their citizenship:

---

[12] Field notes, Tancítaro, August 2018; La Unión, July 2018. For an analysis of similar strategies in the lime sector in Michoacán, see Omar García-Ponce and Andrés Lajous, "How Does a Drug Cartel Become a Lime Cartel?" *Washington Post*, May 20, 2014.

[13] Edson (FG_MCN27), berry producer, focus group, La Unión, August 2018.

[14] Uriel (FG_MCN71), berry producer, focus group, La Unión, August 2018.

[15] Paolo (FG_MCN9), berry producer, focus group, La Unión, August 2018.

[16] Interview with Jesús (MCN14835), community member, La Unión, September 2018.

What does this say about the rule of law? What does it say about the state's responsibilities, about whether it fulfills them? That there was no rule of law and that in that moment we didn't matter at all to the government [*al gobierno le valiamos madre*].[17]

A berry producer whose son was taken by the police until the producer turned over a late extortion payment described how that experience affected his relationship to the state:

Do you know what that is like? You don't see that in your country [*Eso no se ve en su país*]. To see that the police, whose salary you are paying, comes to do the work of the criminals, drives your son away in the car that you paid for and puts them in a cell that you also paid for. But the only crime committed was that I didn't have enough to pay [the criminal tax] that month—something that should have been an embarrassment to the government. What did that tell us? That we were alone, without a government to help.[18]

The nature of relations between agricultural sectors and criminals in my field sites thus shifted as the latter's time horizon grew shorter. But, although victims began mobilizing to resist extortion, collective vigilantism unfolded in distinct ways across the two cases.

5.2 VARIETIES OF COLLECTIVE VIGILANTISM

This section traces the contrasting processes and mechanisms that yielded centralized and decentralized collective vigilantism in Tancítaro and La Unión. I argue that faced with both criminal actors with short time horizons and criminal capture of the police, the contrasting nature of the political economies helps explain this variation.

5.2.1 Criminal Capture of Municipal Police Forces

The war on drugs in Mexico cuts across jurisdictions despite being a federal policy. Technically the federal government and its security apparatus, namely, federal police and the armed forces, are responsible for combating organized crime and the illegal drug trade. But in reality, the responsibility is distributed across distinct levels of government. Because organized crime is a territorially grounded phenomenon at the subnational level (Trejo and Ley 2020), it is municipal forces who are most exposed to DTOs on an everyday basis. Yet, these are precisely the parts of the security apparatus in Mexico that have the most limited institutional capacities, characterized by scarce financial resources, inadequate training, and outdated and ineffective equipment (Sabet 2012).

Limited police capacity, when faced with the coercive power of DTOs, can facilitate criminal capture. This is particularly the case in a context such as Mexico where there is a long history of collusion between security institutions

---

[17] Interview with Ramon (MCN959), berry producer, La Unión, July 2018.
[18] Interview with Félix (MCN2), berry producer, La Unión, August 2018.

TABLE 5.1 *Mexico: Perceptions of municipal police corruption among business firms and the general population (2012–18)*

	Mexico		Michoacán	
Year	Business firms	General population	Business firms	General population
2012	70.1	71.3	71.6	73.9
2014	66.2	66.3	75.7	65.1
2016	68.4	66.7	71.4	56.6
2018	69.0	69.1	72.4	66.2

Sources: Data from Encuesta Nacional de Victimización de Empresas (National Survey on Business Victimization, 2012–18) and the Encuesta Nacional de Victimización y Percepción sobre Seguridad Pública (Nacional Survey on Victimization and Perceptions of Public Security, 2012–19).

and drug traffickers (Astorga 1995). Sizable portions of both business firms and citizens perceive the municipal police to be among the most corrupt government institutions in Mexico, as shown in Table 5.1. While the percentages across these two populations are largely equivalent at the national level, there is a noticeable gap between the two in Michoacán. Table 5.1 shows that as of 2014, perceptions of corruption were substantially higher in Michoacán among business firms relative to the general population. The survey data does not enable us to establish the reason behind this difference, but it could reflect the presence of competing criminal organizations in Michoacán that were capturing and using municipal police forces to extort business firms.

Over time, municipal police became more deeply involved in the mechanics of extortion, collecting both victims and money to turn over to criminals. Stories of victims, who reported extortion to police only to receive threatening phone calls from the DTO minutes later warning them to keep quiet, were common in both localities.[19] The police thus represented an active threat to victims' resistance if they were to find out about it, which prompted victims to instead leverage the structures they used to coordinate everyday market activities to resist extortion.

5.2.2 An Encompassing Political Economy in Tancítaro's Avocado Sector

While Michoacán became the primary supplier of avocados to the United States and several other foreign markets in the late twentieth century, avocados had been grown in the region since the mid-twentieth century (Gallardo et al. 1987). However, producers faced a 1914 US ban on the import of Mexican avocados. The ban was intended to prevent pest infestation, but California avocado

---

[19] Field notes, Tancítaro, August 2018 and La Unión, September, 2018.

growers also supported it as a way to fend off foreign competition (Paz-Vega 1986). The North American Free Trade Agreement (NAFTA), however, required that signatory states harmonize sanitary and phytosanitary (SPS) measures to facilitate cross-border trade.[20] Michoacán's avocado sector could access the US market as long as it met SPS requirements enforced by the Animal and Plant Health Inspection Service (APHIS), a division of the United States Department of Agriculture (USDA). This set the stage for intense organization building between the Mexican state and avocado sector (Stanford 1998; 2002).

Between 1992 and 1994, Mexico's Dirección General de Sanidad Vegetal (National Plant Health Directorate, or DGSV) worked with avocado producers and packing houses to implement pest surveys that adhered to USDA-approved scientific protocols. To gain ground-level information from the avocado sector, however, federal and state authorities needed municipal-level data. Hence they established Plant Health Boards (Juntas Locales de Sanidad Vegetal, or JLSVs) that oversaw production, harvesting, and certification processes in avocado-growing municipalities. In 1997, avocados from Michoacán were allowed to be imported into nineteen northeastern US states. But to this day, local avocado sectors must continuously monitor and certify local production and export processes in coordination with APHIS officials based in Michoacán. This means that the capacity of the JLSVs to effectively coordinate sectoral actors within their municipalities is critical for keeping collective access to lucrative foreign markets, particularly given the potential for cross-contamination of pests among orchards.[21] All municipal avocado producers that supply packing houses with avocados for export must be members of their local JLSV, endowing the organization with a high degree of membership density.

The JLSV in Tancítaro also had a robust hierarchical decision-making structure that was led by a president, a secretary, and a treasurer. Beneath them was a committee made up of representatives from each of the communities in the municipality that conveyed information from the organization to the producers. The organization also oversaw a team of agronomists and technicians who assessed local production and exports. The JLSV received some funding from the federal and state governments, but its primary revenue source was dues that individual members paid for every hectare of land that they used for avocado production. In 2013, for example,

---

[20] SPS measures are defined as "mandatory technical requirements adopted by nations to protect the health and lives of humans, animals, and plants from risks associated with disease, pests, and contamination of foodstuffs, and to prevent damage caused by the establishment or spread of pests. Sanitary measures relate to human or animal health, whereas phytosanitary measures relate to plant health" (Waite and Gascoine 2013, 2–3). NAFTA was renegotiated in 2018 and became the United States Mexico Canada Agreement.

[21] Even producers who sell exclusively to domestic markets still have to join and are subject to the same inspections to encourage uniform application of SPS protocols so as to avoid cross-contamination (Stanford 2002, 304).

nearly three-quarters of the JLSV's budget came directly from individual membership dues (Tancítaro JLSV Annual Report, 2013).

This high level of organizational capacity was accompanied by strong ties to local governing authorities. Organizational cohesion is a key component of the "instrumental" power that economic actors use to influence politics in ways that favor their interests (Doner and Schneider 2000; Fairfield 2015; Lindbloom 1977; Schneider 2008; Vogel 2003). For the avocado sector, sustaining ties with and influence within municipal governments ensured that local authorities protected the sector's interests. In Tancítaro, the JLSV's leaders regularly worked with municipal authorities to collectively lobby agencies and authorities at the state and federal levels for financial resources to develop and maintain local infrastructure necessary for the avocado sector. The power of the JLSV also extended into electoral politics, with several members having held a variety of local elected and appointed positions, including the municipal presidency and posts in the municipal cabinets.[22] It bears noting that this overlap between private and public sectors cut across partisan lines: JLSV leaders from both the PAN and the PRD were members of local government at different points in time. This overlap was also structural, in so far as community-level representatives that linked individual communities with the JLSV were often simultaneously working for the municipal government as *Encargados del Orden* (Keepers of Order) – community-level elected positions in Michoacán in charge of maintaining local order, directing residents to local government services, and otherwise serving as a link between municipal government and the communities within them. The economic spillover generated by the avocado sector also benefited local government insofar as it flowed into local service, transport, and retail sectors. Thus local government and the avocado sector in Tancítaro exhibited strong ties under the encompassing political economy.

The encompassing political economy in Tancítaro does not mean that the avocado sector was free of cleavages. I identified two overlapping cleavages during my field research: socioeconomic and partisan. The first was evident in tensions between small- and large-scale avocado producers. The average avocado producer in Tancítaro owned approximately five hectares of land, while large-scale producers could own several dozen hectares or more. Moreover, some of the largest producers also owned the local packing houses. A perennial source of tension was the demand from small-scale producers that the packing houses pay higher prices for their avocados. Packing house–owners, in turn, claimed that fluctuations in what they paid reflected fluid market conditions. Despite this cleavage, however, both large- and small-scale producers largely worked through the JLSV to resolve intra-sectoral grievances that took various forms, from heated

---

[22] One of the most notorious acts of violence by the Knights Templar took place in 2012 when it set on fire one of the packing houses in Tancítaro in retaliation for the owner's failure to pay the criminal tax. In addition to owning the packing house, the owner had also been the municipal mayor in the late 1990s.

arguments during official meetings to temporary work stoppages as a tactic to pressure packing houses to pay higher rates for avocados. As one small-scale producer told me:

Our meetings in the *Junta* [JLSV] can sometimes be very tense, with very strong disagreements. But everyone knows that that's what the *Junta* is for. All of us created the *Junta* ... before avocados were a way to live. No matter the size [of the producer] ... our livelihoods would be at risk if we didn't maintain the *Junta*. We didn't work so hard to see it fall apart.[23]

The class cleavage overlapped with the partisan cleavage. Wealthier producers tended to support the right-of-center PAN while small-scale producers largely aligned with the left-of-center PRD. This partisan cleavage stemmed from the broader history of the rise of *Cardenismo* in Michoacán. In 1988, Cuauhtémoc Cárdenas, son of famed President Lázaro Cárdenas (1934–40), lost what was widely seen as fraudulent presidential elections while representing the left-wing Frente Nacional Democrático (National Democratic Front, or FDN), the predecessor to the PRD. This electoral debacle set in motion intense political conflict in Michoacán, particularly during the 1989 municipal elections that were bitterly fought between the PRD and the PRI and which involved political violence (Calderón 1994).

Yet, along with the class cleavage, partisan differences within the avocado sector were relegated to the background during mobilization to resist criminal extortion. To be clear, the cleavages did not vanish. They instead temporarily receded to the background as the need *and* organizational means for centralized coordination of collective vigilantism came to the foreground. As I show in Chapter 6, once security conditions eased somewhat, these cleavages would once again rise to the surface in ways that affected the sector's efforts to sustain order.

5.2.3 A Segmented Political Economy in La Unión's Berry Sector

Michoacán's berry sector, which is spread across twenty-one municipalities, accounts for 95 percent of the country's berry production, the majority of which is exported to the United States.[24] But unlike the avocado sector's encompassing political economy, the berry sector in La Unión is segmented with vertical and horizontal cleavages among actors in the commodity chain on the one hand, and weak ties between the sector and local governing authorities on the other hand.

Whereas NAFTA provided a focal point for collective mobilization and organization building in the avocado sector, it had the opposite effect in La

---

[23] Interview with Amelio (MCN1200), avocado producer, Tancítaro, July 2018.

[24] See "Mexico: Michoacán, Leader in Blackberry Production," *FreshPlaza.com*, August 31, 2018, and "New berry fever in Michoacán, Jalisco, and Baja California," *FreshPlaza.com*, April 6, 2016. Berries are the third-most exported commodity from Mexico behind beer and avocados (González-Ramírez et al. 2020, 4).

Unión. Much of Michoacán's berry-growing zone originally produced sugarcane in the twentieth century with support from the federal government (Chollett 2009). Yet, following NAFTA, the US sugar industry transitioned its overproduction of corn into high-fructose corn syrup that Mexico imported while exports of Mexican corn declined as global prices dropped. Local cane producers in La Unión thus pinned their hopes on new crops: berries. But the architects of the berry market were multinational corporations (MNCs) rather than local producers working with government authorities.

As NAFTA was being finalized, several berry sector MNCs from Chile and the United States opened facilities in parts of Michoacán, including La Unión. The MNCs were attracted by propitious local growing conditions, including temperate weather, geographic proximity to the United States, and the ability to grow blackberries nearly year-round to satisfy foreign consumer demand during winters. But unlike avocados, blackberries have a very limited shelf life, must be refrigerated immediately after harvesting and throughout the export process, and are susceptible to damage given their high water content. Berries from Michoacán are thus normally transported to the US border less than forty-eight hours after being picked in the fields (González-Ramírez et al. 2020). These technical complexities had political ramifications because satisfying them required localized sectoral coordination by vertically integrated export firms with the capacity to swiftly and efficiently package and transport the fragile commodity. The MNCs that arrived in Michoacán thus each had their own research, packaging, storage, export, sales, and international distribution capacities under one roof. The MNCs configured the local berry market in ways that outsourced risk to producers while precluding collective mobilization among them.[25]

Berry exporters own little land for the purpose of production and instead rely predominantly on contract farming.[26] Each season local producers who rent or own farmland commit to growing set amounts of berries for individual export firms at predetermined prices. The exporters, in turn, provide individual producers with their trademarked and genetically modified berry varieties as well as loans and lines of credit – often with high interest rates – for production expenses, requiring landowners to put up their land assets as collateral.

Export firms charge producers for packaging their berries in clamshells directly in the fields and transporting them in refrigerated trucks to climate-controlled storage facilities.[27] The export firms can reject berries that do not meet export standards, and they may withhold payments until the products are successfully delivered and accepted at their foreign destinations. The export

[25] On the historical political economy of Michoacán's export berry sector, see Feder (1977).
[26] Some export firms own small amounts of land that they use as nurseries to experiment with different varieties of berries.
[27] These charges range from 10 to 20 percent of the final payments. Telephone interview, berry export firm representative (LU319), Guadalajara, May 2019.

firms thus exert what Gereffi, Humphrey, and Sturgeon (2005) term "captive governance" of the commodity chain, which is marked by a strategically sustained asymmetry in market power among actors.[28]

Sectoral segmentation extends into cleavages between individual export firms, who have few incentives to coordinate collectively given intense rivalry and fierce protection of proprietary berry varieties. In 2010, berry export firms across Mexico established the Asociación Nacional de Exportadoras de Berries (National Associations of Berry Exporters, or Aneberries), which focuses much of its work on marketing berries to foreign consumers. But as several representatives of the export firms who are also members of Aneberries indicated, their fierce competition does not allow for *local-level* cooperation.[29]

In addition to the divisions between producers and exporters, among the latter there was also a cleavage between producers of different sizes, specifically the handful of large-scale berry producers who owned and rented considerable amounts of land and the majority small-scale producers who worked on their own small plots of land or rented them out. The strong production capabilities of the large-scale producers enabled them to secure better prices from the export firms. But small-scale producers were also segmented. Several small-scale berry producers made individual attempts to establish municipal-wide associations that would encompass small producers. These efforts, however, consistently failed as variation in the pricing among export firms incentivized competition between small groups of producers that reduced incentives for coordinating with each other.[30]

Within La Unión, this segmentation manifested in multiple and competing associations of berry producers. Some associations represented producers located in different parts of the municipality. Both large and small producers had their own individual associational organizations. Another cleavage developed between producers who either owned or rented land. The 1917 Mexican Constitution established ejidos to offer individuals and small groups usufruct rights under which they could use land and profit from production processes without having individual private ownership. Between 1930 and the late 1970s, the federal government transferred half of the country's land base to the ejido sector (Perramond 2008, 356–58). In 1992 modifications to Article 27 of the Mexican Constitution – which established the ejido system – allowed individual ejidatarios to obtain land titles and subsequently sell, rent, or sharecrop their land – attracting both domestic and foreign investment. Today, many large berry producers own or rent ejido lands, while smaller

---

[28] Gereffi, Humphrey, and Strugeon (2005, 84) define captive governance as a situation in which "small suppliers are transactionally dependent on much larger buyers. Suppliers face significant switching costs and are, therefore, 'captive'. Such networks are frequently characterized by a high degree of monitoring and control by lead firms."

[29] Telephone interview, berry export firm representatives (LU319), Guadalajara, Mexico, May 2019.

[30] Field notes, La Unión, July 2018.

producers rely on their own small plots. The result of these multiple cleavages was wide variation in the nature and capacity of the berry sector's multiple organizations. Some were formal organizations that operated on the basis of institutionalized rules and decision-making structures, whereas others functioned as the projects of individual producers that straddled the border between formal entities recognized by export firms and informal groupings.[31] In either case, efforts to generate a sector-wide producer association consistently failed to overcome these cleavages. Taken together, these aspects of the segmented political economy would influence the structure, practices, and trajectory of collective vigilantism in La Unión in ways that contrasted sharply with how they unfolded in Tancítaro.

Compared to the avocado sector, local-level linkages between the berry sector and governing authorities are comparatively thin. In part, this reflects the timing of the two sectors' emergence. The proposal to export Mexican avocados to the United States consumed much of the agendas of bilateral working groups between Mexican and US government authorities during NAFTA negotiations. Both sides recognized local-level organization building as being critical for satisfying export requirements and continuously maintaining access to the US market, hence leading to the creation of municipal JLSVs.[32] By contrast, prior to NAFTA the United States was already importing berries from Chile, Guatemala, and Mexico (Calvin, Foster, and Solorzano 2002). Between 1989 and 1993, Mexico represented 90 percent of US imports of fresh and frozen strawberries, with production sites in Michoacán, Baja California, and Guanajuato (Bertelsen 1995, 19–20). MNCs that arrived in La Unión in the 1990s thus did not face the same regulatory hurdles as in the avocado sector – a point evident in the fact that Mexican berries are only assessed for potential SPS issues by US authorities once they have already arrived at US ports of entry.[33] This lack of regulatory oversight within Mexican territory – unlike the constant stringent local inspections of avocado production and export sites in Tancítaro – coupled with the need to quickly transport berries out of the country almost as soon as they are picked translated into a weaker local interface between the berry sector and governing authorities. The vertically integrated nature of the export firms also limited the need for building sector-wide organizations as each firm oversaw its own microcosm of actors necessary to compete in the sector.

---

[31] Field notes, La Unión, July 2018.

[32] Organization building was not limited to the local level. Shortly after NAFTA was ratified, the USDA demanded that the avocado sector build an overarching state-level organization to help coordinate certification processes. This led to the formation of the Asociación de Productores y Empacadores de Aguacate de México [Avocado Producers and Exporting Packers Association of Mexico] (APEAM).

[33] Email communication from USDA APHIS, Phytosanitary Issues Management, Office of the Deputy Administrator, June 8, 2020.

5.3   CENTRALIZED COLLECTIVE VIGILANTISM

In 2012, in Tancítaro, some members of the avocado sector as well as commercial business owners and community members held secret meetings to discuss ending criminal extortion. But the Knights Templar identified those individuals, kidnapped them, and hung their dead bodies in public as a warning to others.[34] Individuals in the avocado sector believed this happened because they tried to mobilize outside of their immediate organizational borders that were susceptible to criminal monitoring:

> We thought about doing something, but we didn't always know who we were talking to: people who were on the other side [*gente que andaba por el otro lado*]. To confront the criminals we needed to be careful and it could only work if we organized among ourselves [referring to the avocado sector].[35]

The avocado sector thus turned to the JLSV as the least risky vehicle for collective resistance given the familiarity among members forged through years of building, organizing, and sustaining the local avocado industry. As I note above, the sector was not immune to the influence of organized crime; some members were forced to hand over to the criminals the organization's data on local producers and packing houses. But victims used histories of exchange and interaction within the JLSV to discern whether fellow members either were loyal to the criminals or forced to obey them. For example, some victims in the avocado sector collected the criminal taxes on behalf of the Knights Templar. We would expect other victims to view such actions as criminal collusion. But to my surprise I found that victims used the JLSV's preexisting ties with these individuals to decide whether this type of behavior was collusive or strategic:

> If [the criminals] kidnapped you or someone else you knew ... and they released you or that person, now you owed them. You might have to work by collecting *cuotas* in your community. You *had* to work for them. And they would call you to meetings, and you *had* to go to the meetings. You had to work, because if not, well, you know. But people close to you—your family, yes of course, but also people you worked with—they knew this ... people knew the difference between a criminal [*malandro*] and someone being forced to work for them because we had spent lots of time working together. How many meetings of the *Junta* [JLSV] had we all attended?[36]

Similarly, another avocado producer who was forced to collect the criminal tax reflected on how his ties within the JLSV helped him convince fellow producers that he was carrying out this task under duress:

> Because [the Knights Templar] let me go [after kidnapping him for several days when he fell behind on paying the criminal tax], I had to do what they said and collect the *cuota* from the other *aguacateros* in my community. Some people got mad. But when I met with

[34] Interview with Marco (MCN3 15), avocado producer, Tancítaro, July 2018.
[35] Interview with Oswaldo (MCN5813), avocado producer, Tancítaro, July 2018.
[36] Interview with Marco (MCN3 15), avocado producer, Tancítaro, July 2018.

them, I explained that I was being forced to do this. Then people understood—because they knew what it was like and because we had been working together and as part of *Junta*. As long as you showed [people] that your hands were tied, that you had no other choice, then there was still trust. But not everyone. Some people were greedy. We knew those collaborated with the *malandros* [criminals] because they wanted to. We had to avoid them [when organizing resistance].[37]

In early 2013, the first widely recognized self-defense forces in Michoacán emerged in the municipalities of Tepalcatepec and La Ruana in Tierra Caliente.[38] In Tancítaro members of the JLSV decided to see if self-defense forces in Tierra Caliente would come to Tancítaro to help launch the municipality's own self-defense group. They traveled to Tepalcatepec and found that the self-defense groups were open to the proposal of helping, but not for free.[39] Here the pooled financial assets of the JLSV (from dues paid by every producer) enabled the avocado sector to enlist outside armed assistance for their resistance:

[The self-defense groups from Tierra Caliente] didn't come here for only their love to clean [*limpiar*]. They needed to be paid. And paid well. So the *aguacateros* from the *Junta* gave them some money there in Tierra Caliente, and they promised to give them more after they came to Tancítaro.[40]

The JLSV also used member dues to purchase weapons, radios, and other equipment – sometimes from criminal groups operating in Tierra Caliente. Once this initial payment was made, the small contingency from the JLSV returned to Tancítaro and began preparations to mobilize collective vigilantism.

During the heightened violence under the Calderón administration, local communities throughout Michoacán were widely critical of the President's party, the PAN. This made cooperation between the avocado sector and the Tancítaro's PAN municipal president during the uprising all the more surprising. Moreover, it was common knowledge that the mayor had been giving the Knights Templar the requisite 10 percent of the municipal budget. Yet, members of the JLSV informed the mayor of the arrival of the self-defense forces from Tierra Caliente and their own mobilization days before the uprising and encouraged him to flee the municipality. This provided the mayor with an alibi to claim ignorance about the uprising when questioned by federal and state authorities, and it enabled him to avoid being punished by the Knights Templar for having allowed collective resistance to emerge.

Moreover, and as further evidence of the strong ties between the avocado sector and local government, the mayor was a former leader in the JLSV and himself an

---

[37] Interview with Raul (MCN950), avocado producer, Tancítaro, July 2018.
[38] For analyses of the emergence of the self-defense group in La Ruana, see Fuentes Díaz and Paleta Pérez (2015) and Fuentes Díaz (2015).
[39] Interview with Vilma (MCN1065), municipal government employee, Tancítaro, July 2018.
[40] Interview with Rafa (MCN1066), municipal government employee, Tancítaro, July 2018.

avocado producer. The local community therefore generally concluded that his handing over of municipal resources reflected obedience to the criminals rather than collusion. Interestingly, both the wealthier members of the avocado sector who were the mayor's PAN co-partisans and the small-scale producers who supported the PRD offered this same perspective.[41] The mayor, who fled to the state capital of Morelia, was able to return to Tancítaro less than a week later and resume his position as municipal president. As I discuss below, from this position he would play a crucial role in providing the municipality's self-defense group with protection from pressures by federal and state authorities.

5.3.1   The Structure of Centralized Collective Vigilantism

To organize collective vigilantism the avocado sector used the JLSV's internal structure. Because some members of the avocado sector were seen as having colluded with Knights Templar,[42] however, JLSV leaders only told those community representatives who they trusted about the arrival of self-defense forces. A day before those forces arrived, JLSV leaders conveyed what was about to happen: "We said that this was going to be all of us doing this together—that it wasn't going to be just some of us. And that they should get ready, because this was the moment … or we would never do it."[43] The morning that the self-defense forces from Tierra Caliente arrived in Tancítaro in November of 2013, JLSV leaders used the organization's records to contact trusted community-level representatives and instruct them to place the avocado producers in their communities on alert.[44]

Avocado producers throughout the municipality built makeshift barricades at the entrances to their communities, organized rotating sets of guards, and used text messaging to inform each other and JLSV leaders if they spotted members of the criminal group near their communities so that the self-defense groups could map and target them. This level of organization was important given that credible threat of reprisal by the Knights Templar. A robust preexisting organization thus provided the avocado sector with ready-made structures that it could use to mobilize resistance to criminal victimization while reducing possible denunciation of their efforts.

5.3.2   The Practices of Centralized Collective Vigilantism

Nearly two dozen members of the criminal group who had perpetrated extortion and associated violence in Tancítaro were captured by the self-defense groups. Accounts of what exactly happened to them varied and changed over time when I conducted follow-up interviews with some

---

[41] Field notes, Tancítaro, July 2018.   [42] Field notes, Tancítaro, July 2018.
[43] Interview with Francisco Javier (MCN711), JLSV employee, July 2018.
[44] Interview with Juan Carlos (MCN08513), municipal government official, Tancítaro, July 2018.

respondents – likely a result of my gradually gaining more trust from the interviewees. Some indicated that the understanding within the local self-defense group was that any criminals who they captured should be killed.[45] Others said that the criminals were kept for several days before being turned over to federal troops operating in the area. Still others said that the criminals were "disappeared," which suggests that victims utilized the very repertoire of violence that the DTO had used to punish them for failing to pay criminal taxes.[46] And while it was a rare practice according to my interviews, still others noted that some of the self-defense forces from outside of the municipality "forgave" members of the Knights Templars if they paid to be *perdonados* [the forgiven]. Being forgiven enabled individual criminals to flee the municipality without being harmed by the self-defense groups or to join the groups as they moved on to other municipalities. Despite this variation in extralegal practices, the majority of people who I interviewed indicated that the local self-defense group removed criminals from the municipality once they captured them, normally by forcing them to flee under threat of violence.

Preexisting tensions among victims in the avocado sector surfaced as victims pursued collective vigilantism. But the encompassing nature of the political economy kept the tensions from erupting into outright conflict that could derail the crucial initial collective efforts to oust the Knights Templar. For example, early in their mobilization some small-scale producers feared that resistance would fracture along the class cleavage and that the self-defense forces who were called in from Tierra Caliente would protect only the wealthier large-scale avocado producers:

SAUL: The ones with fifty, sixty hectares [of avocados], some started calling—they were desperate—and urged the leaders [of the JLSV] to send men and weapons to them first. There was worry that the leaders would do what they were asking, because the ones asking are the ones with the most land, the most money ... But fortunately we continued with the plan...[47]

MARCO ANTONIO: What was my worry? That instead of being one united movement, that this big exporter would have his group [of armed men], this big orchard owner would have his group [of armed men], and like that and like that. But it didn't happen that way. Because this began with the *Junta*. It was coordinated not by any one person, but by the *Junta*, and we are all part of the *Junta*—even though the big producers sometimes wish we weren't! [Laughs.] It's not that the *Junta* is perfect, but it's what all of us ... the *aguacateros*—small and big—have used to work with each other and resolve our differences [with regard to activities in the avocado sector].[48]

One of the wealthier large-scale avocado producers in Tancítaro admitted that some large-scale producers did request that the self-defense groups attend to their lands first during the initial part of their mobilization. But he also indicated

---

[45] Field notes, Tancítaro, July 2018.   [46] Field notes, Tancítaro, July 2018.
[47] Interview with Saul (MCN2011), avocado producer, Tancítaro, July 2018.
[48] Interview with Marco Antonio (MCN1900), avocado producer, Tancítaro, July 2018.

that the JLSV's leaders realized that they had to avoid letting the mobilization fragment along class lines: "it couldn't be that way. If we had done that, then everything would have lost legitimacy. And without legitimacy, people would not work together. We needed all of the producers and the exporters working together—the big and the small ones."[49] A small-scale avocado producer stressed the importance of the JLSV in ensuring that the interests of large-scale producers during the initial mobilization of collective vigilantism were not favored over that of smaller producers:

Here the [JLSV] is strong. But that does not mean that things here are perfect. There are conflicts between producers, communities, some of the exporters ... but that's normal, right? But if there are disagreements, people follow the rules, we raise our concerns at meetings, we propose ideas, debate solutions. To have fights and disagreements ... is normal. Without the [JLSV] we could not have launched a movement that had this level of discipline, that developed and executed a plan, and most *aguacateros* would not have supported if it had been otherwise. It was everyone together, because if not, then the *malandros* would have come back to impose themselves on us.[50]

This illustrates how an encompassing political economy can prevent salient cleavages from fracturing resistance precisely when victims are beginning high-risk mobilization against powerful criminal actors.

Collective vigilantism in Tancítaro also entailed acts of informal justice wherein elements of the avocado sector mimicked formal legal trials to dispense justice for victims of the criminal group. Most of the "cases" that the local self-defense group addressed involved instances in which the Knights Templar had forcibly taken avocado producers' lands, sometimes as punishment for failure to pay extortion taxes, and in other cases because the criminal groups wanted the lands in order to sell avocados themselves. Members of the JLSV "investigated" several of these cases following a roughly similar procedure. They would visit the community along with a local lawyer to address potential legal questions.[51] Together with local avocado sector representatives to the JLSV, informal oral testimonies would be elicited from community members either for or against the aggrieved party's claim. After some deliberations and discussions, a "verdict" would be issued. Thus informal justice as part of centralized collective vigilantism mimicked formal legal procedures as seen in other cases of vigilantism in places such as South Africa (see Minnaar 2001, 39). But it distinguished itself along two dimensions: its institutionalized nature and its interlinkages with formal legal procedures as part of achieving restitution. That said, as I discuss in Chapter 6,

---

[49] Interview with Lorenzo (MCN30119), JLSV employee, Tancítaro, July 2018.

[50] Interview with Alvaro (MCN033656), JLSV employee, Tancítaro, July 2018.

[51] Because the Knights Templar would force people to sign over their lands, several of these edicts under informal justice, in turn, were codified into formal property rights by local lawyers, who would help to draft legal documents to transfer land titles back to their rightful owners. Interview with James (MCN6660), lawyer, Tancítaro, August 2018.

as local security conditions improved, informal justice, along with other extralegal practices by the self-defense group, would succumb to the resurfacing of class-based and partisan cleavages.

5.3.3 The Trajectory of Centralized Collective Vigilantism

Victims in Tancítaro's avocado sector harnessed the JLSV and strong ties to local government in order to deflect threats to the sustainability of collective vigilantism from both the state and rival criminal organizations. The Governor of Michoacán at the time, Fausto Vallejo Figueroa (2012–14, PRI), ordered state police to several municipalities, including Tancítaro, to coordinate with federal troops in setting up roadblocks to contain the self-defense groups. This threatened violent confrontation between the state and victims, which the latter feared would undermine the growing public support that self-defense groups enjoyed at the time. JLSV leaders thus coordinated with community-level representatives throughout the municipality to have female family members physically place themselves at the front of the self-defense groups when they were traveling down roads where state police and federal troops were stationed:[52]

The women opened a path for [the self-defense groups]. The government ... the military, the *verdes* (the "greens," referring to the color of military uniforms), wanted to stop the *autodefensas* from entering and moving in the municipality. It was tense, because the ones from Tierra Caliente were less cautious and simply wanted to go through the military. But the *aguacateros* ... brought order to the issue. How did they do it? They put women from the communities at the front of the self-defense groups on the roads. The *aguacateros* gave the women an order: "You push forward, against the soldiers, but never hit the soldiers, only push them so that we can advance."[53]

Federal troops threatened to disarm the self-defense groups, but centralized coordination again enabled victims to neutralize this threat by stationing women and even children on roads to block the troops:

How are you going to take our weapons and leave those *cabrónes* alone? If you want to help us, go look for those *cabrónes*! We can tell you where they are—forty to fifty of them. Go look for them. The old women, the *viejas*, they were mad and on top of the soldiers, telling them to go and *chinga* [fuck off]. Women, because they are women, the soldiers weren't going to hurt them ... like children too.[54]

The avocado sector also used its preexisting organization to prevent criminal co-optation of resistance. This was a risky task given that rivals to the Knights Templar – including the Viagras and the CJNG DTOs – had infiltrated the self-defense groups throughout Tierra Caliente. But it was a particularly perilous challenge in Tancítaro because the avocado sector had knowingly recruited

---

[52] Interview with Marco (MCN315), avocado producer, Tancítaro, July 2018.
[53] Interview with community member (MCN0117), Tancítaro, July 2018.
[54] Interview with Raul (MC950), avocado producer, Tancítaro, July 2018.

self-defense groups from Tierra Caliente who were receiving help from known drug trafficking organizations. This help ranged from financial assistance to weapons to foot soldiers from the criminal groups fighting alongside the Knights Templars' victims.[55] Criminals offered these resources to the self-defense groups in Tierra Caliente in exchange for allowing them to take over the illicit drug trafficking routes and markets in the municipalities where the Knights Templar were ousted. In the case of Tancítaro, the avocado sector was aware of this threat of criminal co-optation:

> ... to be honest, I won't say that everyone [in Tierra Caliente] was pure. There was Hipólito [Mora], there was Dr. Mireles, but there were also lots of other people whose intentions ... well, we didn't know about completely. There were the *Viagras*, the *Americano* ... alongside people who were not narcotraffickers. But even if they weren't poor they were not all bad. The *Abuelo* sent his people ... and he's a narcotrafficker, but in my opinion, he's not bad because he hasn't caused damages to the communities where his group has operated. He sent people to work with us as part of the movement to free ourselves of organized crime.[56]

Hipólito Mora and Dr. José Manuel Mireles were among the public leaders of the self-defense forces who emerged in La Ruana and Tepalcatepec. The *Americano* refers to Luis Antonio Torres, a leader of a self-defense group based in Tierra Caliente who worked with the Viagras and other criminal groups. The *Abuelo* is Juan José Farías Álvarez, another self-defense group leader who worked with the CJNG to produce and traffic methamphetamines. Enlisting outside help ran the risk of simply replacing one criminal extorter for another.

To avoid this outcome the avocado sector relied on the strength of the JLSV, specifically the intra-sectoral ties that facilitated communication among disparate members to collectively confront potential efforts at incursions by rival criminal groups. At the same time that they were fighting the Knights Templar, producers were also monitoring the self-defense forces who had arrived from Tierra Caliente to see if they tried to "take control of the *plaza*," as Oswaldo explained:

> So, there was a moment when the ones from Tierra Caliente had to go and we had to take the reins. *We* are the autodefensas ... we are, *not them*. They were here because we organized and paid for their services. There was a man who arrived here in my community after we had "cleaned" it ... he was from the group from over there [in Tierra Caliente] and this man arrived, and he said: "I am the one that will help here now. I am the *jefe* [boss]." This happened in other parts of the municipality too. Once again, a *jefe de plaza* coordinating his people in each community ... like the *malandros* that we had just expelled? No! I contacted [lists the names of other avocado producers] and they came along with maybe forty or fifty *aguacateros* from the municipality, all well-armed, and we told [the men from Tierra Caliente]: "Well, no, we don't have *jefes*. The jefes are

---

[55] The Viagras had once been assassins and drug transporters for both the Familia Michoacana and the Knights Templar.

[56] Interview with Marco (MCN315), avocado producer, Tancítaro, July 2018.

everyone—each one of us is a *jefe* in his community." We asked the main *cabrón* how much we owed him and his men, and that he had to leave after we paid. They left, angry, but that's the difference between here and other municipalities where this occurred and where the *jefes* stayed . . . but they don't have anything to do here. And then later you saw conflicts among those who gave us a hand . . . *cuotas*, kidnappings, awful things again. They wanted the *plaza* here to do the same. And that's what we have not permitted.[57]

Oswaldo's statement is instructive for several reasons. First, he makes clear that the avocado sector did not see itself as outsourcing security to self-defense forces from Tierra Caliente. This was not a case of the private sector using its financial resources to purchase private security. Actors in Tancítaro's avocado sector viewed *themselves* as the self-defense forces in their municipality, and the outside self-defense forces as a tool that they collectively enlisted to help catalyze their own mobilization. Second, as I show later in the case of the berry sector's resistance in La Unión, criminal co-optation of victims' resistance can contribute to the continuation of insecurity, crime, and, once again, criminal extortion. Oswaldo indicates that the avocado sector in Tancítaro was aware of this possibility even as it invited groups affiliated with rival criminal organizations to help them launch collective resistance. Yet, the avocado sector was able to prevent co-optation in part because it could draw on pooled assets – the result of an encompassing political economy – to pay criminal actors to not remain in place. Of course, such payments would not stave off the likelihood that rival DTOs would recapture territory; instead, again as indicated by Oswaldo, the carrot of victims' financial payments was accompanied by the stick of victims' threats of coercive force, both of which were coordinated under the sector's core organization.

Close linkages to local government were crucial for the sustainability of the collective resistance early on. First, as noted earlier, criminal capture of the police was seen as a threat to the avocado sector's efforts. When members of the avocado sector alerted the municipal mayor to the coming collective mobilization, they asked for help in neutralizing the municipal police (i.e., thwarting their efforts to alert the Knights Templar or even turn their weapons against the self-defense groups, including the locals who were forming their own group). Before fleeing the municipality, the mayor thus instructed municipal police to conduct patrols in the outskirts of the municipality far from where the self-defense groups from Tierra Caliente would be entering. Second, the mayor and the local self-defense group coordinated to minimize local disruptions in everyday life that could attract criticism and prompt interventions from state or federal governments. Shortly after returning to the municipality, the mayor issued a public statement in conjunction with the local leaders of the self-defense group indicating that they would work together to ensure resumption of basic public services,

---

[57] *Jefes de plaza* are individuals working for DTOs that oversee the organization's activities within a municipality. Interview with Oswaldo (MCN5813), avocado producer, Tancítaro, July 2018.

including reopening schools that had been closed when the fighting began as well as local government offices and the JLSV.[58] The latter was particularly crucial because personnel from the APHIS office of the USDA had stopped visiting the municipality amid the violence, which forced producers and exporters to stop working since the avocados could not be packaged and exported without certification from APHIS personnel. But by coordinating to establish order, the mayor and the self-defense group enabled this key economic sector to resume, and further projected a return to "normalcy" that would keep the municipality off the radar of the state and federal governments that were demanding the self-defense groups disarm and disband.

5.4 DECENTRALIZED COLLECTIVE VIGILANTISM

Decentralized collective vigilantism in La Unión can be traced back in part to four berry producers who were extorted by the Knights Templar. As in Tancítaro, the four berry producers traveled to Tierra Caliente seeking help from self-defense forces. But unlike in Tancítaro, the berry producers were not representatives of a single sectoral organization. Each was instead the leader or part of the leadership of an individual organization that represented the interests of distinct groups of berry producers. These organizations differed along the dimensions of size (large or small), land tenure (rent or own), location within the municipality, and the specific export firms with which they contracted.[59]

One of the producers, Leopoldo, was the leader of a small organization whose membership included about a dozen small-scale neighboring berry producers. Leopoldo had established the organization in the mid-2000s with the intent of it becoming a municipal-wide representative of all small-scale berry producers. But many producers were reluctant to join because they feared that the export firms would punish collective mobilization, which stunted the organization's growth. A second berry producer, Carlos, had landholdings for small-scale berry production as well as livestock ranching. He had been one of several leaders of a berry producer–organization that also failed to attract a critical mass of producers. Both Leopoldo and Carlos nonetheless stayed on as the leaders of their respective organizations, which pooled resources among what members they did have to collectively invest in farming equipment, fertilizer, and the "macro tunnels" in which berries are grown to keep the fragile fruit protected from inclement weather and thus extend their shelf life. Felipe had been a sugarcane producer in the 1990s before the sector collapsed. He and other sugarcane producers shifted to berry production and formed an organization to represent their collective interests

---

[58] "Alcalde de Tancítaro se Reúne con Autodefensas" *Milenio*, November 19, 2013.
[59] These types of organizations are often referred to as *Sociedades Rurales* (Rural Societies), though there are multiple types of Rural Societies depending on their origins and objectives.

with Felipe as its leader. Most of the individual producers in the organization that Felipe led had collectively worked ejido lands for several decades. Finally, when I arrived in La Unión, the last producer, Roberto, was in jail in the state capital on charges of assaulting a government employee. Roberto headed a family in La Unión with a long history in the agricultural sector that included growing sugarcane and berries as well as livestock ranching. Roberto led a small organization of berry producers who either worked for him on his family-owned lands or farmed on neighboring lands. All four berry producers left La Unión in 2013 after the Knights Templar threatened violence for failure to pay the criminal tax.[60] And all four returned to La Unión at the end of 2013 to organize individual groups of armed men who waited for self-defense groups from Tierra Caliente to arrive in the municipality in early 2014. The four men drew primarily on the members of their respective organizations to populate their self-defense groups. Interviews with former members of each of these groups as well community residents indicated that group leaders did not coordinate with each other either in Tierra Caliente or upon their return to La Unión – a development that reflects the segmentation of the political economy in the berry sector.

My field work also revealed that the export firms that controlled the berry sector did not mobilize or participate in the self-defense groups or their extralegal activities. Two factors help explain their lack of participation. First, because of their status as MNCs, the firms sought to avoid taking actions that would draw negative attention to themselves. Interviews with former management-level employees at two berry export firms indicated that once the self-defense groups emerged in La Unión, foreign owners quietly and informally warned their local management-level employees not to get involved in the ensuing violence.[61] Indeed, several of the export firms in La Unión relocated upper management personnel to the neighboring state of Jalisco, which is the second biggest challenger to Michoacán in berry production. This strategy of relocating personnel aligns with what evidence we have of MCNs in Mexico targeted for criminal extortion. MNCs operating in parts of Mexico that, like Michoacán, have been sites of intense state–criminal conflict as well as criminal competition have, at times admitted to having paid criminal extortion to DTOs for years without ever reporting it to authorities. The reason for not reporting such activities is to prevent damage to "their public image and share prices."[62] Likewise, much like export firms in La Unión that relocated personnel to reduce their exposure to criminal violence, other major MNCs have relocated or temporarily closed their factories amid

---

[60] Field notes, La Unión, October and September of 2018.

[61] Telephone interviews, (MCN02909) and (MCN02901), former managers at berry export firms, Morelia, Michoacán and United States, May 2020.

[62] Ioan Grillo, "Mexico's Drug Cartels are Making Millions Robbing Multinational Corporations," PRI (*Global Post*), April 14, 2015.

extortion-related violence.[63] The ability to outsource risk to producers without having to invest capital in the fixed asset of land enabled export firms to reduce their physical vulnerability by shifting personnel to other relatively less violent localities. More broadly, the segmented nature of the berry sector's political economy thus meant that export firms where the majority of the rents generated by the sector are concentrated would not contribute to the mobilization against the Knights Templar. As noted in Chapter 2, this would compound the uneven distribution of assets across groups of victims and which, in turn, would encourage competition and conflict among them.

Comparatively thin ties between the berry sector and local governing authorities meant that collective vigilantism also unfolded without the close coordination with local government that we saw in Tancítaro. As in Tancítaro, it was common knowledge in La Unión that the mayor, also a member of the PAN, was handing over a part of the municipal budget to the Knights Templar. But unlike in Tancítaro, the absence of a core organization to structure sustained interaction between municipal authorities and the berry sector led to a very different interpretation of the mayor's actions. Under the segmented landscape, the mayor's payments were widely interpreted as evidence of collusion with the criminal actor rather than of being under duress to ensure survival.[64] Hence there was no warning given to the mayor of impending mobilization by victims. Instead the mayor went into hiding within La Unión the day that the self-defense groups both from Tierra Caliente and from within La Unión surfaced, only to appear later and demand that victims disband – again casting a sharp contrast with the more cooperative relations between the mayor of Tancítaro and victims in the avocado sector.

5.4.1   The Structure of Decentralized Collective Vigilantism

Five different self-defense groups operated in La Unión in 2014. As shown in Table 5.2, four out of the five groups (labeled as Groups A through E) were led by the four aforementioned berry producers. Group E came from Tierra Caliente and was led by a farmer and livestock rancher backed by the Viagras.

Initial efforts to centralize collective vigilantism failed in La Unión. It had become common practice for public leaders of the self-defense forces from Tierra Caliente to establish governing councils (or Consejos Ciudadanos de los Autodefensas [Self-Defense Group Citizen Councils]) in the municipalities they entered as a way to "help make certain that the *autodefensas* remained

---

[63] In Mexico's southern state of Guerrero, increased levels of extortion and related violence perpetrated by the Knights Templar led both the Coca-Cola and Pepsi MNCs to shut down and ultimately relocate their bottling facilities. See Mark Stevenson, "No Coke, No Pepsi: Bottlers Leave Mexican City Hit by Crime," *Associated Press*, June 13, 2018.

[64] Field notes, La Unión, July 2018.

TABLE 5.2 *Self-defense groups operating in La Unión, Michoacán*

Group	Leader	Occupation of leader	Size of group
Group A	Leopoldo	Local berry producer	~80 men
Group B	Felipe	Local berry producer	~50 men
Group C	Roberto	Local berry producer and livestock rancher	~60 men
Group D	Carlos	Local berry producer	~100 men
Group E	Juan	Non-local farmer and livestock rancher	~200 men

Sources: Interviews with members of Groups A–E; field notes, La Unión, August and September 2018. Aligning with my argument about the consequences of segmented political economies for the structure of collective mobilization, there was variation in coercive capacity across the five groups. The self-defense groups varied in size from fifty to several hundred members, though this would change over time as some groups absorbed others while still others attracted more recruits. Groups A, B, and C were the smallest and had comparatively limited resources, which meant that their members did not receive money for their participation and had to bring their own weapons. By contrast, Group D led by Carlos was the largest locally based group largely because when Carlos visited Tierra Caliente he secured money and weapons from the CJNG to establish and build his self-defense group.[65]

a force from and for the people."[66] In Tancítaro, no council was established given tight centralized oversight by the avocado sector. By contrast, public leaders of the self-defense groups from Tierra Caliente considered it necessary to establish a council in La Unión given the lack of coordination across the multiple armed groups:

We could see it already, that the people [in La Unión] needed organization. Imagine that you enter a territory where people have guns and there are groups and some work with each other but others have conflicts and you don't know who is with you and who is against you ... that is a very dangerous situation and the best way to avoid a disaster is to organize everybody under a single command.[67]

The members of the council were announced in a public meeting in La Unión's main plaza. Among these were the five leaders of Groups A through E along with several other berry producers, a journalist, two schoolteachers, and the owners of a few local restaurants and a grocery store. Interviews in La Unión with a diverse range of people revealed no consensus regarding how people were named to the council.[68]

The leaders of La Unión's smaller self-defense groups (A, B, and C) initially supported the council as a way to keep the larger groups (D and E) from using

---

[65] Interview with Moisés (MCN8002), member of Group D, La Unión, September 2018.

[66] Interview with self-defense group leader from Tepalcatepec #2 (MCN17), Morelia, August 2018.

[67] Interview with self-defense group leader from Tepalcatepec #1 (MCN1042), Morelia, July 2018.

[68] Field notes, La Unión, August 2018.

their superior size and coercive capacities to dominate how collective vigilantism would be carried out.[69] More importantly, it was common knowledge that Groups D and E were backed by rival criminal groups, and there was fear of more violence emerging from criminal competition through the proxies of the self-defense groups. The leaders of Groups D and E, by contrast, not only resisted participating in the council but actively sought to undermine it, as one civilian member of the council explained:

Of the [council's] members, some of us who were not *autodefensas* wanted it to be something of the people to help ensure that the self-defense groups didn't get out of control. And meanwhile Carlos and Juan [leaders of Group D and E, respectively] were already trying to subvert it because each one wanted to be *the* leader of the self-defense groups [in La Unión].[70]

The full slate of council members never met again after that first day in the plaza as conflicts surfaced among the individual self-defense groups almost immediately. The initial key objectives of the smaller groups (A, B, and C) were to survive and end extortion by ousting the Knights Templar. However, the uneven distribution of money, men, and weapons and the challenge posed by the larger more capable groups would ultimately prompt competition for these resources and deviation from these objectives. By contrast, the two larger groups (D and E) backed by rival criminal organizations immediately set out to fill the governance void and claim the territory up for grabs in the wake of the ousting of the Knights Templar.

5.4.2   The Practices of Decentralized Collective Vigilantism

The uneven distribution of coercive power across the five self-defense groups and the lack of a mechanism to coordinate among themselves led to their use of distinct and countervailing practices that had differential effects on local order. All five groups engaged in violence against the Knights Templar. But the leaders of the smallest self-defense groups (A, B, and C) opted for a more *defensive* posture that reflected their relatively limited coercive capacity and, more broadly, lack of ties to the other sectoral actors who were mobilizing. Instead, they chose to keep close to the areas where their leaders' and members' lands were located. As a former member of self-defense Group A stated:

We were not many, did not have many guns, only some of us had high-caliber weapons. It would have been something different if we had talked to each other and coordinated. But it wasn't like that. And I was not going to send my men—people I knew and whose families I knew—to be killed. After we cleaned our area, we stayed there, monitored who came and went—that was our part.[71]

---

[69] Interviews with members of the Consejo Ciudadano de los Autodefensas de La Unión (MCN149105 and MCN1414), November 2018.

[70] Interview with Jesús (MCN14835), community member, La Unión, September 2018.

[71] Interview with Marcelino (MCN38), member of self-defense Group A, La Unión, October 2018.

By contrast, the two large self-defense groups (D and E) who counted on backing of rival criminal groups pursued an *offensive* strategy under which they leveraged their greater numbers to both oust criminals and begin to establish territorial control. As one member of Group D explained: "We went out in small patrols, kept in communication with our radios and the moment we saw [a criminal] everyone was alerted and whoever was closest would go to help. That way we made our way throughout the *entire* municipality."[72] Whereas centralized collective vigilantism in Tancítaro limited the uneven provision of security in the crucial early stages and execution of centralized collective vigilantism, decentralized collective vigilantism in La Unión led Groups D and E to actually compete against each other from the outset to provide security to local agricultural producers. This again echoed the practices that the Knights Templar and its predecessors had used to build legitimacy by providing locals with benefits. The following story from one berry producer illustrates this dynamic:

One day some of Juan's [Group E] men arrive and offer to put a few men in places around my farms to keep things calm. But they asked for money—it was a lot [of money]. The very next day some of Carlos' [Group D] men arrive to ask if Juan's men had been there and what they had said. I told them everything, and then Carlos' men offered to do the same for nothing. It seemed strange then—now I understand it—but then in that moment it seemed strange. I thought: "What the fuck? Don't we have a single movement here? Isn't this supposed to be about establishing order and not fighting with each other?"[73]

As in Tancítaro, collective vigilantism in La Unión also entailed efforts to provide informal justice. Initially, the leaders of the three smaller self-defense groups (A, B, and C) wanted the council to coordinate the provision of informal justice.[74] Victims sought assistance from the council in regaining lands that the Knights Templar had forced them to sign over to either a member of the criminal group or sometimes to another community member who was colluding with the DTO.[75] The latter cases were particularly challenging because the community member was usually still in La Unión and so could contest the accusation but also faced becoming the target of revenge attacks.[76] The leaders of the three smaller self-defense groups attempted to direct victims to collective meetings among the three of them and other members of the Citizens Council. But the leaders of the two larger self-defense groups began working directly with victims to resolve their conflicts, which undermined this effort to centralize the provision of informal justice. By working directly with

---

[72] Interview with Moisés (MCN8002), member of Group D, La Unión, September 2018. Emphasis added.

[73] Interview with Uriel (MCN71), berry producer, La Unión, July 2018.

[74] Interviews with Jesús (MCN14835), community member, La Unión, September 2018 and Santiago (MCN1414), berry producer and council member, La Unión, November 2018.

[75] Interview with Marcelino (MCN38), member of self-defense Group A, La Unión, October 2018.

[76] Interview with Jesús (MCN14835), community member, La Unión, September 2018.

victims, Groups D and E reduced the legitimacy of the Citizens Council and bolstered their legitimacy as purveyors of order in the municipality. Furthermore, both groups used their relatively superior coercive capacity to resolve grievances without going through the motions of holding informal trials and collecting testimonies. As one individual that had been a member of Group D explained:

Well, there was a lot of demand from people, from the aggrieved, who had been forced to turn over orchards, farming equipment, even their houses and cars, when they couldn't pay [the criminal tax]. There was so much demand, a lot. Because in the courts the process would take too long or they would want evidence that was impossible for the aggrieved to provide. That was when we could help them.[77]

This led to conflict resolution becoming a lucrative business for both groups as they charged victims to help them solve their conflicts. But it also encouraged the smaller self-defense groups (A, B, and C) to eventually join this informal market and sell their own comparatively limited coercive power to resolve grievances.[78] Eventually this inter-group competition led to the dissolution of the Citizens Council, as one member described it:

Well, later there were people ... who began to charge for fixing cases. And so some people saw it as a business. They tried to hide it, tried to do maneuvers. But you know, between heaven and earth nothing is hidden ... everything is known [*del cielo a la tierra no hay nada oculto ... todo se sabe*]. And so we dismantled [the council]. The one who gave money got his problem fixed. And all we [in the council] got were complaints. So better to end the fucking council [*Entonces mejor que se acabe el pinche Consejo*].[79]

Decentralized vigilantism also led different self-defense groups to approach the question of forgiveness of former accomplices of the Knights Templar in contrasting ways that satisfied their distinct needs and objectives. The three smaller self-defense groups did not forgive criminals for fear that they would inform on them to the Knights Templar who were still operating in the neighboring municipalities.[80] By contrast, Groups D and E did forgive former accomplices. To be forgiven, the accomplice could not have killed or disappeared someone – though how this was determined was unclear even among members of the two groups.[81] Criminals also had to surrender material goods they had obtained from extortion. But crucially, the forgiven were also required to join the ranks of the larger self-defense groups. Forced recruitment thus followed forgiveness, which incentivized the two self-defense groups to forgive as many criminals as they could in order to bolster their sizes

[77] Interview with Moisés (MCN8002), member of Group D, La Unión, September 2018.
[78] Field notes, La Unión, October 2018.
[79] Interview with Santiago (MCN1414), berry producer and council member, La Unión, November 2018.
[80] Field notes, La Unión, September 2018 and November 2018.
[81] Field notes, La Unión, September 2018.

and coercive capacities.[82] In brief, while in some instances the individual group's practices aligned and reinforced each other, at other times they worked at cross-purposes.

5.4.3 The Trajectory of Decentralized Collective Vigilantism

The case of resistance in La Unión is illustrative of how decentralized collective vigilantism is vulnerable to derailment and co-optation. The Commission for Security and Comprehensive Development in the State of Michoacán, which President Enrique Peña Nieto established in January of 2014, sought to channel self-defense groups into a Fuerza Rural Estatal (State Rural Police) that would work in an auxiliary role to support state police and, on occasion, federal authorities in providing order.[83] The strategy was widely seen by members of the self-defense groups as an effort to "institutionalize" and neutralize them given their public accusations of collusion between elements of the federal and state governments and organized crime. The state strategy, however, succeeded in fragmenting the self-defense groups as some opted to join the Rural Police while others refused to do so – with elements of organized crime found in both camps.[84]

The leader of Group B, Felipe, accepted the state's offer and he and his men joined the Rural Police. By contrast, most of the men in Group C, led by Roberto, joined Carlos in Group D in 2014, shortly before Roberto was arrested by federal troops for assaulting a government employee. The leader of Group A, Leopoldo, disbanded many of his men – some of whom also joined Group D – but most of whom retreated to their lands and berry farms. Having gained men, Carlos used his increased coercive capacity and the dissolution of the Citizens Council to challenge his remaining rival, Group E, led by Juan and his backers in the Viagras. But Juan opted not to fight for control of La Unión and instead departed with his several hundred men to a neighboring municipality. Respondents gave conflicting reasons for why Juan chose to retreat. Some suggested that the CJNG and the Viagras had made a deal to parcel out the municipalities between themselves and restart drug production and trafficking sooner rather than later. Others indicated that the growth of Carlos's group and growing local complaints about Juan as an outsider in the municipality led Juan to move on.[85]

As the last self-defense group left standing in La Unión, Carlos's Group D began to repay the CJNG by resuming the production and trafficking of

---

[82] Interview with Hector (MCN50), member of self-defense Group B, La Unión, November 2018.

[83] There is a long history of such auxiliary forces in rural Mexico, including the Guardia Rural (Rural Guard) and the Cuerpo de Defensa Rural (Rural Defense Corps).

[84] "Fuerzas Rurales Infiltradas por Delincuentes," video, *Quadratín Agency*, January 24, 2016. www.quadratin.com.mx/municipios/regiones/Fuerzas-rurales-infiltradas-delincuentes/.

[85] Field notes, La Unión, August 2018. The idea of a pact between the CJNG and the Viagras seems unlikely given the fierce rivalry between the two DTOs.

methamphetamines. At the same time, Group D continued running patrols and checkpoints throughout the municipality while, most crucially, refraining from extortion. As Chapter 6 shows, maintaining the balance between drug trafficking and providing order would be difficult to sustain in the long term. Yet, most of the people who I spoke with described this combination of activities with a degree of nostalgia for the criminal groups of the past who had managed to run the drug trade in relative peace. One member of Group D described this arrangement himself:

What you have to understand is that drugs are not a problem. Look at how long people here have grown drugs, like marijuana, like poppy . . . and nothing happened. There were no killings and no *cuotas*. People didn't even know that the drugs were here if they weren't growing them. It was all managed with restraint. But the [federal] government ended that when they got involved, and look at what happened: all those awful things began right then . . . No one will charge the *cuota* here again. People can go on with their lives and work without being afraid that someone is going to demand money, and rape or kill them if they don't pay. Never again. That was the deal and that's what will keep happening here.[86]

5.5   CONCLUSION

Aligning with the argument developed in Part I of this book, this chapter's comparison of the two cases of resistance to criminal extortion in Michoacán illustrates why we need to consider the nature of local political economies in trying to decipher puzzling variation in the nature of resistance to criminal victimization. In Tancítaro, the encompassing political economy enabled the avocado sector to mount centralized collective vigilantism. Here victims redirected an organization from conducting relatively mundane market activities to instead overseeing a campaign of violence against criminal actors. The centralized nature of resistance in Tancítaro precluded its derailment by the state or co-optation by rival criminal groups. To the contrary: tight linkages between the sector and local government facilitated coordination between the two that, in the initial phase of mobilization, provided the latter with protection from criminals and state actors opposed to the self-defense groups. By contrast, the segmented nature of the political economy in La Unión's berry sector made it difficult to realize the same level of coordinated resistance despite attempts to do so. Collective vigilantism in La Unión instead consisted of multiple and competing groups. Decentralized collective vigilantism yielded conflicting sets of practices despite the shared overarching objective of ending criminal extortion by the Knights Templar. The decentralized nature of collective resistance proved porous to the influences of both state and criminal actors.

[86] Interview with Vicente (MCN8003), member of self-defense Group D, September 2018.

The analysis of the processes and mechanisms that yielded distinct forms of collective vigilantism also enables me to address several potential confounding factors. One such confounder is that perhaps the political opportunity structure (Meyer and Minkoff 1994; Tarrow 1994) differed across the two cases in ways that account for the subsequent variation in collective mobilization to resist criminal extortion. But there are several reasons why this has limited explanatory traction. In both Tancítaro and La Unión, the same political party – the PAN – was in power in local government during the time leading up to and during collective vigilantism. If one of the municipal presidents had been from the same political party as the one that controlled the governor's office during this time, the PRI, then we might hypothesize that variation in partisan power could have led to differential levels of support from the governor's office for dealing with local crime that could then help explain variation in the observed forms of resistance. But this potential explanation falls short because both municipal presidents were from the same party. Another potential confounding factor might be that the local governments had different relations to local criminal groups (e.g., either colluding with or opposing criminals groups). But here again both municipal mayors provided criminals with valuable municipal public funds in the time leading up to victims' resistance. This shows that the conventional binary classification of political authorities as either corrupt or not corrupt is insufficient to capture the range of perceptions and understandings that victims view as the choices that confront populations in territories under criminal control. This chapter instead shows that victims differentiate between when different actors willfully comply with criminals or are instead forced to obey them. I find that victims did not view all municipal presidents as satisfying the conventional definition of "corrupt." This subtle difference has substantial implications for how we study the politics of crime – a point I return to and expand on in the book's concluding chapter.

An additional factor we could consider is the history of civilian mobilization in response to political threats. Scholars identify how the legacy of conflict influences patterns of political behavior over extended periods of time (Balcells 2012; Lupu and Peisakhin 2017; Weintraub, Vargas and Flores 2015). In the specific case of resistance to criminal extortion in Michoacán, Osorio, Schubiger, and Weintraub (2020) argue that the history of armed collective mobilization in the early twentieth century against the federal government's anti-clerical policies – the *Cristero* rebellion – explains territorial variation in the rise of self-defense groups nearly a century later. Attention to such historical legacies provides an important insight into a factor that could influence the incidence of armed resistance. However, explaining variation in where self-defense groups did or did not emerge cannot account for variation in the particular type of mobilization that victims pursued – the focus in this chapter and, more broadly, this book. Whether victims in Michoacán embarked on collective vigilantism that was centralized or decentralized in nature requires unpacking the contemporary political and economic conditions in each locality, as shown here.

Finally, we could also hypothesize that the nature of the grievances among victims might help explain variation in the strategy of resistance. Some scholars suggest that crimes that violate deeply held social norms, such as sexual violence, may increase support among victims for extralegal violence (Fuentes Díaz 2015; García-Ponce, Young, and Zeitoff 2019). But the comparative analysis offered in this chapter shows that while victims' wives and daughters in both localities were targeted as part of the process of criminal extortion, the victims still varied in their specific form of resistance. This finding underscores the importance of both comparative study of resistance and attention to the structures within local political economies that channel grievances into action.

6

The Coproduction of Order

In 2018, one of Tancítaro's municipal government officials asked me whether I had experienced any crime during my time conducting research in the municipality. I replied that I had not. He smiled and explained why:

Here the *autodefensas* and the government work hand in hand. They emerged and ended the disaster that we were living in. To keep those conflictive times from coming back—because they are always out there—we work together, shoulder to shoulder: the government and the *autodefensas*.[1]

By contrast, a municipal official in La Unión provided a more sobering perspective on the period of order their municipality was experiencing after the Knights Templar had been ousted:

Things are delicate right now. Here the [self-defense] groups weren't organized, people did not cooperate with each other. No one here took 100 percent control of the situation, and then one group [referring to self-defense Group B led by Carlos] has been trying to impose itself. [We] had to accept that this group existed, even though the state and federal governments told [us] that it could not exist! There was an equilibrium, where the groups helped and the government did other parts for security. We divided security. But now one group has gotten involved in politics, and they won the last [2018 municipal] elections with their candidate. Now they have people working in the [municipal] government ... and at the same time, they manage the *plaza* [referring to the local illicit drug trade]. But at least until now, they have done it the right way, the way that narcotrafficking is supposed to work: produce, transport, and export, and that's it. They don't mess with society, not with citizens and not with [agricultural] producers—no *cuotas* and violence, which is what was suffocating us. But now, like any group, they want more power, and they are taking it. I fear that it's a delicate moment here, very delicate.[2]

---

[1] Interview with Rafa (MCN1066), municipal government official, Tancítaro, July 2018.
[2] Interview with Teo (MCN4848), municipal government official, La Unión, August 2018.

As Chapter 5 showed, centralized collective vigilantism in Tancítaro and decentralized collective vigilantism in La Unión varied in their structures, practices, and trajectories. But both variants of collective vigilantism ended extortion by the Knights Templar. Crucial to this outcome was "arresting" or chasing off members of the municipal police forces. Yet, because elements of the Knights Templar and other drug trafficking organizations in the areas surrounding both municipalities remained active, the threat of criminal actors reimposing criminal extortion persisted. Under these conditions victims turn to the coproduction of order to prevent victimization using a combination of practices, including extralegal ones. As I indicate in Chapter 2, coproduction of order consists of sustained formal and informal agreements and practices coordinated between victims and governing authorities to prevent victimization by criminal actors in ways that simultaneously bolster and undermine the rule of law. Yet, the quotes from municipal government officials above illustrate how the nature of coproduction varied across the two cases. This chapter traces this variation to differences in the local political economies and the distinct legacies of the collective vigilantism that these political economies generated.

In the next section, I show that collective vigilantism in Tancítaro and La Unión changed the strategic conditions that had shaped victims' initial strategies of resistance by producing "bottom-up" purges of local police. Section 6.2 then uses the 2015 and 2018 municipal elections in Michoacán to trace how victims and politicians pursued divergent forms of coproduction in my field sites. I show how variation in the local political economies affected the abilities of victims to impose the terms of coproduction. In Tancítaro the avocado sector and local government pursued centralized coproduction through which crucial decisions on how to produce order were made jointly by relying on the sector's single core sectoral organization and the long-standing ties between the sector and local government. In contrast, the segmented nature of the organizational landscape in La Unión and the legacy it imparted in the form of competing armed groups of victims with comparatively weak ties to local government fostered a more competitive political environment. This was reflected in decentralized coproduction across multiple actors competing violently against each other but also within the municipal political arena. The conclusion summarizes the empirical analysis.

6.1 RESISTANCE TO CRIMINAL EXTORTION AND ENDOGENOUS CHANGE

The conflictive settings in which actors operate can change over time as they make gains against their rivals. Civil war studies in particular show that attention to such endogenous dynamics helps to explain why and when actors' preferences shift in ways that "override prewar political, social and economic factors" (Kalyvas 2008a).[3] I find that collective vigilantism can also produce endogenous changes in the strategic contexts in which victims resist victimization. In the cases of Tancítaro and La Unión, this endogenous change took the form of victims ending criminal capture of municipal police – what I term "bottom-up" purges of the police. This shift in victims' strategic context introduces the potential for victims to shape the coproduction of order in coordination with governing authorities.

6.1.1 Bottom-Up Purging of the Police

In both Tancítaro and La Unión, among the first steps that self-defense groups took at the start of collective vigilantism was to neutralize municipal police who, as I established in Chapter 5, had been captured by the Knights Templar.[4] The self-defense groups occupied the local police headquarters and confiscated the weapons and ammunition of local police agents. Many police agents fled, while the self-defense groups physically assaulted municipal police they caught trying to escape as punishment for having facilitated criminal extortion. Thus both variants of collective vigilantism caused bottom-up purges of local police institutions.

Unlike conventional "top-down" purges whereby governments dismiss either parts of or entire corrupt police forces, victims organize and orchestrate bottom-up purges as part of their resistance. Collective vigilantism thus changes the strategic conditions that shape victims' initial strategies of resistance. In particular, bottom-up purges not only remove a core threat to their mobilization, but, in doing so, also generate local security vacuums that actors then have incentives to shape.

Mayors in Mexico appoint directors of Public Security [Directores de Seguridad Pública Municipal], who plan, organize, and direct municipal police activities. Mayors are thus the elected authorities most proximately responsible for overseeing municipal police forces to ensure local order. Hence it is mayors who must rebuild municipal police forces after they have been purged. However, in the wake of collective vigilantism municipal mayors are unable to do so freely because they face armed victims who also have their own incentives to shape the way that local order is produced. More broadly, governing authorities in Mexico also face the challenge of building order in settings in which municipal police forces generally lack the institutional capacity to confront organized crime.

---

[3] Kalyvas (2015a, 45) provides a revealing example of the Islamic State of Iraq and Syria (ISIS): "the endogenous dynamics of conflict have played a key role through 'positive resource shocks' in the form of sudden capture of massive quantities of heavy weaponry. For example, when ISIS took Mosul in June 2014, it captured 1,500 Humvees, 52 M198 Howitzers and much more. In other words, ISIS benefited from a rare constellation of very weak yet heavily endowed opponents."

[4] Interview with Marco (MCN315), avocado producer, Tancítaro, July 2018.

For victims, the emergence of new municipal police forces represents both a threat and an opportunity. It is a threat because victims believe the autonomy of any new local police from criminal organizations would be short-lived given the limited institutional capacity of Mexican municipal police. In Tancítaro and La Unión, the Knights Templar continued operating in surrounding municipalities, the DTO's leaders were still free despite ongoing state efforts to arrest them, and there were constant rumors circulating in both municipalities that the *Templarios* were planning to recapture the municipal *plazas,* punish the members of the self-defense groups, and reimpose extortion.[5] In Tancítaro, the avocado sector was united in opposing the construction of a new municipal police force without first changing what victims perceived as a key condition that had enabled criminal capture of the police:

FREDY: [The government] began creating a municipal police, but then what? They weren't going to be different from what we had before. That was the weak point in the municipality before we took up arms, and it was going to be again with a new police. The easiest thing for a criminal to do is to buy a poor police officer.[6]

WALTER: The police that the municipal government was building was well on its way to becoming a disaster—the same low salaries as before, the same bad equipment as before. So we would get what we had before . . . the criminals would infiltrate them and take over and impose the *cuota* again. One has to be realistic from the perspective of the police officer and the common citizen. For the police agent, of course if someone offers you two or three times your salary to look the other way, it's logical that they accept—more so if the one offering you the money also has a gun to your head. And for the common citizen, why turn to the police if they cannot do it or if it will take forever [to resolve concerns]? It's easier to go to the criminals who can take care of things right away.[7]

Both statements echoed a concern I heard repeatedly from victims in Tancítaro: that weak police institutions were easy prey for criminal capture. But the second statement also highlights that victims in Tancítaro recognized the danger of allowing a security vacuum to persist because it would encourage demand for the private supply of order and protection that criminal actors had satisfied time and again as part of establishing territorial control.

Self-defense group leaders in La Unión also opposed establishing a new municipal police force, though the reasons differed across the multiple groups in existence. Both Felipe, the former leader of self-defense Group B and now commander of the local Rural Police, and Carlos, the leader of self-defense Group D backed by the CJNG, believed that any new municipal police saddled with limited institutional capacity would be easy prey for criminal capture. But

---

[5] Throughout late 2014 and into 2015, federal military troops worked with a small number of self-defense groups in Michoacán to form an elite squad called the G-250 whose sole purpose was to locate the leader of the Knights Templar.

[6] Interview with Fredy (MCN6019), avocado producer, Tancítaro, August 2018.

[7] Interview with Walter (MCN2055), avocado producer, Tancítaro, August 2018.

each had additional reasons to oppose the construction of a new municipal police force in La Unión that reflected their conflicting interests in how to bring about local order.

A new municipal police could have complicated Carlos's ability to coordinate drug production and trafficking in La Unión on behalf of the CJNG – unless he could influence how such a municipal police force operated. In other words, Carlos and his men needed to capture the municipal police, much like the criminals who they had helped to oust had done before them. By contrast, Felipe viewed the construction of a new municipal police force as another source of competition for his own power as the leader of the Rural Police. As I show below, Felipe thus pressured local governing authorities to allow his men to serve as the primary purveyors of order in La Unión.

Victims in Tancítaro and La Unión believed that extralegal practices were necessary to prevent the return of criminal extortion and associated violence – even if they required violating the formal rule of law. As Fredy, an avocado producer in Tancítaro, made clear: "What all of this [resisting extortion] made clear to us is that the security of the municipality requires that we do things that go against some parts of the rule of law, but supports other parts of it—like guaranteeing public order and ensuring the right of people to live their lives without fear of having some criminal charge you money to let you and your family live."[8] Yet, the contrasting political economies and the divergent forms of collective vigilantism that followed from them would result in very different forms of coproduction.

6.2 VARIETIES OF THE COPRODUCTION OF ORDER

Coproduction refers to "the process through which inputs used to produce a good or service are contributed by individuals who are not 'in' the same organization" (Ostrom 1996, 1073), wherein the different organizations are located in state and society.[9] Much existing research views the state as the first mover in coproduction wherein the state has the power to allow for and shape citizen participation, as well as to discourage it as way to preserve its own power (Ostrom 1996, 1075–78). The emphasis is therefore on how society can inform and collaborate through spaces that the state permits. This dynamic is evident in analyses of community policing initiatives (Frühling 2012; Fung 2006). Garland (2001) argues that under community policing society is "responsibilized" as to how it can support state efforts to improve security conditions. Grabosky (1992, 266) notes that collaboration between state and society in contexts of insecurity is an opportunity for the state to use citizen inputs to build its own capacity to "monopolize" the provision of order. The

---

[8] Interview with Fredy (MCN6019), avocado producer, Tancítaro, August 2018.
[9] Such public–private coordination can satisfy gaps in the provision of goods and services while structuring the governance of the related policy domains (Evans 1996; Fox 1996; Tendler 1997).

assumption underwriting these approaches to coproduction is that the state enjoys a position of relative strength where it initiates and dictates the terms of coproduction.

But what happens when the balance of power between the state and society is less favorable to the state? One such context is where the autonomous, but low-capacity, police are the very result of collective resistance by victims. Analyzing coproduction in Tancítaro and La Unión shows that societal actors – in these cases armed groups of victims – can exert more power in the process of the coproduction of order than existing literature allows. Yet the forms of coproduction in the two cases also varied considerably.

6.3 CENTRALIZED COPRODUCTION OF ORDER

For Tancítaro's avocado sector, the 2015 municipal elections were an inflection point for either securing the gains it had realized in establishing order or backsliding to the extortion and associated violence they had fought against. Ensuring continued order would require close coordination among members of the sector and between it and the next municipal government. Federal and state authorities had declared self-defense groups illegal in Michoacán. But Tancítaro's self-defense group had no intention of disbanding with organized crime threatening a return to the municipality.[10] The self-defense group needed the municipal government as an ally with which it could work through formal *and* informal channels to safeguard local order. Or as Marco, an avocado producer who participated in the emergence of the local self-defense group, explained: "There are things that the law cannot do and that the state cannot do. But these are things that somebody needs to do to maintain security. They are not legal, not allowed by the state, but they are necessary if we want to not have what happened to us before happen again."[11]

Here the encompassing political economy with strong links within the avocado sector but also between it and local government facilitated a centralization of the coproduction of order. The sector again relied on the JLSV to coordinate the sector's activities as the municipal elections drew near. Members of the organization proposed identifying a single candidate to run for municipal president with the backing of the avocado sector. They saw this as a way to prevent partisan cleavages from erupting into conflict that could weaken the avocado sector's collective ability to put into power a municipal government that would be friendly to the continued existence of the self-defense group. The agreement on the need for a joint candidate does not mean that the process to select a "unity candidate" was free of conflict or divisions. As one municipal government employee reflected:

[10] Interview with Oswaldo (MCN5813), avocado producer, Tancítaro, July 2018.
[11] Interview with Marco (MCN315), avocado producer, Tancítaro, July 2018.

Not everyone agreed with the idea of a single candidate. But I do think it was necessary at that time. It wasn't that we had security guaranteed right after the *autodefensas* emerged —to the contrary, there was a general belief that the *Templarios* or another [criminal] group could try to take the municipality again at any time. And so what was needed was for the municipal [government] and the *autodefensas* to work together in ways that are quiet ... but effective.[12]

Over the course of several months and dozens of meetings, members of the avocado sector rejected a number of proposed candidates who failed to secure a majority of support.[13] The fact that these deliberations did not break down into outright partisan factionalization, however, further illustrates how an encompassing political economy can prevent preexisting cleavages from breaking down into outright conflict during mobilization. The deliberations within the avocado sector led a majority to settle on a single candidate who was amenable to the sector's collective interests.[14]

The candidate, Arturo Olivera Gutiérrez, was a member of the PRI who had previously served as municipal president from 2002 to 2004. Once agreed upon, avocado sector leaders worked with municipal party officials from the PRI, PAN, and the PRD in lobbying state-level party organizations to have Arturo run as the representative of a multiparty coalition. In return for supporting the unity candidate, each party would receive an equal number of appointments to the municipal cabinet. Yet, the cohesion that had characterized centralized collective vigilantism and then coproduction did show signs of strain on the eve of the elections. Several wealthy producers and packing house–owners suddenly declined to support Arturo and instead threatened to nominate their own candidate for municipal president. Yet, again the encompassing political economy characterized by close coordination among sectoral actors enabled it to avoid a major rupture as members made the case that fragmentation at this critical moment would generate an opening for organized crime to recapture the municipality by leveraging partisan differences. Ultimately Arturo ran for mayor with the backing of the three major parties and won the 2015 municipal elections.

The avocado sector's political support, however, required that Arturo coordinate closely with it on crafting, enacting, and overseeing local order in ways that both pushed against and violated the rule of law. Upon assuming office Arturo declared that he would collaborate with the avocado sector to prevent criminal groups from reentering the municipality – a decision that clearly contradicted the federal and state governments' demands that self-defense groups in Michoacán disband and disarm. Thus by harnessing their collective power and mobilizing it through a single sectoral organization, Tancítaro's avocado sector successfully intervened in local electoral politics. In doing so, it laid the groundwork for the election of a mayor who was both

---

[12] Interview with Rafa (MCN1066), municipal government official, Tancítaro, July 2018.
[13] Field notes, Tancítaro, July 2018. [14] Field notes, Tancítaro, July 2018.

indebted to the sector for its electoral support and amenable to working closely with it – and often on its terms – in the coproduction of local order.

6.3.1   The Structure of Centralized Coproduction

The structure of coproduction in Tancítaro was centralized, with decision-making concentrated in the hands of the avocado sector and the municipal government led by the mayor. The very existence of the self-defense group, much less its coordination with local government, defied federal and state authorities' declarations that by 2014 self-defense groups would have disbanded or been transitioned into the Rural Police. But in Tancítaro the avocado sector's involvement in local security matters did not look the same as it did in 2013, when the sector's self-defense group openly patrolled the municipality in pickup trucks overflowing with heavily armed men. Having ousted the Knights Templar, the avocado sector now had to get back to work. As producers returned to their orchards, the JLSV resumed communicating with producers and exporters about potential pest infestations and harvesting schedules as well as with the USDA's APHIS personnel to resume exports. But alongside these mundane sectoral activities, it also maintained intra-sectoral communication to prevent the incursion of criminals linked to DTOs into the municipality: "What worried us was that people from outside … strangers … would try to come into the municipality and take control and establish a *plaza* again. If that happened, then the next thing would be the *cuotas* and, then everything else would follow." [15]

Self-defense group members used two-way radios to keep in touch with each other on security matters. Soon after arriving in Tancítaro I noticed many men wearing two-way radios clipped to the front of their shirts or belts. In the course of an interview I was conducting with one avocado producer, his radio squawked into life with someone yelling that "two trucks filled with men" had just driven into Tancítaro from the neighboring municipality. He began to excuse himself to go intercept the vehicle, a handgun strapped to his waist and partly hidden beneath an untucked shirt, but then someone on the radio reported that members of the self-defense group had already stopped the two trucks and it turned out that the men were simply headed to a wedding celebration. He sat back down to finish the interview and noted with a smile: "As you can see, we continue to be organized and present here. Nothing enters the municipality without us knowing about it. That's how we brought order to the municipality." [16]

The centralized structure of coproduction consisted of both formal and informal arrangements between the municipal government and the avocado sector. The formal component entailed jointly constructing the municipality's new police force and filling the void left in the wake of the bottom-up purge that

[15] Interview with Ramiro (MCN808), JLSV employee, Tancítaro, October 2018.
[16] Interview with Marco (MCN315), avocado producer, Tancítaro, July 2018.

victims had carried out. The mayor and the avocado sector agreed to share the costs of building a municipal police force with a high level of institutional capacity: the JLSV would provide 47 percent of the municipal police's annual budget, while the municipal government would be responsible for the remaining 53 percent. The funds from the JLSV came from a new annual tax on local avocado production that the organization's members agreed to pay. The JLSV transferred those funds directly to the mayor's office, where they were pooled with funds from the municipal budget as well as standard financial subsidies provided by the state government to support municipal public security initiatives and institutions.[17]

But informally the avocado sector also leveraged its position of strength in order to influence how local government would construct, maintain, and operate the municipal police. Municipal authorities and the avocado sector jointly established criteria for who could become a municipal police agent. Only people who had lived in the municipality for at least a decade were eligible to apply as a way to reduce the potential that people from outside the municipality with potential links to organized crime would penetrate the police force.[18] Local government officials and members of the avocado sector interviewed each applicant as well as the applicant's local family members. The municipal authorities and the avocado sector jointly hired former Mexican military personnel to train the new police force, including undergoing extensive physical tests. In 2014, nearly one hundred people applied to become part of Tancítaro's new municipal police, called the Cuerpo de Seguridad Pública de Tancítaro (Public Security Force of Tancítaro, or CUSEPT), but less than one-third survived the grueling screening and training processes. The combination of public and private financial resources enabled the building of institutional capacity by doubling monthly police salaries from MXN 2,500 monthly to MXN 5,000 (approximately USD 260). The police also received an array of new weapons, trucks, and bulletproof vests – high-quality equipment normally not available to municipal police forces in Mexico. But the avocado sector and municipal authorities also relied on a set of extralegal practices that shaped how these formal dimensions of the coproduction of order were produced and sustained.

6.3.2 The Practices of Centralized Coproduction

Despite rigorous training, sophisticated equipment, and substantial salaries, the CUSEPT was not the sole provider of order within the municipality. Like any

---

[17] All municipalities in Michoacán can request funds from the state government to invest in local security, including police salaries, weapons, and training. The funds are distributed to state governments by federal authorities through a 2.35 percent tax on the annual federal budget. State governments are then responsible for disbursing the funds to their municipal governments. The funds are coordinated through the Fortalecimiento de los Municipios y de las Demarcaciones Territoriales del Distrito Federal.

[18] Field notes, Tancítaro, July 2018.

other municipal police force in Mexico, the CUSEPT assumed responsibility for everyday order within the municipality. But the question of who would deal with potential incursions by organized crime exemplifies the uneasy balance between legal and extralegal arrangements as part of the centralized coproduction of order.

Armed self-defense group members continued to operate checkpoints on both critical roads within Tancítaro but also at points of entry into the municipality. This gave them a powerful vantage point from which to oversee and regulate flows of people and goods in and out of the municipality – all without formal state sanctioning. From the perspectives of members of the avocado sector, these checkpoints were key nodes in a surveillance web they maintained throughout the municipality to detect potential incursions by organized crime from neighboring municipalities.

Why did the avocado sector and local government invest sizable resources to build and maintain a highly functional municipal police force but not have it be the primary defense from the organized crime that actively operated on the fringes of the municipality? The local government and the avocado sector purposely allowed for ambivalence regarding who was responsible for the question of confronting organized crime. This enabled the avocado sector to maintain informal authority and influence in municipal security, with the tacit consent and cooperation of local government, despite the self-defense group being technically illegal. One avocado producer explained how coproduction thus entailed the piecing together of distinct private and public sector actors in a complex arrangement that straddled the legal and extralegal in ways that they perceived as the only solution to a context marked by the threat of organized crime:

We [referring to the self-defense group] believed that the [municipal] police were absolutely necessary for the security in the municipality. But the police can't do everything or be everywhere. Imagine if [the police] see a group of men driving into the municipality with assault rifles [*cuernos de chivo*]. The police can't deal with that. And even if they stop them, then what? Arrest them? When there's only four or five in a police truck and the *malandros* are coming in dozens? And if they go to jail . . . they'll be out the next day and back here because of the laws and the judges that say there is not enough evidence. No. That's where we do our part for security. There are things [the municipal police] and the law cannot do, things that the law doesn't let them do, but we can do them.[19]

By building a new high-capacity police, both the avocado sector and the local government also prevented political interference in local security matters from parts of the state above the municipality, specifically from state and federal authorities. As noted above, municipal governments in Mexico are expected to establish and oversee municipal police forces. At the same time, the self-defense

---

[19] Interview with Jesús David (MCN113011), avocado producer, Tancítaro, August 2018.

groups were also supposed to have disbanded. By establishing a high-capacity police force, centralized coproduction formally satisfied the first requirement, but the informal arrangement between local government and the avocado sector allowed for the self-defense group to remain in place. This interweaving of the formal and extralegal as part of coproduction helps account for the initially puzzling response I received in Tancítaro on several occasions when I asked both government officials and members of the avocado sector whether the self-defense group still existed: "It exists, but it does not exist [*Si existe, pero no existe.*]"[20] More broadly, it illustrates the generalized notion in Tancítaro that maintaining local order required more than the state could provide because criminal organizations continued to threaten the victimization that capture of the state-sanctioned police had previously facilitated.

6.3.3 The Trajectory of Centralized Coproduction

Over time centralized coproduction in Tancítaro began to break down. The sources of this breakdown were interrelated and threefold. The first emerged from the difficulty of keeping in place a mutually agreed-upon arrangement between formal and informal practices. The second source of strain was the challenge of maintaining distance from organized crime, which wielded significant power in Michoacán. The final strain was associated with the resurgence of preexisting cleavages within the avocado sector.

During my interviews with members of the avocado sector as well as local government officials, it was not uncommon for respondents to appear visibly proud when they spoke about the CUSEPT. Yet, interviews with some members of the CUSEPT indicated that all was not harmonious between local government and the avocado sector. One member of the CUSEPT admitted that there was growing resentment about the informal veto that the avocado sector exercised over their institution. Another acknowledged the challenge of being dependent on, and at times subordinate to, an illegal armed group as part of maintaining the rule of law.[21]

The avocado sector, meanwhile, justified its continued involvement in local security matters because it believed that the CUSEPT was only able to impose order up until the point allowed by the constraints imposed on it under the rule of law. Members of the avocado sector argued that any resentment with its continued involvement in local security matters ignored the important, though admittedly fragile, benefits generated by the local security landscape that they and municipal authorities had jointly crafted:

Today no one pays *cuota* in the municipality . . . *no one*. No one has to keep their eyes on their feet when some fucking criminal walks past them on the street. Girls aren't disappeared for days because you didn't have enough to pay [the criminal tax]. You

---

[20] Field notes, Tancítaro, July 2018.   [21] Field notes, Tancítaro, August 2018.

have your job, and we have ours. If we are divided, then we cannot keep the municipality safe.[22]

In Michoacán the long-standing presence of powerful criminal clans and organizations has long complicated the ability to draw a clean border between the legal and illegal in the political and economic realms (Maldonado 2010). This dynamic is evident in my analysis of the connections between the avocado sector and organized crime as well as the sector's mobilization to resist extortion. It is therefore not surprising that over time "shielding" the municipality from organized crime – a term that both municipal authorities and members of the avocado sector used to describe what they had accomplished – began to erode. This became evident when one tried to reconcile two seemingly irreconcilable phenomena: the tight control that the self-defense forces exerted throughout the municipality along with the heavily armed CUSEPT on the one hand, and the presence of a vibrant local consumer market for illicit drugs on the other hand.

In parts of Tancítaro, one could obtain a variety of illicit drugs for personal use, including marijuana and crystal meth. In recent years, the municipal government had started to invest in drug treatment and prevention programs amid growing public concern over increased drug use in the municipality. These trends, however, were difficult to reconcile with the presence of capable and heavily armed public and private armed actors combating organized crime.

When I asked members of the self-defense group about this paradox, they explained that it was part of a purposive strategy of not stopping drugs for *personal use* from entering the municipality through their checkpoints. From the avocado sector's perspective, confiscating the drugs was not in their interest because doing so could spark conflict with whichever criminal organization the narcotics belonged to: "Those are delicate situations. We cannot be like the military confiscating shipments [of drugs.] And of course, the military comes in, confiscates, and leaves, but then the fights between criminals is what they don't see. We live here. So we need a different approach."[23] This different approach entailed tolerating an illicit drug market for personal consumption that, according to locals, was coordinated by local youth who purchased the drugs outside of Tancítaro and brought them into the municipality to sell to community residents. But the long-term sustainability of this arrangement, and specifically the ability to keep a local drug market divorced from the robust regional drug trafficking markets, did not elicit much confidence in many of the people who I interviewed. In reality, local drug markets rarely operate independently of DTOs given their utility for generating revenue and further strengthening organized crime's control over territory.

Finally, the cross-party alliance forged during the 2015 elections broke down in anticipation of the 2018 municipal elections as preexisting class and partisan

---

[22] Interview with Jesús David (MCN113011), avocado producer, Tancítaro, August 2018.
[23] Interview with Noe (MCN7835), JLSV employee, Tancítaro, July 2018.

cleavages returned to center stage in local politics. The members of the avocado sector who had been at the forefront of these efforts in 2015 did initially propose a similar unity government in 2018, but resistance from all three political currents within the avocado sector ultimately derailed these discussions. In part this reflected the reduced sense of threat that the sector perceived relative to the security context during the 2015 elections. Victims believed that the self-defense group and its coordination with the municipal government had transformed Tancítaro into an "oasis" in a "sea of insecurity" [referring to the rest of Michoacán].[24] One avocado producer who was still actively involved in the self-defense group acknowledged that though DTOs were present in neighboring municipalities, the absence of extortion within Tancítaro had fostered a "lack of urgency [*falta de urgencia*]" regarding intervening in the municipal elections. A leader in the municipal PRD organization explained:

In that moment [referring to the 2015 elections], all you had to do was look in [name of neighboring municipality] or [name of neighboring municipality] to see that the *maña* was rearranging itself. The *autodefensas* had hit [the criminals], yes. Now [the criminals] were going to try to reclaim the territories . . . the *plazas* they had lost . . . by capturing the [political] candidates. An alliance [among the parties] was something reasonable *at that moment*. Today things are different. Today the municipality is shielded [*blindado*], and so we can have politics like normal again.[25]

Yet, because the period of relative order in Tancítaro was widely attributed to the close coordination between the municipal government and the avocado sector, subsequent municipal authorities faced potentially high political costs if they attempted to veer away from coproduction. Partisan lines that overlapped with class lines in Tancítaro's avocado sector thus dominated the 2018 elections, with small-scale producers supporting the PRD and wealthier producers aligning behind the PAN. The PAN candidate won the election by less than one hundred votes.[26] Yet, some parts of centralized coproduction of order persisted. In 2019, the newly elected mayor representing the PAN sustained the arrangement regarding local policing between the avocado sector and the municipal government, including the informal distribution of security between the CUSEPT and the self-defense group.

Yet, for the reasons that I discuss above, the long-term sustainability of centralized coproduction was far from certain. The resurfacing of intragroup tensions fostered critical reflections on the ways in which resistance to criminal extortion had unfolded in Tancítaro. For example, in discussions with small-scale producers, they noted there had been issues during mobilization of collective vigilantism that they interpreted as reflecting preexisting cleavages.

---

[24] Field notes, Tancítaro, July 2018.
[25] Telephone interview, Cynthia (MCN85001), member of the PRD municipal committee, Tancítaro, January 2019.
[26] Based on results consulted on the website of the Instituto Electoral de Michoacán (iem.org.mx).

These issues included who among the avocado producers were given access to particular types of weapons. Several of the wealthier producers were able to obtain firearms using their own money while not all smaller producers had access to weapons purchased with funds from the JLSV, and thus had to rely on personal weapons, often shotguns or handguns. According to other small-scale producers, there were also controversies with informal justice under collective vigilantism. After some lands that had been taken by the Knights Templar were returned to an array of landowners, both small and large, the cases of several large expanses of avocado orchards were never resolved, with suspicion that some of the larger producers opted to keep the avocado-producing lands themselves. Interviews with larger producers indicated that the controversy was not clear – with some of the people whose lands had been taken did not want to reclaim them because they had left the municipality. Other large-scale producers indicated that the lands were never actually stolen and that the people claiming them had not owned them in the first place – instead these were personal disputes, sometimes between family members, that some parties sought to resolve through the informal justice provided under collective vigilantism. In brief, the centralized coproduction persisted, but its robustness waned over time as security conditions improved and cleavages that had been subsumed during collective vigilantism and the early period of coproduction resurfaced in the political landscape.

6.4 DECENTRALIZED COPRODUCTION OF ORDER

The 2015 and 2018 municipal elections were also critical opportunities to shape local order in La Unión. But unlike in Tancítaro, the berry sector in La Unión was not organized under a single sectoral organization through which to intervene in electoral politics. Decentralized collective vigilantism, a result of the segmented political economy, had left in its wake two armed groups whose leaders had both overlapping and conflicting incentives to shape order. Whereas the avocado sector in Tancítaro coordinated with political authorities to shape the nature of coproduction, the process leading to coproduction in La Unión was contentious and ultimately yielded uneasy alliances between armed groups of victims and political entrepreneurs competing for power.

In 2015, Felipe, former leader of self-defense Group B and now commander of the local Rural Police, and Carlos, leader of Group D and backed by the CJNG, each intervened in local elections by supporting opposing candidates for municipal president. Felipe – a long time member of the PRD – supported Hugo, the PRD's candidate for municipal president.[27] And echoing Trejo and Ley's (2020) finding that organized crime in Michoacán largely backed the PRI during the 2015 elections, Carlos threw the support of his self-defense group behind the PRI candidate for municipal president, Rodolfo. The armed groups' coercive

---

[27] Field notes, La Unión, August 2018.

capacities made them strategically useful for both candidates' electoral ambitions, though the candidates harnessed these resources in different ways.

Felipe accompanied Hugo on the campaign trail in public displays of support that embodied the complex amalgamation of informal and formal power that characterized Michoacán's Rural Police. Blurring the line between private and public force, news stories of Hugo's rallies showed Felipe wearing his government-issued uniform and weapon alongside some of his men in plain clothes carrying personal weapons. But as one government official who served during Hugo's tenure as municipal president explained: "Of course people wanted a candidate that could help the municipality to progress. Insecurity was . . . one of, if not the, main issue. It was because of what we had experienced with the *maña*. People wanted to see a candidate that could bring order. And for that, having people see Felipe's support was important."[28] At the same time, during his campaign speeches, Hugo would often refer to Felipe and his men not as the Rural Police, but instead as the municipality's "legitimate self-defense group [*autodefensas legítimas*]."[29] In doing so, Hugo avoided reminding voters that Felipe's men were technically part of a state institution that was deeply unpopular among large portions of the local population for its association with state and federal efforts to "institutionalize" – and thus neutralize – the self-defense groups. But this label also enabled Hugo to indirectly communicate that unlike Carlos's men, the group led by Felipe was not working for a criminal actor. By this point it was common in Michoacán to differentiate between three types of self-defense groups: those that were "legitimate" – meaning they were part of the original self-defense groups and did not have links to organized crime; those that were "illegitimate" – meaning that they too had been part of the original self-defense groups but had been compromised as they accepted support from criminal actors; and those that were "false" – referring to those that consisted primarily of criminal groups pretending to be victims so as to advance their illicit interests under the facade of the self-defense movement.[30] By naming Felipe's self-defense group as "legitimate," Hugo reminded voters of the group's comparatively earnest origins while simultaneously – but carefully and implicitly – raising concern about the nature of Carlos's group and its intentions as an extension of the CJNG.

By contrast, the alliance between the PRI candidate, Rodolfo, and self-defense Group D was comparatively less visible. Carlos did not accompany Rodolfo to public events on the campaign trail and his support was largely limited to encouraging members of Group D to vote for the PRI.[31] Some believed that Carlos was too busy fulfilling his commitment to the CJNG to

---

[28] Interview with Harold (MCN4849), municipal government official, La Unión, May 2019.
[29] Interview with Harold (MCN4849), municipal government official, La Unión, May 2019.
[30] Field notes, La Unión, July 2018.
[31] Interview with Sergio (MCN8001), member of Carlos's self-defense Group (B), La Unión, September 2018.

restart local drug production and trafficking, primarily methamphetamines.[32] His absence from public campaigning may have also reflected confidence in the PRI's ability to win the election given criminal support for the party throughout the municipality, but also because several of Rodolfo's family members had been high-level elected officials and party organizers at the state level for the PRI. But the discreet nature of the alliance between the PRI candidate and self-defense Group D shifted as the race tightened to a three-way contest between the Hugo, Rodolfo, and the PAN candidate in the days leading up to the 2015 elections. Hence Carlos's men began intimidating the PRD and PAN campaigns, including stationing their trucks filled with armed men outside the houses and campaign headquarters of the two candidates. Representatives from both the PRD and PAN campaigns also indicated that people began refusing to open their doors or come to publicly advertised meetings in different parts of the municipality – with rumors swirling that self-defense Group D had threatened them not to do so. But by this late in the election, Group D's tactics fell short in securing victory for their preferred candidate. Hugo, the PRD candidate backed by the leader of self-defense Group B, narrowly won the municipal elections in June of 2015. The key challenge that the segmented political economy and decentralized collective vigilantism left for the newly elected municipal president, however, would be structuring, enacting, and sustaining order in a way that balanced the formal authority of local government and the continued presence of competing armed groups that represented combinations of personal, state, and criminal interests.

6.4.1 The Structure of Decentralized Coproduction of Order

Even before taking office, Hugo attempted to exert his authority as mayor-elect in establishing the terms of coproduction of order. He did so by telling supporters, including Felipe, that he would appoint a long time acquaintance as director of Public Security in La Unión – an individual with no ties to either of the armed groups operating in the municipality. Although Felipe had openly declared that he wanted to be the director, Hugo bypassed him. This strategic move signaled that Hugo, as the elected leader of local government, would not allow the armed groups to dictate the terms of the coproduction of order. But in response to Hugo's decision, Felipe soon issued threats against not only the individual who Hugo proposed for director of Public Security but also the mayor-elect himself as well. Tense negotiations between Hugo and Felipe – including a stand-off in a public plaza where dozens of former members of Group B who were now part of the Rural Police physically confronted the mayor-elect – led to a compromise: Felipe would become subdirector of Public Security, and the Rural Police would accompany an emerging local police in maintaining order within the municipality. By all accounts, this was

---

[32] Interview with Jesús (MCN14835), community member, La Unión, September 2018.

an unorthodox move as municipalities in Mexico typically have individual municipal-level police forces separate from other security institutions. The proposed arrangement would allow Felipe autonomy as his Rural Police force would shape local order alongside a nascent municipal police force that the local government was building, but without reporting directly to the mayor. In striking this deal, Hugo avoided further confrontation with Felipe. This again underscores that like decentralized collective vigilantism, the decentralized coproduction of order in La Unión did not feature the close and cooperative linkages between local government and armed victims.

The agreement between Hugo and Felipe also provided the mayor-elect with political dividends that underscore the importance of disaggregating the state when analyzing the politics of crime. By allowing Felipe and the Rural Police to assume a role in local policing, Hugo also prevented the politically risky move of having political forces from outside of the municipality dictate the terms of local policing. In 2014, the federal government had passed legislation establishing the Mando Unico (Single Command), an initiative under which all of Mexico's municipal police forces would be centralized under state-level police forces in each of the country's thirty-two states. From the perspective of the federal authorities, this would constrain links between local-level police and DTOs. Yet, in Michoacán this was widely derided as another way for the state government to place police personnel from outside of the municipality into their territories, including people potentially linked to DTOs. By instead naming the Rural Police as part of the municipal security structure, Hugo deflected outside intervention in local security matters in so far as he could claim that there was no need to have La Unión's police join the Mando Unico given the enhanced security capacity resulting from coordination with the Rural Police. But doing so also increased the number of armed actors involved in the coproduction of local order and dispersed power and authority over local security without a clear understanding of the responsibilities of the individual actors.

Soon after the 2015 municipal elections, it became evident that there was a lack of clarity about which level of government the Rural Police in Michoacán were technically reporting to. The federal government had initially provided the Rural Police with weapons, trucks, and uniforms in a highly publicized unveiling ceremony in May of 2014, but just days later it was already unclear which level of government would provide for its ongoing budgetary needs such as paying salaries and benefits. Federal authorities indicated that it was the state government's responsibility, but state legislators countered that under existing laws, the Rural Police could not technically exist as a state-level security force.[33] Soon parts of the Rural Police across the state of Michoacán went on strike, decrying that this lack of government support had come at a critical moment: elements of the Knights Templar still active in Michoacán had begun

---

[33] According to the debate in Michoacán's state legislature, the Rural Police force could not legally exist because it did not fit under existing legislation as a state-sanctioned security force.

assassinating former members of self-defense groups who had become Rural Police agents.

In La Unión, Felipe – now filling the dual role of subdirector of Public Security and commander of the local Rural Police – was forced to ask his officers to use their own cars and trucks to patrol the municipality.[34] The lack of resources forced Felipe to also outsource aspects of everyday policing to a small group of older men who had been part of his self-defense group, but who had opted to return to growing berries in their orchards versus becoming part of the state's security apparatus. This group of former *autodefensas* revived the Monday afternoon meetings in the municipal plaza where members of the Citizens Council had briefly met before disbanding amid infighting. With his men in the Rural Police already stretched thin given the lack of resources, Felipe began this parallel extralegal mechanism through which community residents could bring their everyday conflicts to the subset of former *autodefensas*.[35] The overarching result was further decentralization of the coproduction of local order to an expanding array of public and private actors with minimal coordination among them.

At the same time, Carlos's self-defense Group D remained armed and operating within the municipality. Having failed to ally with the successful mayoral candidate, Group D operated on the fringes of the arrangement between the municipal government and the Rural Police and the array of smaller actors operating around them. Carlos and his men focused on their illicit interests, mounting methamphetamine labs throughout the municipality. But this did not mean that Group D ceased to provide security. Instead Carlos and his men continued to fulfill this function by remaining vigilant about the incursion of rival criminal organizations. Publicly Carlos framed this as a necessary strategy to stop the criminal groups who coveted the lucrative *plaza* of La Unión from potentially resuming extortion and associated violence. But it was also widely, yet tacitly, recognized that Group D was now an extension of the CJNG, and, as such, defending the municipality from rival criminal groups was as much about keeping control of the *plaza* for itself as it was about preventing extortion by another criminal group. But, as I discuss below, this entailed Group D engaging in practices that would ultimately lead to conflict with municipal authorities and other actors within the decentralized coproduction of order.

6.4.2   The Practices of Decentralized Coproduction of Order

La Unión's municipal president recognized the challenge of having Carlos's group operating freely throughout the municipality.[36] This challenge reflected

---

[34] The issue of which level of government was responsible for maintaining the Rural Police force was never fully resolved before the entire entity was technically disbanded in 2016.

[35] Field notes, La Unión, September 2018.   [36] Field notes, La Unión, August 2018.

the decentralized nature of coproduction in La Unión. As Group D monitored and policed the municipality's borders to prevent the entry of criminal groups aligned with the Knights Templar or other DTOs, it also controlled the flows of illicit narcotics in and out of the municipality on behalf of the CJNG. As Gladys, a local journalist, noted:

That group [referring to Group D] counted on many, many men, and all connected using radios and cell phones. If one of them saw something suspicious, in ten minutes you would have several hundred men with their guns in their trucks ready to attack. There were police here in the municipality [referring to the Rural Police], but they were nothing compared to Carlos's group.[37]

Gladys's commentary on the discrepancy in the coercive power between the Rural Police and self-defense Group D alluded to broader conflicts that unfolded between the two actors. On several occasions, the Rural Police and the self-defense group clashed on the municipality's borders as each sought to assert territorial control in an increasingly fragmented security landscape.

Municipal authorities, including the nascent municipal police and the Rural Police, lacked incentive to intervene in Group D's drug trafficking efforts. As long as the drug trade did not degrade into extortion and associated violence, it did not threaten to produce the kind of disorder that victims had sought to end through collective vigilantism. As a result, the municipal government actually urged Felipe to not interfere with self-defense Group D's extralegal activities, including the drug trafficking. A municipal official in Hugo's administration explained the logic of this decision:

What we had was a time bomb. The legacy of the lack of organization in the municipality was armed groups that did not speak to each other but that had some things in common. Both wanted the municipality to be secure, although one of them had reasons beyond not wanting to see the *cuota* come back. [The municipal government attempted] to organize the situation, but it didn't work.[38]

Felipe and the Rural Police obliged the municipal president for a short period before challenging self-defense Group D, including setting up rival checkpoints near those organized by Group D on roads leading in and out of the municipality. Residents began to complain of having to make two stops – one at each barricade – as one bus driver recounted: "It was comical. You stopped at the barricade that the *autodefensas* [referring to Group D] were running and right there from your bus you could see the next barricade down the road and see the uniformed [referring to the Rural Police] waiting as well."[39] The decentralized structure of coproduction in La Unión thus extended into the range of formal and extralegal practices, and the strained nature of the interaction between the actors presaged its unsustainability.

---

[37] Interview with Gladys (MCN6507), journalist, La Unión, June 2018.
[38] Interview with Mercedes (MCN4800), municipal official, La Unión, August 2018.
[39] Field notes, La Unión, June 2018.

6.4.3   The Trajectory of Decentralized Coproduction of Order

In April of 2016, the Rural Police was disbanded in Michoacán when federal authorities admitted failure after being unable to secure a steady supply of resources and funding from the state government. But soon after yet another police institution, the Policía Michoacana, was announced. All members of the Rural Police who passed background exams were transitioned into the new state-level police force. Felipe was again named commander of the newly created local division of the Policía Michoacana and continued functioning as a local police institution in La Unión alongside the small municipal force. But the tensions associated with the decentralized nature of coproduction increasingly manifested in violent clashes between the new state-level police force led by Felipe and self-defense Group D.

These tensions reached a boiling point in the summer of 2016 when armed men kidnapped Felipe as he left to carry out his normal patrol duties. His body was found several days later with signs of extensive torture. Many in the municipality with knowledge of what had happened indicated that Carlos, likely following the CJNG's orders, had finally ordered Felipe's assassination to clear the way for him to become more directly involved in local security matters and the production of drugs without interference.[40]

Group D subsequently assumed a more prominent role in shaping local order while simultaneously enabling the continuation of the local drug trade. Carlos pressured Hugo to furnish him with a more influential role in the governance of local order. Hugo was forced to appoint people close to Carlos to local government positions from which they could oversee local security issues. Two of Carlos's lieutenants in Group D were named "security advisors" to the municipal government, while another lieutenant was ultimately hired to replace Felipe as head of the Policía Michoacana in La Unión. But it was the 2018 municipal elections when Group D mobilized to more directly wield control over local government.

Carlos and his men threw their support behind the PAN's candidate for municipal president, Sebastian. The alliance between Sebastian and Carlos still did not rely on the two appearing together at public events or campaigning together. Instead Carlos's self-defense group systematically intimidated Sebastian's political opponents and voters. From the start of their campaigns, men from Group D staff physically intimidated and threatened staff members for the PRI and PRD candidates. News coverage during the election reported armed groups of men who had historically voted for the PRD and the PRI appearing in the municipality's districts to warn residents to vote for the PAN instead. In one incident, armed men from Carlos's group kidnapped the PRI candidate along with their manager and released them only several days later. The PRI campaign manager subsequently resigned and moved out of Michoacán, while the PRD

---

[40] Field notes, La Unión, June 2018.

candidate stopped holding campaign events.[41] Sebastian won the 2018 municipal elections with a wide margin of victory – several thousand votes over his closest competitor.[42]

Under Sebastian, Carlos's influence in local governance increased substantially, as evident in the selection of several of Carlos's men for local cabinet positions and as the director of Public Security in La Unión. But as one of Carlos's closest confidants in Group D argued, coordination with local government was "good for everyone" because it meant that no "*bad* criminal groups" would be able to enter the municipality and victimize the population:

SERGIO: You must see by now, you've learned about how things are here now. Does anyone here say they have to pay the cuota?

EM: No.

SERGIO: Does anyone say that there are kidnappings [*levantamientos*] anymore?

EM: No.

SERGIO: There it is—there is peace in the municipality. That's all people wanted.[43]

6.5 CONCLUSION

This chapter shows that collective resistance can produce endogenous shifts in the contexts within which victims mobilize. Despite engaging in distinct forms of collective vigilantism, victims in Tancítaro and La Unión made neutralizing local police who had colluded with criminals a key objective early in their mobilization. These "bottom-up" purges of the local police shifted a key element of the context in which victims operated. It opened the door to the possibility of local governments establishing new and autonomous, but low-capacity, police. In both cases victims feared that a low-capacity coercive arm of the state would again provide an access point for organized crime to reenter the municipalities. Victims responded by pursuing the coproduction of order. Yet, coproduction varied across the two cases.

In Tancítaro victims once again used their organizational resources to engage in a centralized effort to bring into power a local government willing to coordinate with what was now an illegal self-defense group. The resulting centralization of coproduction produced a high-capacity coercive arm of the state. But here, it was constrained by its origins as part of an informal arrangement that enabled victims to continue using extralegal practices accorded to them as part of centralized coproduction.

By contrast, in La Unión the segmented political economy and the decentralized collective vigilantism it yielded contributed to competing efforts

---

[41] This information is based on conversations with several of the candidate's campaign workers and local news coverage.

[42] Data accessed at: iem.org.mx. Accessed on October 12, 2018.

[43] Interview with Sergio (MCN8001), member of Carlos's self-defense Group (B), La Unión, September 2018.

to shape the nature of coproduction. This took the form of different groups of victims and politicians forming competing coalitions to secure power and shape local order. Decentralized coproduction was strained as some victims built formal ties with local government and others were sidelined from this arrangement but continued to wield coercive power. The latter used this power to both support and undermine different parts of the rule of law.

More broadly, these cases also illustrate one of the potential downsides of the coproduction of order. Evans (1996) shows that coproduction, or state–society synergy, can produce positive developmental outcomes under two conditions: when states have autonomous bureaucracies that are embedded in society. This combination enables states to benefit from the input, resources, and support of social groups, while still preserving the state's freedom to autonomously articulate and enact decisions. But lacking this bureaucratic autonomy, coproduction becomes less an exercise in the use of state–society synergy to generate positive outcomes and more a reflection of uneven power dynamics between states and society. Coproduction thus sits on a continuum bookended by the ideal-types of state autonomy and state capture. In both Tancítaro and La Unión, the ability of victims to end their victimization and oust their criminal victimizers gave them a powerful combination of legitimacy and coercive power vis-à-vis local authorities. This allowed victims to impose the terms of the coproduction of order, though importantly, variation in the organizational cohesion of victims and its resulting legacy following collective vigilantism produced different processes of coproduction. This chapter analyzes these different processes of coproduction, showing how they involved both contrasting practices of political competition and distinct arrangements of formal and extralegal practices that simultaneously upheld and eroded the rule of law.

7

Summing Up and Next Steps

This book set out to deepen our understanding of a phenomenon that I encountered in different parts of Latin America, but one that is largely overlooked in existing research: victims using contrasting strategies to resist victimization at the hands of armed criminal actors. Research on criminal politics in Latin America focuses on when and how the interactions between states and criminal actors in the illicit drug trade produce different patterns in the frequency and modalities of lethal violence – important outcomes given the threat that criminal violence poses for development and democracy (Ayres 1998). This book broadens the analytic lens to include victims as critical actors who shape patterns of crime, violence, and victimization. I develop in-depth case studies using data collected in sites of past and ongoing criminal victimization via extortion and associated violence in Colombia, El Salvador, and Mexico. I examine how different configurations of three variables generate different processes and mechanisms that lead to distinct strategies of resistance: the time horizons of criminal actors, local political economies, and the criminal capture of the police. The resulting strategies have divergent structures, practices, and trajectories, with broader implications for everyday political life. In this concluding chapter I first briefly summarize the argument. I then identify the broader contributions of the analysis. Next I outline tasks for future research. The final section identifies the policy implications derived from the analysis and findings.

7.1 SUMMARY OF THE ARGUMENT

7.1.1 Criminal Time Horizons

I argue that the time horizons of criminal actors influence not only their preferences and behaviors but also those of their victims. The focus on criminal actors' time horizons both aligns with and extends important insights forged in classic and recent analyses of the incentives that shape the behavior of armed actors, all of which build on Mancur Olson's (1993) distinction between stationary and roving bandits. Stationary bandits cooperate with civilians to foster long-term productivity of the populations they govern, while roving bandits engage in predation to maximize rent extraction in the short term because they discount the future. Scholars of civil wars have harnessed this theoretical point to theorize the behaviors of rebel groups, specifically their choices in whether and how they govern populations in the territories under their control in wartime settings (Arjona 2017; Mampilly 2012; Sánchez de la Sierra 2020). I import these insights from the study of civil wars to the politics of crime, highlighting a crucial point of overlap as a fruitful bridge for dialogue and future research. But I also extend the line of inquiry by considering how the time horizons of criminal actors not only shape their behaviors but also influence the preferences and behaviors of their victims.

Criminal actors with long time horizons enjoy a position of strength that increases victims' perceptions that they will suffer punishment if they attempt to end their victimization. This is because in the absence of either state crackdowns or criminal competition, the criminal actor has a robust grip on local territory, strong networks of informants, and it can use its coercive capacity toward its challengers without having to divert resources away from defending itself from the state and/or rivals. At the same time, the long time horizon enables criminal groups to provide populations with benefits to elicit obedience, including access to critical goods and services ranging from financial assistance to protection. Under these conditions victims are therefore more likely to attempt to negotiate their victimization via everyday resistance, as I showed in Chapter 3.

By contrast, state crackdowns and/or criminal competition shorten criminal actors' time horizons. Here the criminal actor must divert resources and invest coercive capacity in fending off its challengers. Given the need to generate more resources, the criminal actor assumes a more predatory stance toward its victims, increasing the frequency and intensity of the strategies of domination discussed in Chapter 2 and analyzed empirically in Parts II and III. This shift in the time horizons of criminal actors changes the preferences of victims, as the benefits of negotiating victimization decrease and the costs of keeping the status quo increase. Under these conditions, all things being equal, victims are more likely to risk pursuing resistance to end or prevent victimization. Yet, while criminal actors' time horizons affect victims' preferences, the ability of victims to challenge criminal actors hinges on their capacity to mobilize collectively.

7.1.2   Local Political Economies

Local political economies shape relations among victims and relations between victims and governing authorities. The first feature aligns with studies in political science that focus on how ties among actors condition their ability to engage in high-risk mobilization. Petersen (2001) shows that preexisting social bonds contained within factory units and college fraternities enabled collective mobilization in Lithuania against armed occupation by the Soviet regime. Arjona (2016, 70–72) finds that civilians used the leadership structures associated with conflict resolution institutions to contest rebel governance in Colombia. Also in Colombia, Kaplan (2017, 34) argues that preexisting community organizations provided the social cohesion that communities harnessed to "retain autonomy, or self-rule" vis-à-vis rebel groups. Varshney (2002) shows that the structure of associational life, specifically the existence or absence of preexisting interethnic associational organizations, affects whether ethnic tensions can be neutralized before producing ethnic violence.[1] Shifting to settings of crime, Bateson (2013) concludes that in Guatemala, where the military organized people into armed pro-government civil patrols, former patrollers revived the skills and the social ties forged during war to collectively punish criminals who were committing everyday crimes. By contrast, where the military did not organize civil patrols, civilian responses were more likely to take the form of individual-level acts of extralegal violence.

Where my book deviates from these important works is by bringing the state into the analysis of mobilization against the threat or use of violence by armed non-state actors. I argue that where victims count on strong ties to the state, specifically local governing authorities, they are more likely to coordinate with them in order to mount, enact, and sustain resistance. Strong preexisting linkages between victims and governing authorities entail channels of communication that each uses to influence the other. Here governing authorities have incentives to cooperate with victims that range from obtaining protection from criminal reprisals to electoral support. This translates into the state engaging in both legal and extralegal practices to accommodate victims. Hence preexisting ties enable the state and victims to coordinate resistance to criminal victimization. This is important because this type of coordination can bolster the capacity of victims to sustain their mobilization. As shown in Chapters 6 and 7, close linkages to local governing authorities enabled victims in Tancítaro to sustain their mobilization while governing authorities received the benefits of order and political support.

By contrast, where these links between victims and governing authorities are weak or nonexistent, the chances of coordination drop considerably. More importantly, the lack of strong ties makes it more likely that victims will interpret governing authorities giving into criminal actors' demands as corruption. Hence victims and governing authorities have tense and conflictive interactions in contexts where linkages between the two are absent. It denies victims political cover from higher levels of the state that may oppose their

---

[1] Varshney (2002) distinguishes these formal associational structures, which he calls "organized" networks, from "quotidian" or "everyday forms of engagement" that may cross ethnic lines but prove less capable of stopping ethnic violence in the face of political actors who want to polarize communities along ethnic lines for political gains.

mobilization as well as clear channels through which to influence local policymaking. As the same time, governing authorities face much more perilous situations vis-à-vis victims, as shown in the case of La Unión in Chapter 6.

In brief, the state plays a key role in how victims mobilize against criminal victimization. The state can be an accomplice and, in the process, blur the lines between legal and extralegal in its own ways. Or, the state can be a target of victims' efforts to end victimization. As I show above, even in contexts in which governing authorities obeyed criminal actors, victims base their differential treatment of governing authorities on whether or not they had preexisting ties to them – a function of the political economy.

7.1.3   Criminal Capture of the Police

We would expect that where the state's security apparatus has a high degree of institutional capacity, armed criminal groups will be less likely to establish territorial control and coordinate their illicit economies because of the higher probability that they and their illicit operations will be dismantled. Here victims can denounce criminals through formal legal channels by turning to police institutions that can and will provide order while upholding the rule of law. In these contexts, victims have little need to pursue strategies of resistance that target the criminal actor. This is why the argument I develop in this book explores the choices that victims make in contexts where the police either are captured by criminal actors or are autonomous but lack the institutional capacity to enforce order while adhering to the rule of law. It is precisely in these settings where victims are more likely to resist victimization by bypassing formal legal channels. When the police are captured by criminal actors, trying to activate the rule of law is either ineffectual at best or risks violent punishment at worse.

Victims will not incorporate into their resistance police who are captured by criminal actors because the police have incentives to denounce victims. Examples of such incentives include financial remuneration by the criminal actor, who threatens to punish the police if they fail to neutralize threats to criminals' territorial control, including rivals, other elements of the state, and victims mobilizing against them. Under these conditions, victims circumvent police, and, depending on the specific strategy of resistance that they pursue, they may even target police as part of their mobilization to end criminal victimization, as shown in the cases of collective vigilantism that I analyzed in Chapter 5.

But the argument in this book also shows that police have incentives to join with and facilitate strategies of resistance that entail extralegal practices. Exceeding the boundaries of the rule of law is no longer outside of the realm of possibility in settings where police either lack the institutional capacity to ensure order while adhering to the rule of law – as evident in my discussion of the survey data of police in El Salvador that I analyze in Chapter 4 – or have to carry out state-ordered crackdowns on powerful criminal groups with limited institutional resources while being violently targeted by the criminal actors. Under these conditions police are more likely to be available to join with and support victims in practices of extralegal violence against a shared enemy – particularly the lower ranks of the police that are disproportionately exposed to criminal violence and also most likely to be negatively impacted by limited police capacity. Here victims do not demand that police engage in procedural justice, but instead help them to punish criminal victimizers using means that violate and weaken procedural justice. Chapter 4's analysis of piecemeal vigilantism in El Salvador showed that police provided valuable inputs (e.g., information and protection from other parts of the state) to carry out and sustain extralegal violence jointly with victims.

Victims also have incentives to collaborate with police, especially when they perceive that powerful armed criminal actors threaten to undermine the ability of autonomous, yet institutionally weak, police to thwart victimization while adhering to the rule of law. In the cases of coproduction in Michoacán that I analyzed in Chapter 6, victims viewed an autonomous, but low-capacity, police as susceptible to criminal influence. But victims also viewed the rule of law as inadequate to safeguard against victimization posed by powerful criminal actors. Hence producing order, from the perspective of the victims, required working with government authorities and police to distribute security responsibilities across multiple actors using both formal and extralegal practices.

7.2 BROADER IMPLICATIONS

The hypotheses that follow from the argument in this book are probabilistic and not deterministic. The empirical analysis was not constructed to test the theory, but instead to illustrate its analytic utility. The in-depth case studies offer a high level of within-case explanatory power. This internal validity results partly from a research design that aligns with recent studies of both political and criminal violence in combining an "ethnographic sensibility" (Schatz 2013) with multisited comparisons of processes and mechanisms (Arias 2009, 2017; Wood 2003). The research design and analysis yields several contributions for the study of the politics of criminal victimization.[2]

The voices of victims of armed criminal groups and how they understand their victimization are relatively absent in much of the existing research on criminal politics.[3] But this book shows that foregrounding victims and their relations with criminals and state actors in our analyses can provide a powerful vantage point from which to study the politics of crime. Unpacking and distinguishing between different forms of criminal victimization reveals

---

[2] See Simmons and Smith (2019) on the contributions of comparative ethnography.
[3] Important exceptions include Auyero and Berti (2016) and Moser and McIlwaine (2004).

dynamics that otherwise go unobserved when we think about crime as only a onetime act. The analysis shows that though material domination is central to criminal extortion, the forced extraction of material rents is also accompanied by criminals' use of social and political practices of domination that facilitate victimization. While we have not previously analyzed these aspects of victimization in depth, victims across my cases underscored their importance in making sense of and processing their experiences with criminal extortion. Contrary to my expectations before I went to the field, I found that for victims of criminal extortion and associated violence in diverse contexts, victimization is not only about criminal actors taking their money under threat of coercive punishment, but also about having to repeatedly endure social and political forms of humiliation and disparagement. Unearthing these additional dimensions of victimization should prompt us to broaden the analytic scope of existing research to include victims' experiences that, while not easily observable, influence how victims make sense of crime, violence, and order and, in turn, shape their responses both at and beyond the ballot box. More broadly, by understanding the meaning of victimization, researchers can facilitate innovation in theory-building by zooming in on the locus of choice (Arjona 2019) to compare seemingly distinct cases.

Unpacking criminal victimization – how victims understand and make sense of their victimization at the hands of armed criminal groups – necessitated theorizing the strategies of domination that criminal actors use to facilitate and sustain victimization. As developed in Chapter 2, I argue that like any governing ruler, criminal groups employ material, social, and political strategies of domination. The empirical analysis in Chapters 3–6, in turn, illustrates these strategies and underlines how they perpetuate criminal extortion. By identifying these strategies, the analysis offers new dimensions along which scholars can compare criminal actors, which, to date, largely emphasize their organizational composition and use of coercive force but overlook the social and political aspects of criminal rule and their consequences.[4]

At its core my analysis complicates the assumption that victims lack agency. I disaggregate resistance – defined as observable strategies outside of the rule of law that victims direct at criminals to negotiate, end, or prevent their victimization – along multiple dimensions to yield a typology of distinct forms of resistance. Taken together this provides a new conceptual vocabulary with which to identify and compare the pathways that lead victims to distinct strategies of resistance. I illustrate the argument's analytic utility in each of the empirical chapters in which I triangulate different data to show how piecemeal vigilantism, collective vigilantism, and the coproduction of order emerge. But considered together, the resulting empirical case analyses enable

---

[4] There is a small but growing number of studies on strategies of criminal governance (e.g., Arias 2017; Lessing and Willis 2019; Magaloni, Franco-Vivanco, and Melo 2020).

us to zoom out and identify overarching similarities in the processes and mechanisms of victimization and resistance across time and space.

I was able to identify these additional aspects of victimization by using multiple methodologies as I engaged with victims to document and then analyze how they made sense of their own victimization. Though the strategies of resistance varied across the cases, the previous chapters show that the factors I identify in the theory of resistance to criminal victimization help us understand how resistance differs with regard to its trajectories, structures, and what practices victims use. Identifying these additional layers of victimization and resistance would have been difficult without carrying out fieldwork in multiple localities and using methodologies that privileged learning about and from the experiences of the key actors in the analysis.

This book's findings should encourage us to broaden how we understand and study the range of potential political consequences that result from criminal victimization. Analyses of the political consequences of victimization focus on the impact of victimization on voting and civic mobilization (Bateson 2012; Dorff 2017; Ley 2018; Visconti 2019). These are crucial outcomes that merit further study. But by centering on how victims experience victimization across multiple contexts, this book also urges us to widen the lens on what counts as "political." Victims in the cases that I analyzed – from the informal vendors who pursued everyday resistance in Medellín to the agricultural producers in Michoacán who engaged in variants of collective vigilantism – all understood the behaviors they undertook as part of resistance (e.g., nonviolent verbal jousting or acts of extralegal coercion) to be inherently political statements. Moreover, as evident in the analysis of the coproduction of order in Chapter 6, the political consequences of victimization can extend well beyond the casting of votes to include exerting informal pressure as well as threatening or using violence against elements of the state to reshape governance. As the analysis of piecemeal vigilantism in Chapter 4 shows, victims can reconfigure aspects of governance through less direct ways by enlisting and supporting core elements of the state – in this case, the police – to pursue and facilitate extralegal actions.

This book also has implications for the ways in which we understand relations between police and communities in contexts of organized crime and violence. Researchers and policymakers urge strengthening police–community ties to facilitate collaboration that could stem and prevent crime while concurrently strengthening the capacity of the police to exercise a monopoly on the legitimate use of violence (Arias and Ungar 2009; Frühling 2012). Underlying efforts to improve community–police relations is an extensive body of research that concludes that whether citizens perceive the police as legitimate or not influences their willingness to cooperate to prevent and/or end criminal activity through formal institutional channels (Tyler and Fagan 2008; Tyler and Jackson 2014). The notion of institutional legitimacy used here is akin to that indicated by Juan Linz (1988, 65): "the belief that in spite of shortcomings and failures ... " a particular institution is "better than any other that might be established, and therefore can demand obedience." According to extant research, people gauge legitimacy based on subjective evaluations of whether the police uphold "procedural justice," meaning that police are neutral in their application of the rule of law and are respectful in their interactions with people (Tyler, Goff, and MacCoun 2015, 85). Everyday experiences with police, in turn, help shape these subjective perceptions (Epp, Maynard-Moody, and Haider-Markel 2014).

Yet, I find that victims of violent crime do not always understand legitimacy, at least as defined above, as a necessary condition to collaborate with the police. This echoes recent studies that depart from the received wisdom regarding the origins and consequences of police legitimacy, much of which is based on experiences in the United States and Western Europe. Recent efforts to gauge whether findings from this literature travel to different sociopolitical contexts unsettle the notion that citizens collaborate with police only on the basis of their perceptions of its perceived legitimacy, as well as the idea that the intent of collaboration is always intended to strengthen the rule of law. For example, Tankebe (2009) analyzes the portability of this hypothesis to the case of Ghana. There he finds that given both relatively high levels of crime and the police's historical role as an instrument to advance and sustain the interests of ruling powers, people decide whether to engage the police based on more utilitarian criteria. People may collaborate with the police not because they believe the police are legitimate but because they have some "minimum threshold" of efficiency to help resolve their particular dilemma or conflict. Crucially, police can satisfy this threshold in ways that sit outside of or contravene the formal rule of law (Tankebe 2009).

Testing my argument would require assessing it in out-of-sample cases. My aim was instead to develop a small-N comparative research design grounded in "rich knowledge of cases and context" (Collier, Brady, and Seawright 2004, 238) in order to gain inferential leverage on the processes and outcomes of interest. Observing and analyzing the dynamics and different dimensions of victimization require shifting to the ground level where these processes unfold and the relevant actors seek to keep them concealed. The approach in this book therefore aligns with the growing call within studies of both criminal and political violence to employ micro-level research designs. The micro-level is where the contrasting sinews of relations between victims, criminals, and state actors can be most readily observed. As Arias (2017) argues, "The complex demands of remaining clandestine and the types of networks produced by those dynamics mean that crime is often easier to understand in the local context." This does not mean, however, that research on criminal victimization should be limited to micro-level research designs. Quantitative approaches to criminal victimization, such as those based on production and analysis of survey data, provide vital insights into the distribution of criminal acts across space and time both across and within countries. Macro-level analysis of criminal victimization helps to establish aggregate trends that provide us with general understandings of the state of crime and violence in the world. Micro-level studies such as the one developed in this book, however, can complement and inform macro-level analyses by generating new forms of granular data, narrowing the gap between concepts and empirics, mapping processes and the workings of causal mechanisms, and establishing a greater degree of internal validity (Kalyvas 2008b).

The analysis of relations between criminals and victims presented this book also yields insights relevant for the broader study of state–society relations. The power dynamics between criminals and victims that I analyze in this book resemble those identified by scholars of more conventional dominant and subordinate relations, ranging from those between capital and labor (Gaventa 1980; Scott 1985) to those between citizens and autocrats (Fu 2018; O'Brien 1996; Wedeen 1999). Among the important shared features across these dyads is contention over asymmetries of power between actors who are seeking to maximize benefits. These benefits, moreover, go beyond the material to include the immaterial (e.g., dignity and respect). Indeed, it is telling how the strategies of social and political domination by criminal rulers in my analysis parallel those deployed by states as analyzed in studies of interactions between marginalized citizens and state bureaucracies, such as social welfare agencies (Auyero 2012; Soss 2002). Similar dynamics are evident in research on the political meanings embedded in the interactions between civilians and another coercive actor: the police. Scholars of civilian–police interactions have shown that the ways in which the police treat civilians, including whether civilians view the police as treating them with respect and dignity, weigh heavily on not only how civilians perceive individual police but the institution as a whole as well as democracy itself (Lerman and Weaver 2014).[5] These and other parallels suggest that future research would do well to build dialogues between studies of the politics of crime on the one hand and the established literature on dominant and subordinate actors and, more broadly, state–society relations.

7.3 FUTURE RESEARCH

7.3.1 Analyzing Victimization beyond Extortion

Future research on criminal politics should differentiate between crimes that are onetime acts and those that are recurring processes. This book focuses on a widespread, but particular, form of criminal victimization: extortion. Moreover, the study centers on the type of extortion by which criminals hold territorial control and engage in regular, face-to-face interactions with their victims. As I noted in Chapter 2 when I discussed the scope conditions, the conceptual parsing of crime and victimization helps to identify the boundaries

---

[5] Seminal studies on the nature and consequences of civilian–police dynamics include Sunshine and Tyler (2003); Tyler and Jackson (2014); and Tyler and Fagan (2008).

of the theory of resistance to criminal victimization. The dynamics of crimes that are onetime acts are likely to be different than those of the recurring phenomena of criminal extortion studied in the book. Having a stranger steal a person's cell phone on a busy city street is qualitatively different from having a criminal regularly visit a victim's business to demand money under threat of violence. A key challenge for future research is therefore to assess the potentially consequential differences that these contrasting forms of criminal victimization have on a range of important outcomes of interest, such as voting behavior, political and policy preferences, and civic mobilization.

What other types of crime beyond extortion might the argument developed here help us better understand? One critical area in need of further study is intimate partner violence (IPV). The World Health Organization (WHO) defines IPV as "one of the most common forms of violence against women and includes physical, sexual, and emotional abuse and controlling behaviors by an intimate partner" (WHO 2012, 1). One out of every three women in the United States has experienced "sexual assault, physical violence, and/or stalking by an intimate partner" during their lifetime (Triantafyllou, Wang, and North 2016). Levels of IPV in Latin America are particularly pronounced. A wave of nationally representative surveys carried out between 2003 and 2009 in twelve Latin America and Caribbean countries found that between one-fourth and one-half of all women reported having ever experienced IPV (Bott et al. 2019, xvi).

But like extortion, the individual physical criminal act of IPV cannot be fully understood without assessing the broader set of interactions within which it is embedded, and which enable and sustain the process of victimization. Female victims of physical and sexual modalities of IPV regularly suffer their own forms of social and political subordination at the hands of their victimizers, including "being insulted or made to feel bad about oneself; being humiliated in front of others; being intimidated or scared on purpose" (WHO 2005, xiii). But we still know relatively little about the dynamics and consequences of these other aspects of IPV precisely because of the conventional understanding of IPV as a criminal act of physical violence (WHO 2005, 37). Aligning with the argument developed in this book, greater attention to the social and political dimensions of IPV could provide greater analytic leverage for unpacking its layered and dynamic nature.

Despite its prevalence, variation in levels and modalities across space and time, and toll on victims, families, societies, and institutions, the literature on criminal politics has largely overlooked IPV. Moreover, better understanding IPV promises insights for the other forms of violence commonly found in the literature on criminal politics. For example, using ethnographic methods, Auyero (2015) shows how organized violence linked to illicit economies, common delinquency, and the physical and emotional abuse of partners and children in households "concatenate" in complex and mutually reinforcing ways in Latin America. While the argument and conceptual insights developed in this book do not apply to all forms of crime, they can help us better understand particularly pressing, yet understudied, types of crime whereby victims and criminals contest varied forms of power in ongoing processes of victimization.

7.3.2 Between Corruption and Conflict

Scholars of political violence argue that the binary of civilian cooperation and non-cooperation with armed actors in wartime settings masks important variation in the nature of civilian behaviors (Arjona 2016; Wood 2003). Aligning with this important point, we also need more attention to analogous distinctions in the behaviors of political and social actors in the study of the politics of crime.

The nature of state–criminal relations weighs heavily on patterns of violence, order, and disorder (Snyder and Durán-Martínez 2009; Trejo and Ley 2020). State–criminal relations influence different aspects of governance, policymaking, and civic mobilization in the spaces that criminal groups control (Arias 2017). But the predominant approach to state–criminal relations as one of either corruption or conflict conceals additional variation in the nature of these relations. The analysis presented in this book suggests that by centering the voices, perspectives, and experiences of victims in our studies, scholars can uncover this variation and be better positioned to theorize its consequences.

In several of the cases that I analyze in this book, victims distinguished between being forced to obey criminal actors and being corrupted by them. In the former instance, victims viewed governing authorities as simply allowing criminals to produce and transport illicit narcotics because they had no other choice – here governing authorities were not corrupt; rather, they avoided challenging criminals in order to avoid being killed. Likewise with regard to extortion, governing authorities were at times seen as obeying criminal actors when they did not actually perpetrate extortion but allowed it to occur.

Similarly we need to consider the multiplicity of potential relations beyond the corruption–conflict binary between members of society and criminal actors. In the analysis of cases of piecemeal vigilantism in El Salvador (Chapter 4), among the people who the handfuls of victims and police jointly targeted for extralegal violence were those charged with handling the money that gangs forcibly collected under extortion, including the relatives of gang members. By contrast, in Michoacán, some of the avocado farmers who collected rents on behalf of criminal groups were deemed by victims to have been obeying criminal actors and not acting for individual gain as part of complicity with the criminals. This perception had concrete implications – it allowed those deemed to have been obeying criminal actors to participate in resistance against them, whereas those who were viewed as having been complicit were not. More research is needed to refine our knowledge of how people make these consequential judgments of complicity versus obedience.

7.3.3 Resistance to Criminal Victimization and Armed Politics

Recent studies highlight the importance of researching how armed groups participate in politics, and particularly elections (Matanock and Staniland 2018). Much of this research focuses on insurgent groups and the armed wings of political parties (Staniland 2017). This book shows that resistance to criminal victimization – particularly that which entails a relatively high degree of collective mobilization – provides fertile empirical terrain for the study of armed politics.

Politicians and partisan politics can intersect with mobilization by victims to resist criminal victimization in different ways. Not all expressions of resistance to criminal victimization may engage with electoral politics in sustained and substantive ways. Groups of victims engaging in collective resistance may develop linkages to political parties or electoral interests over time rather than at the outset. In the cases that I analyze in Michoacán in Chapters 5 and 6, victims initially organized and enacted collective vigilantism without being directed by politicians or political parties. But they then became deeply enmeshed in local politics as they shifted to a strategy of coproduction, whereby both victims and politicians saw benefits in allying to secure power.[6]

Groups of victims contesting crime may also become more involved in formal politics depending on their relations with governing regimes. In the Cape Flats of South Africa, the group known as People Against Gangsterism and Crime (PAGAD) emerged in the mid-1990s to put an end to drug dealing coordinated by street gangs – at times by setting fire to the houses of known drug dealers. The group initially steered away from politics, and the African National Congress-led provincial government largely declined to stop it. It was only when PAGAD began building linkages to the competing Pan Africanist Congress party that the ANC government moved to dismantle PAGAD in 2000 (Fourchard 2011, 617). The case of PAGAD suggests that elements of the state will seek to dismantle groups of victims when they pose a threat to the political status quo. But states may also seek to capture groups contesting criminal victimization if the groups enjoy some degree of popular support and can therefore help politicians win elections and fend off political opponents. This seems to have been the case with the Bakassi Boys, a vigilante group in Nigeria who over time was sought out by local politicians and state governors that used them to fight crime, earn popular support among voters, and intimidate their political and electoral opponents (Reno 2006, 34–38). In other words, resistance by victims can prompt contrasting state responses that merit further investigation.

Political actors may not always wait for groups of victims to emerge before trying to parlay popular support for the use of extralegal violence into political power. Thus, politicians may start their own armed groups to combat crime,

---

[6] Matanock and Staniland (2018) differentiate the political strategies of armed groups by whether they run their own candidates and whether they make public their policy preferences.

but primarily to reap political dividends. In parts of Nigeria, for example, state governors have been known to arm vigilante groups (Reno 2006). In the Philippines then-mayor of the city of Davao and current president Rodrigo Duterte was alleged to have enabled the organization and operation of the Davao Death Squad – a group of police, criminals, and former communist insurgents – that killed alleged criminals and drug dealers. President Duterte (2016–) has made state support for vigilantism a central component of his governing strategy, but there is increasing evidence that these groups are used in targeted ways to weaken and eliminate political opponents.[7]

The confluence between the politics of crime and armed politics is an important area of future research with many broader implications. For example, scholars have begun to explore the direct and indirect ways that criminal actors outside of the formal political system influence electoral outcomes and then use varying levers of power to shape policymaking in ways that favor impunity and illicit interests (Arias 2017; Albarracín 2018; Hidalgo and Lessing 2015). Analyzing different types of organized manifestations of resistance to criminal victimization by victims, however, also offers opportunities to develop fruitful dialogues with emerging research on armed politics. More research is needed to understand when and how political actors use mobilized resistance to criminal victimization as vehicles for political power, and likewise, the conditions under which victims do the same. Cross-regional analyses that compare these aspects of armed politics could be particularly powerful ways to explore the causal weight of diverse explanatory factors while building needed dialogue between scholars who have different regional foci.

7.3.4 Criminal Governance and Order

Criminal actors engage in forms of governance that produce order within the territories that they control (Arias 2006, 2017; Magaloni et al. 2020). Much of this research places state–criminal relations at the center of the analysis. This book broadens our lens to bring victims into the picture, which shows how shifts in the nature of criminal–victim relations can reconfigure local orders in both subtle and dramatic ways. The evidence analyzed in Chapter 4, for example, suggests that the handfuls of victims and police who engaged in piecemeal vigilantism prompted gangs to retaliate by monitoring and killing people associated with piecemeal vigilantism. The evidence available to me on how the gangs in these cases responded is limited relative to the collective body of evidence on why and how victims pursued piecemeal vigilantism. Further research is needed to understand the broader range of potential responses that criminal actors may elect when confronted with resistance by victims. This can provide additional insights into the dynamic nature of local orders and reveal

---

[7] Nick Aspinwall, "Duterte Turns Death Squads on Political Activists," *Foreign Policy*, June 10, 2019.

new patterns of contestation and retaliation that go unobserved when we start with the premise that victims lack agency.

A key task for future research is therefore identifying more cases of resistance to criminal victimization. This can enrich our empirical understanding of criminal rule while providing a stronger basis for more comparative studies. One challenge for increasing the number of observations, however, is locating cases in the first place. In some instances, such as cases of collective vigilantism, the signals associated with this type of resistance are fairly visible given the relatively large-scale collective mobilization among victims and practices of extralegal violence. Though, as this book shows, the critical task of then differentiating the important differences between forms of collective vigilantism requires in-depth analysis in different localities. Uncovering and analyzing comparatively "quieter" strategies of resistance, such as everyday resistance, poses its own set of challenges. As shown in the analysis of everyday resistance in Chapter 3, learning from victims and the ways they understand their victimization *and* resistance is key to making legible and analyzing the logic and practices of everyday resistance. In this particular case, focus groups allowed me to "see" some of the hidden transcript (Scott 1990) of resistance among informal vendors that I could then use to identify and make sense of practices of everyday resistance. The typology and argument developed here can help in future efforts to collect, classify, and compare more cases of resistance. Additional support for the argument will result when additional observations fit within the ideal-types developed in this book and are shown to result from processes indicated by the theory of resistance to criminal victimization. Where out-of-sample cases do not fit in the conceptualization or result from different pathways, this too will allow us to refine the argument and, more broadly, better understand the ways in which victims resist criminal victimization.

We also need to collect more cases of *failed* resistance. I identify instances in nearly each one of my cases in which victims attempted some form of resistance only to have their efforts ended by criminal actors who either threated or used violence. In Michoacán, for example, the emergence of self-defense groups and collective vigilantism starting in 2013 drew much attention in both Mexican and international media. But as I discuss in Chapter 6, victims had tried to collectively resist extortion on prior occasions. These failed attempts are not likely to capture public attention or that of the media, but they are important empirical observations that suggest that the nature of victim–criminal relations in contexts of criminal rule might be a great deal more contentious than we conventionally assume. Identifying additional unsuccessful attempts at resistance to criminal victimization would provide a more complete empirical picture of order under criminal governance and enable us to better understand the conditions under which victims enact specific strategies or, conversely, are unable to do so.

A broader implication from this discussion is that we are likely to see multiple forms of order with varying levels and types of contention across space inside cities, regions, and countries. Future research should evaluate the interrelations between these distinct orders as well as how they aggregate at varying scales. The generation of order in one locality may lead to factors that foster disorder in other localities. In the cases of Tancítaro and La Unión, for example, both collective vigilantism and the co-production of order prioritized ousting and keeping specific criminal actors out of their municipalities. Criminal groups consequently sought to sustain their territorial hold and illicit markets, including extortion rackets, in neighboring municipalities. How order is constructed in one place thus has spillover effects for security conditions in adjacent spaces. Likewise the inability to resist victimization in those adjacent spaces kept the threat of revictimization alive, which further encouraged victims and government authorities to sustain their complex combinations of legal and extralegal practices. Future studies should assess the interlinkages between orders at multiple scales to generate aggregate understandings of political and criminal realities. This underscores the importance of mapping and analyzing the micro-level dynamics of resistance to criminal victimization for scholarship as well as policymaking.

Finally, the analysis and findings of how criminal actors intervene in everyday aspects of political, social, and economic life suggest important points of overlap with the growing research on rebel governance in the civil war literature (Arjona 2016; Arjona et al. 2015). One such connection concerns the strategies that armed non-state actors deploy as part of building not only power but also legitimacy. Mampilly (2015) finds that rebel groups use "symbolic expressions of power" toward instrumental ends, including sustaining territorial control and eliciting obedience and even loyalty from civilians. I find that in the distinct contexts across my cases, criminal actors also relied on symbolic tools as part of their repertoire of practices intended to reduce the cost of maintaining territorial control by subjugating their victims without solely relying on sheer force. This highlights the need for more dialogue on the tools of domination that rulers utilize across domains of study that have largely remained isolated from each other.[8] One specific query concerns whether the differential presence and meaning of the state across settings of civil war and intense criminal violence means that armed non-state actors invoke the state in different ways as part of their symbolic practices. For example, whereas criminal actors in the cases that I analyzed strategically proclaimed their capture of the state – usually but not exclusively of the police – in civil war settings rebels appear to instead mimic the state's behaviors and even the practices and symbols of nationalism, such as anthems and flags and public commemoration of fallen comrades in arms. More broadly, greater attention to the strategies of domination that criminal actors use beyond coercive force should prompt scholars to take seriously if and how populations on the ground, including both victims of criminal groups and their members, view criminal groups as political actors that embody shared

---

[8] See Kalyvas (2015) for an important exception.

meanings for distinct purposes. Doing so should also catalyze greater debate regarding the binary distinction often drawn between rebels and criminals where the former are analyzed as inherently political actors while the ambitions of the latter are seen as restricted to material enrichment.

7.3.5 The Political Economy of Crime and Development

Each of the cases that I analyze in this book highlights a shared theme: the intersection between the political economy of development in Latin America and the politics of crime. The cases in Colombia and El Salvador involve economic sectors struggling to survive amid economic changes and marginalization wrought in part by trends and transformations of local and global economies. In Medellín the vendors operate on the margins of the formal economy in a city where the informal sector nonetheless employs nearly 44 percent of the economically active population.[9] And small-scale farmers in El Salvador are being left behind by the country's shift away from its historical dependency on the primary sector as part of market reforms. By contrast, the victims in the cases in Mexico embody the broader efforts in that country to more deeply entrench their domestic economies in global markets – in these instances by building enclave agricultural economies in the avocado and berry sectors in response to growing consumer demand in US, European, and Asian markets. Analyses of the political economy of development assess the ways in which these types of economic trends generate socioeconomic and political upheaval in the form of growing inequality; the reconfiguration of links between states, capital, and labor; and the cohesion of political parties (Murillo 2001; Portes and Hoffman 2003; Roberts 2002; Weyland 1996). In addition to these important outcomes, however, this book shows that we also need to assess how macro-economic transformations associated with the political economy of development influence, and are themselves shaped by, processes of crime, violence, and resistance to criminal victimization.

Here my analysis joins with a small, but growing, body of work that cuts across subfields within political science as well as boundaries across different disciplines – all of which share a focus on the ways in which global economic transformations are filtered through domestic political and socioeconomic realities to reconfigure dynamics of order, conflict, and violence. Some scholars in this line of research focus on the rise of the private security industry as a force in global governance (Abrahamsen and Williams 2010) as well as urban- and neighborhood-level politics (Samara 2011). Others analyze how global commodity booms, such as vanilla from Madagascar (Osterhoudt 2020) and iron ore from Mexico (Glass 2020), can unleash new dynamics of violence involving criminals, communities, firms, and states. Scholars also

---

[9] Viviana Suárez L., "La Informalidad en Medellín Alcanzó el 43,8%: DANE." *El Colombiano*, March 14, 2019.

analyze the ways in which private sector interests influence public sector responses to crime and violence in major developing world cities in Latin America (Caldeira 2000; Larkins 2015; Moncada 2016) and Africa (Bénit-Gbaffou, Didier and Morange 2008).

Among the challenges for future research is to assess when macro-economic shifts are more or less likely to engender different forms of crime and violence. For example, Osterhoudt (2000) shows that the growing global demand for vanilla from Madagascar has prompted spikes in levels of theft that has largely materialized in the form of individuals who sneak into fields under cover of night to pick small amounts of the vanilla beans to sell for high prices. By contrast, growing global demand for Indonesia's oil palm in recent decades has also prompted an increase in theft, though here its social organization has taken the form of so-called oil palm mafias consisting of fairly organized criminal groups that coordinate not only theft but also manipulate pricing structures in the sector to their advantage (Kenny, Shrestha and Aspinal 2020). How does the intersection between global commodity booms and preexisting local dynamics of crime yield contrasting politics of crime in terms of the organizational structure of its protagonists? Likewise more research is needed to understand how crime dynamics impact macro-level economic conditions, including the price of goods being extorted by criminals and when firms opt to absorb the costs of crime by passing them down to their employees and other firms to whom they outsource particular activities.

7.3.6 Back to Victims

By bringing victims of crime squarely into the analysis of resistance to criminal extortion, this book reveals new and dynamic layers of criminal victimization. But there is more research to be done along these lines. One task for future research is to analyze when victims choose different responses to similar forms of criminal victimization. Why do some opt to resist, for example, while others opt to exit? Both criminal extortion and drug-related violence have been shown to contribute to migration from Mexico to the United States (Rios 2014). Yet, following the start of Mexico's war on drugs in 2006 many business firms in the border city of Ciudad Juárez relocated to the United States during a period of intense insecurity, including extortion, while others remained and opted to work with police and government authorities to reduce crime (Moncada 2016; Morales, Prieto, and Bejarano 2014). What accounts for this variation? Analyzing differences in overarching responses to crime can help us understand additional dimensions of criminal politics. Victims who opt to exit, for example, may remain involved in the security conditions of the places they fled because of social and familial ties, and they may provide money to support local formal and extralegal anti-crime initiatives. Victims who exit contexts of victimization may vote from abroad in elections back home, with their past experiences at the hands of criminals being one of the factors that shape their partisan preferences.

A second task is to further unpack the shifts that happen at both the individual and communal levels once victims engage in different strategies of resistance to criminal victimization. How does negotiating with criminal victimizers on an everyday basis impact one's political subjectivity over time? Certainly the informal vendors in Medellín who I analyze in Chapter 3 used everyday resistance as a way to negotiate material and non-material aspects of their victimization, including affirming their self-worth as individuals and as citizens. James Scott (1990) argues that hidden and everyday forms of resistance can accumulate over time to provide the foundation for more visible and explicit forms of resistance against dominant forces. But one wonders if constant exposure to social and political domination over extended periods of time can have the opposite effect of demobilizing individuals by fostering cynicism about the potential for change. Absent changes in the variables that I identify in my argument, it appears difficult for victims in atomized political economies in particular that also face police captured by criminal actors to pursue collective forms of resistance.

Likewise, how does engaging in strategies of resistance that entail using extralegal practices influence one's political subjectivity? During my interviews with members of the self-defense groups in Michoacán, they consistently noted with evident pride that the experience of having fought criminals had made clear to them that they would never again allow criminals to extort, hurt, or humiliate them. Does the process of picking up weapons and coordinating and enacting violence change how victims come to see their role in society and politics? Certainly the analysis in Chapter 6 shows that victims mobilized to shape local order by securing and influencing formal politics in order to advance their varied interests vis-à-vis criminal actors.

Another shift that merits additional research is at the communal level. In the cantons in El Pilar and Cienfuegos in El Salvador, as rumors spread of small groups of farmers and individual police carrying out the occasional killing of a gang member, individual community members asked the group for help in killing their own victimizers. How does witnessing this form of resistance in one's community affect future discussions about local security, how threats are interpreted,[10] and responses to potential future victimization? Do individuals again turn to piecemeal vigilantism in these contexts? As a judge who oversaw one of the cases that I analyzed in El Salvador told me, "Now that we are punishing these people [referring to the participants in the extermination group], others will see that this type of behavior is not tolerated."[11] But at the same time, it is worth researching whether victims that see the state punish piecemeal vigilantism but struggle to punish criminal actors may instead foster more support for resistance that contravenes the rule of law.

---

[10] Bateson (2013) argues that experiencing wartime violence can enhance sensitivity to new threats in post-conflict settings and thus contribute to vigilantism.

[11] Interview with Judge #1 (ESV011), San Salvador, July 2019.

7.4 POLICY IMPLICATIONS

In this section I distill the policy implications from my analysis and findings. These implications are relevant for how states, policymakers, business, and citizens think about and respond to criminal violence in the developing world. I focus on three key policy implications: the need for more innovation in measuring criminal victimization; constructive ways for the private sector to become involved in citizen security policymaking; and the benefits and drawbacks associated with state responses to both criminal extortion and victims' varying strategies of resistance.

7.4.1 Measuring Criminal Victimization: The Need for More and Different Indicators

A basic, but fundamental, need for policymakers is more and different indicators of criminal victimization. Developing more granular data on criminal victimization at the subnational level is particularly important because the dynamics of crime can vary dramatically within countries. These indicators need to capture not only the frequency of crimes but also the different parts of the process of victimization. Broad policy measures based on aggregate data that measure solely the frequency of crime are likely to miss this important subnational variation in the different aspects of victimization. At best, such policy initiatives will prove ineffective in particular territorial localities. But at worst, the disjuncture between the policies and the nature of local criminal victimization could antagonize and contribute to more or new forms of victimization. For example, across the cases analyzed in this book, hardline state measures targeting criminal actors contributed to important shifts in the nature of relations between criminals and victims that, in some instances, sparked new dynamics of violence and insecurity. Indicators of the process of victimization based on more holistic measurements could help policymakers to better understand these and other potentially unintended consequences of hardline security measures. This way policymakers could better weigh the full potential costs and benefits associated with particular policy measures before implementing them, and they could be better prepared to respond to the consequences of these measures during or immediately after they are implemented.

Generating new measures will require creative thinking about ways to overcome the challenges of the standard survey measures of victimization. Sensitive topic surveys, such as crime victimization, are vulnerable to underreporting bias. Experimental survey designs provide one promising way to mitigate underreporting. Complementing surveys and survey experiments with ethnographic fieldwork can help refine large-scale measures of victimization.[12] In this book, observational engagement with

---

[12] See Thachil (2018) on the use of ethnographic fieldwork to improve surveys.

the populations of interest, as well as interviews and focus groups, helped me to better understand that victimization consisted of multiple dimensions beyond the physical act of the forced extraction of money. Surveys could incorporate questions using vignettes and other techniques to indirectly, but more accurately, capture these important aspects of victimization. Participant drawings could further provide innovative indicators either alone or incorporated into more aggregate measures. Certainly carrying out fieldwork and developing and implementing new measures pose resource costs, including time and money. But these new measures could provide policymakers with more complete understandings of the patterns, dynamics, and consequences of criminal victimization, allowing for more targeted policy interventions. Using methods other than the standard per capita rates of particular criminal acts to communicate crime trends can also help the public to better grasp the extent of criminal victimization and avoid unfounded or disproportionate fear of victimization and perceptions of insecurity.[13]

7.4.2 Business in the Politics of Security Policymaking

In my previous research on the political economy of urban violence, I used a top-down approach to analyze how business communities in major developing world cities influence the nature and trajectory of the political projects that cities launch to tackle urban violence (Moncada 2016). In this book I use a bottom-up approach to analyze the ways that businesses resist victimization at the micro-level in varying ways as victims of criminal extortion with equally different implications for society and governance. Together these analyses show that business is a key factor in criminal politics in Latin America.

One implication for policymaking is that the private sector should be incorporated into security policymaking as part of initiatives to tackle crime and criminal violence. The private sector can offer important inputs for policy efforts along these lines, including capital and information. Moreover, incorporating the private sector into policymaking processes may disincentivize their inclinations to bypass the rule of law and pursue extralegal measures.

Prior to bringing the private sector more squarely into policymaking efforts, however, careful attention must be paid to the nature of the political economies among firms. Where segmented landscapes are evident, policymakers should seek to ensure that all relevant parties are included in the policymaking process, lest those left out become "spoilers" of any resulting policy initiatives. Working with existing business associations to foster a more encompassing landscape

---

[13] Groff et al. (2005) use a randomized experimental study to assess how receiving information on crime via tables versus different kinds of maps has differential effects on the public's fear of crime.

could help the private sector to more effectively make its concerns heard and acted upon by policymakers.

But incorporating businesses without addressing local policing can also backfire. For example, fostering greater organizational cohesion among business firms without taking concrete steps to end criminal capture of the police is a recipe for collective vigilantism. By breaking the hold of criminal actors on police and building the capacity of police, policymakers can invite more constructive forms of private sector participation in security policymaking. Vesting the private sector with transparent policymaking processes can encourage it to keep police and government officials accountable for local security conditions while adhering to the rule of law.

7.4.3 State Responses to Criminal Extortion

Extortion takes a significant toll on their victims financially but also emotionally. Using multiple forms of data, this book shows that important features of victimization include how criminals humiliate and belittle their victims. Victims repeatedly highlighted these aspects of criminal extortion as part of sharing their experiences and understandings of victimization and resistance. Repeated criminal extortion renders citizenship hollow, and predatory interactions with criminal actors are enabled by both the capture of the police and when victims perceive governing authorities as complicit, or when criminals taunt victims by pointing out how the state fails to respond to their victimization and uphold their basic right to live in safety. States should take steps to stem criminal extortion. But the policies to do so must consider several of the aspects of criminal extortion highlighted and analyzed in this book.

Criminal actors use extortion to build and sustain territorial control. Criminal actors justify their territorial presence by relying on violence and other extralegal practices to coordinate other illicit activities. But regular face-to-face interactions associated with extortion allow criminal actors to obtain information about potential threats, monitor local populations, and thus keep a tight grip on their territory. The financial rents generated through extortion can enhance their coercive capacity and ability to challenge or co-opt state authority and sovereignty.

Since extortion is central to the ability of criminal actors to operate and survive, they may interpret state efforts to stop extortion as having much broader and even existential implications. Tackling extortion should therefore be part of a broader intervention that simultaneously addresses linked illicit economies. Moreover, it is important for policymakers to recognize that the nature of extortion can vary across space and time. Interventions to dismantle extortion are substantively different when criminal actors are operating under long, rather than short, time horizons. These differences will likely require different types of state interventions and involve different stakeholders. Policy efforts targeting extortion under long time horizons, for example, will need to overcome potential pushback from social actors who view the racket as a source of more beneficial and "effective" outcomes (e.g., informal justice) than analogous formal state institutions.

A heavy-handed, hardline approach to combating extortion might be not only insufficient but possibly counterproductive because it signals a lack of state awareness of the reasons why social actors turn to criminals for justice and security under extortion. This is particularly relevant in settings where criminal capture enabled extortion. Instead, policymakers should invest in institutions and mechanisms that resolve local conflicts and satisfy security needs expeditiously and impartially. Introducing these types of reforms prior to launching punitive measures may enable states to weaken the grip of criminal actors on local populations.

Policymakers face difficult choices in responding once victims have already begun resisting their victimization using extralegal means. Attention to variation in the structure and practices associated with different strategies of resistance can help policymakers weigh the benefits and drawbacks of potential responses. In cases of piecemeal vigilantism, a key concern is that elements of the police are participating in and facilitating extralegal violence. Putting an end to piecemeal vigilantism can send a signal that other parts of the state will not tolerate such behavior by either victims or police. But as shown in this book, piecemeal vigilantism develops in contexts where criminals control territories that feature low-capacity autonomous police. State responses that only clamp down on piecemeal vigilantism without addressing the underlying limited police capacity may spur backlash from other police and incentivize them to engage in extralegal violence. Thus states should see piecemeal vigilantism as an indication of a deeper problem rather than a one-off occurrence. States should acknowledge how limited police capacity fosters this particular strategy of resistance and coordinate with the police – both its leaders and rank-and-file agents who are most vulnerable to violence from criminal actors and hence most susceptible to partnering with victims to carry out piecemeal vigilantism – to address it.

Where states face more organized collective resistance, like in Michoacán, they are initially inclined to "formalize" this resistance, as occurred with efforts to transform self-defense groups into Rural Police. This is an attractive way to defuse conflictive situations without addressing underlying issues, including limited institutional capacity. But formalizing collective vigilantism is not a promising long-term solution, a point that is evident in experiences as contrasting as Nigeria (Meagher 2007) and Colombia (Grajales 2017). In the short term, it can have negative repercussions that vary across cases depending on the specific structure of collective vigilantism. States must recognize the various ways that actors organize and enact collective vigilantism across space and tailor their responses to account for these differences. Taken together, this underscores the need for more research on the strategies of resistance to criminal victimization to inform both scholarship and policymaking.

APPENDIX

Researching Resistance to Criminal Extortion

Studying the illicit poses no shortage of challenges. How can a researcher both identify and make legible something that operates on the basis of concealment, like criminal extortion? And as this book shows, different strategies of resistance are also associated with different levels of illegality, which also raises methodological and ethical challenges. Because everyday resistance, such as that pursued by the informal vendors in Medellín, does not entail victims violating the rule of law, I was able to study it by triangulating data collected through a number of different methods, including direct individual- and group-level interactions with victims as they reflected on their victimization and resistance, as well as direct observation of the practices of resistance. By contrast, the piecemeal vigilantism that victims in localities in El Salvador pursued is illegal and hidden. In Tancítaro the centralized nature of both collective vigilantism and the coproduction of order facilitated identifying its contours and protagonists, as well as collecting associated data. People involved in the process of resistance in this case welcomed the opportunity to share their experiences and stories with me. By contrast, the decentralized nature of collective vigilantism and the coproduction of order in La Unión was comparatively more difficult to map given the plurality of actors and interests involved, as well as the ongoing production and trafficking of illicit drugs. An overarching challenge while conducting the research for this study was carrying out field research and writing the results of my analysis while prioritizing the safety and security of participants, vulnerable populations and research assistants. Engaging in this type of research also required that I consistently confront and consider different dimensions of my own positionality and its implications for the research process and data collection and analysis, and my findings. This Appendix builds on the discussion of the research design and methodology in Chapter 2 to provide additional information on how I approached the research process, including securing access to sites and individuals who are difficult to reach, the challenges and limitations of the methods that I used to collect data, and the measures I took to minimize the risks to the participants in the project, my research assistants, and myself.

RESEARCH ASSISTANTS AND ACCESS IN THE FIELD

The ways in which a researcher gains access to field sites and populations have downstream effects on the research process with regard to who participates, the forms of data one is able to collect, and the findings from the analysis (Edwards 2013; Fujii 2017). This is particularly the case when conducting research in contexts of insecurity and violence, where there can be ample distrust of outsiders as well as mosaics of hidden or illicit interests and loyalties illegible to those unfamiliar with the local contexts. I therefore thought carefully about how to gain access to the populations I wanted to engage in this study to collect the necessary data, and the types of trade-offs I needed to make between maximizing access and ensuring the security of the research participants, research assistants (RAs), and myself. I ended up working with three RAs as well as two occasional informal interlocutors. In identifying the RAs and interlocutors my first priority was to select individuals that as much as possible could be seen as "neutral" and holding no clear affiliation or loyalty to a particular social group or political party. My aim was to work with individuals that would seem innocuous to the diverse populations I was targeting for interviews and focus groups, to ensure the safety of both RAs and that of the research participants. The second and related priority was to identify individuals that had contact with a diverse range of populations so as to minimize limiting my access to other populations by virtue of working with individuals seen as favoring one particular actor.

In Medellín I hired two part-time staff members of a small nonprofit organization that worked on human rights in the city center. Their work brought the two individuals into regular contact with a variety of different actors in the city center, including the population of vendors that I studied. After several in-person meetings during which I explained my research project and data collection objectives, they joined the project and introduced me to several of the informal vendors in the market where I conducted my research. The RAs also knew several individual members of the criminal groups that coordinated extortion in the city center, including in the market where I was working. These relationships had been built over time as the RAs were familiar with the families of several of the members of the criminal group and had watched them grow up over the years. This enabled me to regularly visit the market without being stopped or forced to leave by members of the criminal group that were often in the market once the RAs vouched for me.

In Michoacán a local resident who was well known and respected in the communities where I was carrying out my fieldwork worked with me as an RA. They had deep social roots in the area that commanded trust and respect from a range of populations, including self-defense group leaders, victims, and former members of criminal groups. After several virtual and in-person meetings during which I again outlined my research project and data collection objectives, they agreed to help me to access these different populations.

In both Medellín and Michoacán I made clear to the RAs that they should let me know if at any point they felt that the people we were approaching for interviews and/or focus groups would threaten their safety or that of the interviewees, or if there were particularly sensitive issues that we should avoid broaching given unacceptable security risks. Each RA received a set amount of money as their remuneration. I indicated to them that the remuneration was not contingent on completing a set number of interviews or focus groups. I did not want them to risk their own security in order to complete a "quota" to ensure getting paid. Without the help of the RAs in both localities I would not have had the level of access that I secured. Had I somehow accessed these populations without the help of the RAs, the people that I interviewed and who participated in focus groups would likely not have spoken to me with the often-disarming level of frankness that they displayed. There was rarely a day during my time in the field when I was not surprised by what someone told me about their experiences with extortion or the things they had done as part of resisting victimization. At times the level of frankness resulted in participants telling me things that I have chosen not to include in this book because doing so would place the participants at risk. The RAs helped bring trust and confidence to my interactions with participants that facilitated this high level of candor.

In El Salvador I did not hire RAs in part because of the legal challenges that they might have faced. In August of 2015 El Salvador's Supreme Court classified both the MS-13 and the two factions of the Barrio 18 as terrorist organizations.[1] Local researchers in El Salvador gave me conflicting opinions on whether any RAs that I was to hire would be vulnerable to arrest for interacting with or even simply working in areas with strong gang presence. But precisely because of these conditions I knew that it would be important to at least find some form of local interlocutors in my field sites – though I prioritized finding individuals that would be less likely to face state prosecution. These came in the form of the pastors of two small evangelical churches in the municipalities in which each of my field sites was located. These individuals were well known by, and respected within, the local communities, including among former and active gang members. I identified the pastors prior to arriving in El Salvador to conduct research, and worked closely with them to secure access to victims of extortion and former gang members that had perpetrated extortion but then left the gangs. In lieu of direct payment – again to avoid potential legal entanglements for the RAs – each pastor accepted a small monetary donation to their churches. In brief, the RAs and interlocutors greatly helped me to build networks of contacts that enabled me to identify and carry out the data collection methods discussed below.

[1] InSight Crime. "Tracing the History of Failed Gang Policies in US, Northern Triangle." December 2015.

INTERVIEWS

In conducting interviews with actors involved in criminal activities, I always avoided asking specific questions about whether they themselves had committed illegal activities (i.e., *Did you "disappear" someone?*). Instead, I asked general questions about what "victims in general" had done as part of their resistance. Yet, in several cases respondents voluntarily offered specific information about their own activities – again in part because they viewed them as justified and necessary to end extortion and associated violence. I believe that people were willing to share this type of information because these had become, to a certain degree, normalized and accepted in some contexts. In Michoacán, for example, it was common to laud the violent practices that self-defense groups had committed as part of collective vigilantism. I decided not to use quotes from individuals when they described the violent acts that they themselves directly committed, and instead refer to such acts as committed by victims in general when I was able to use other interviews and secondary data to triangulate and establish that these had indeed been common practices.

Because this is a multisited project, I was not embedded in a single site for an extended period of time. But I had to rely on several strategies to sustain and continue building trust when I was not in the field that would enable me to secure interviews in conflictive settings. I did so primarily via electronic communication, specifically WhatsApp. My strategy was to demonstrate to research participants that I was engaged with their everyday realities even when not physically in the field. To that end I spent regular periods of time when I was out of the field reading up on local news in my field sites from several sources: (1) online newspapers; (2) social media accounts of local radio and television channels; (3) the Twitter feeds of local politicians, business owners, community members, and self-defense group leaders and members; and (4) other social media feeds of relevant government agencies. I also checked-in regularly with my RAs via telephone to converse about ongoing issues and new developments in each locality. I then used this information from across these different sources to reach out to people to ask them for interviews or their participation in focus groups. This helped to signal to participants that although I was not embedded in their local setting, I was carefully following what was happening there. As part of these conversations, I avoided asking about the specific behaviors or practices of the people I was communicating with – my aim was not to endanger them by having them leave a digital record of their activities or opinions on their cell phones. Instead, I purposefully kept the online conversations broad and general.

I did not attempt to establish representative samples of interview respondents given the conflictive and violent nature of the field sites, including the presence of armed criminal actors. I instead took every possible step to interview a wide range of people. The analysis draws on 127 interviews from across the field sites. Sixteen of these interviews – the majority of them in Michoacán – were carried out by an RA using pre-established questionnaires. A small number of the interviews for each of the cases took place via telephone or email inside or outside of the field sites with people that had knowledge of local dynamics. I conducted more than one interview with sixteen individuals across the field sites. More broadly, I also engaged in informal and unplanned conversations with many of the people from the larger sample. Though I did not record these unplanned conversations and did not take notes during them, many provided important insights and additional contacts. A list of the interview respondents is provided below.

The majority of individuals that I interviewed were victims of extortion, followed by politicians, community members, civil society leaders, and former criminals. Nearly all interviews were recorded on digital devices. RAs were instructed not to record interviews and instead only take handwritten notes. At the start of each interview I made it clear to the participant that I was recording only to ensure that their statements were accurately represented in my research. I stressed that all interviews were anonymous and that I would be the only person with access to the recordings and any notes that I took during the interview with my pen and pad. I also indicated to participants that it was okay if they preferred not to be recorded, and that I would turn off the recorder and would not take notes. However, no one declined to be recorded. After each interview, I immediately encrypted the interviews on my recording device, which was usually an iPad, though on several occasions I had to use my phone when the iPad was not available. The encrypted recordings were then automatically uploaded to an online storage provider that was also password-protected. After confirming that the file had been uploaded correctly, I then immediately deleted the original recording.

Though the interviews are a key part of the evidence for the analysis in this book, as Fujii (2010) notes, researchers must consider the issue of veracity (or the lack thereof) when conducting interviews in settings of conflict – particularly with its victims and perpetrators. Here the risks associated with divulging sensitive information run high. To address this concern, I took several steps. I triangulated information collected from the interviews with data from separate sources, including interviews with individuals from populations other than direct victims or perpetrators of criminal victimization. I extensively consulted media archives and local as well as national government documents, including several official requests for information covered by freedom of information acts. Following Fujii (2010), I approached the silences, evasion, and occasional deception that accompanied some of the interviews as "meta-data" to be reflected upon and used as part of theory-building. Just as importantly, early on in my research I took these types of behaviors as indications of the need to figure out ways to address respondents' apprehensions and concerns about answering the types of questions that I was asking them, or, better said, *how I was asking them*. This often led me to reflect on the meta-data early in the research project in order to try and better understand the complexity associated with how people in my field sites viewed and understood concepts such as victims, victimization, and resistance – and therefore enabled me to rephrase and reformulate my questions to them as well as develop new ones that could better dialogue with their lived experiences and understandings in ways that made the interview process less daunting for them and more productive for the project.

FOCUS GROUPS

During the research process it became evident to me that using the same methods in each locality was not going to be feasible. The nature of resistance varied across my cases in ways that also had legal implications for my respondents. For example, whereas in Medellín everyday resistance did not entail the use of violence or other illegal practices, in Mexico victims had taken up arms illegally against their victimizers and, in the process, engaged in varied forms of violence that violated the rule of law. In Medellín victims seemed more at ease and forthcoming in the focus group setting alongside fellow victims. By contrast, in Michoacán victims favored one-on-one interviews – though I did carry out one focus group with a group of victims. In El Salvador, I relied primarily on interviews given the reticence of victims to join in focus groups, though I did manage to organize a focus group with local police in one of the field sites. I conducted focus groups in Colombia with a total of forty-nine individuals, in Mexico with eleven individuals, and in El Salvador with five individuals.

Focus groups can help to establish a temporary space where vulnerable populations may be more at ease discussing sensitive topics given their social nature relative to one-on-one interviews. Though focus groups are often used to interview several individuals simultaneously, Cyr (2016) identifies two other forms of data that they generate. Attention to group-level dynamics enables researchers to see how a subject population collectively understands contentious or "thick concepts" (Coppedge 1999). This enabled me to see that victims understood both their victimization and resistance as *multidimensional* in nature. This was particularly evident early into the process of conducting focus groups with informal vendors in Medellín. Six vendors in the room were visibly tired of my questions about how often and how much they paid under the extortion racket – my attempt to understand what I assumed was the key aspect and extent of their victimization. One vendor finally (and thankfully) motioned for me to stop. He explained:

It's not only that I have to pay every Saturday. That hurts me … all of us, of course it does. But that's only *one* part of the problem: something bigger with the Convivir (term used for the groups that coordinate protection rackets in Medellín's downtown). When [the criminals] take the money from me, I don't stop being a victim. *He* doesn't stop being a victim (pointing at a vendor sitting across from him). *She* doesn't stop being a victim (pointing at a vendor sitting beside him). Like them, I am a victim 12 hours a day and seven days a week (the average work schedule for a vendor)—every single time I step foot in the market, I am a victim.[2]

Attention to the interactions between focus group participants can also provide insights into how social processes unfold – something difficult to achieve using interviews alone. This allowed me to observe and analyze how strategies of resistance were collectively discussed and, in some cases, even rehearsed and performed by victims beyond the gaze of their victimizer.

In the focus groups with victims, I was always careful not to indicate that my project was concerned specifically with understanding resistance by victims. Indeed, I never used this word when describing my work or reacting to what people were saying during the focus groups. This ensured that the method itself did not prime people to think of their actions as resistance and thus frame it that way to align with the objective of my project.

I coordinated and carried out nine focus groups in Medellín, one in Michoacán, and one in eastern El Salvador in the department of San Miguel. Focus groups lasted an average of 1.5 hours. In Medellín the focus groups took place in a small hotel meeting room far from the informal market where the vendors worked, and each participant received a small cash payment (USD 15) given that they were taking time away from their work to participate. I worked with my RAs in Medellín to coordinate transportation for those vendors that needed it. Taxis would pick up those vendors that required transportation at locations other than the informal market so as to not draw unwanted attention. In Michoacán the focus group took place in an office space that I rented out for the day. In El Salvador the focus group with police officers took place in a small hotel meeting room.

I began each focus group by explaining the benefits and risks associated with participating and also asked participants if it was okay for me to record the conversation. I again indicated that the recordings were only to ensure that I accurately documented what they said, and I promised not share the recordings with anyone. I also indicated that while I would never reveal what any specific individual had said by name, I could not guarantee that once the focus group ended others in the room would adhere to the same rule. After providing participants with all of this information, I then told them that they were free to leave and not participate at any point in the focus group, and/or not answer any of the questions posed during the focus group. Only after receiving verbal confirmation that they understood and consented did I then continue. I followed the same protocol as with the recordings from the interviews where the digital recording was immediately encrypted on the recording device before being uploaded to an online and password-protected storage system. The original recordings were then deleted from the recording device. Tables A1 through A3 provide details on the composition of the focus groups.

---

[2] Mario (MDE_FG1_911), informal vendor, focus group, Medellín, July 2016.

TABLE A1 *Focus groups with victims of criminal extortion in Medellín, Colombia*

Focus group number	Men	Women	Total participants
1	2	3	5
2	2	3	5
3	4	2	6
4	1	4	5
5	3	3	6
6	2	3	5
7	1	4	5
8	3	2	5
9	4	3	7
Total:	22	27	49

TABLE A2 *Focus group with police in El Salvador*

Focus group number	Men	Women	Total participants
1	5	0	5
Total:	5	0	5

TABLE A3 *Focus group with victims of criminal extortion in La Unión, Michoacán*

Focus group number	Men	Women	Total participants
1	11	0	11
Total:	11	0	11

PARTICIPATORY DRAWING EXERCISES

As part of the focus groups with victims in Medellín, I also conducted participatory drawing exercises. Scholars have used participatory drawings to study how people experience and interpret violence (Auyero and Berti 2016; Moser and McIlwaine 2004; Wood 2003). I used this methodology as a way to prevent the voices of the most vocal individuals in the focus groups from biasing the resulting data. My concern was that the perspectives of individuals who were not as vocal during the focus groups would not be reflected in the final analysis. As such, toward the end of each focus group I gave participants blank sheets of paper, pencils, and pens, and asked them to draw something in response to the following prompt: "Please think about the place where you work every day. Now draw what you feel generates either insecurity, security, or both in this place."

After about ten minutes once everyone had finished their drawings I invited each participant to share their drawing and explain it to the group. Drawing exercises enable participants to exercise agency in defining part of their contribution to the research process and can help researchers elicit data on sensitive and emotional dynamics (Kearney and Hyle 2004, 376). While most participants engaged in the group discussions, others remained comparatively quiet, but then enthusiastically described their drawings to their fellow group members. The exercise thus helped participants to express sentiments that they otherwise had elected not to share through the conversation portion of the focus groups.

I explicitly asked participants to not include information in their drawings that could serve to identify them, other specific individuals, or the location of the informal market. But several did so anyway. Some did so inadvertently by including the names of nearby streets, shops, landmarks, and their own names or those of neighboring vendors. Others did so purposefully and told the group that they did so because they wanted people to know what was happening to them. In those cases, I was either unable to use the drawing in this book or, where possible, redacted that part of the drawing in order to use the part that did not reveal potentially identifying information (after contacting the author of the drawing to ask if this would be acceptable to them). Before focus group participants left the hotel meeting room I made a copy of their drawing using a portable scanner.

I also proposed the participatory drawing exercise with the focus group of victims in Michoacán, but after several individuals expressed reluctance to do so – in part again I suspect because many had engaged in violent illegal activities as part of their resistance – I opted not to use this method. In El Salvador I did not propose the participatory drawing exercise with the police officers given that the backdrop of recent arrests of local police implicated in extrajudicial violence made for a somewhat tense environment.

JUDICIAL RECORDS

In the case of El Salvador, I was able to secure access to judicial files on two groups of victims and police that had engaged in piecemeal vigilantism. The files were part of a special investigation launched by El Salvador's *Fiscalía General de la República*. The FGR's office initiated the investigation in 2013 in response to growing concern that members of El Salvador's PNC were engaging in extralegal violence against gang members. Over the course of the next two years a small group of investigators in the FGR's office looked into these allegations, several of which produced arrests and subsequent trials in specialized courts in El Salvador called *Juzgados y Tribunales Especializados* that only process legal cases that involve organized crime or which are particularly complex in nature.[3] I accessed these files after numerous months of filing formal requests with the specific courts where the trials were taking place and several meetings with the judges that were overseeing the cases. During these meetings I explained the objectives of my study to the judges, answered their questions, and requested permission to view the hardcopy files. I then spent several weeks in different courts reading through the files and taking detailed notes on files that each contained over fifteen hundred pages.

The judicial files offer remarkably detailed information on the structure and practices of the two groups. This information had several origins. Both judicial files contained some transcripts of conversations between participants in the groups obtained via official wire taps of their cell phones, transcripts of conversations carried out over text messaging, and summaries of cell phone conversations produced by judicial investigators and state prosecutors. Wire taps represent a unique and "relatively neglected source of data" (Campana and Varese 2012, 27) in the study of organized crime. The data from the wire taps in this case have both strengths and weaknesses. There is no reason to believe that the participants were aware that their conversations were being monitored and documented, which means that they likely did not engage in "self-censorship" and hence their discussions provide realistic insights into the activities of and participants in the extermination groups. Full sets of transcripts for all monitored conversations, however, were not available for public release, meaning that the sample of conversations is incomplete. Not all individuals that participated in the extermination groups had their cell phones tapped, which means that transcripts do not provide "wide group coverage" (Campana and Varese 2012, 16–17). But I supplement these transcripts with additional data from the judicial files to partially mitigate these weaknesses.

Both files contain anonymized reports from witnesses to several of the acts of violence that the groups carried out. Some witnesses lived in the areas where the groups carried out violent practices, and others happened to be with the targets of those practices. In one set of files the reports include detailed confessions from one of the group's participants who become a cooperating witness for the FGR's office in return for leniency in their sentencing. The judicial files also contain detailed reports by state investigators into the activities of the groups, including on each of the groups' participants. I triangulated this unique data with insights secured through fieldwork in the communities where the groups carried out their violent activities, interviews with the judges that oversaw the cases, and interviews with some of the FGR's investigators.

---

[3] The *Juzgados y Tribuanles Especializados* in El Salvador were established in 2006 under Legislative Decree No. 190, also known as the "Law Against Organized Crime."

ETHICS

The data collection strategy for this project followed the research proposal submitted to and approved by Barnard College's Institutional Review Board.[4] As part of adhering to the principles of informed consent I relied on oral consent given the high level of risk associated with both providing participants with paper documentation as to their participation in the project and with carrying this documentation with sensitive identifying information on my person while in the field.

Studying the illicit and interacting with actors that had engaged in criminal activities of varying types pose ethical challenges. At no point did I participate in criminal acts, nor did I witness violent criminal acts. I did, however, regularly observe a number of nonviolent criminal acts, including the selling and purchasing of illegal narcotics and their consumption in public settings, civilians carrying high-caliber weapons technically available only to military personnel, and patrols by armed non-state groups. I never shared information about what I had seen with law enforcement or any government agencies or representatives.

As noted above, the consent procedure was oral to reduce the risk for participants. In focus groups and interviews I explained that the objective of my research was to understand crime and insecurity in different parts of Latin America for a book that I would publish in the United States. I informed participants that I would be speaking with a wide variety of people, including victims, criminals, politicians, and civil society representatives, but that all individual-level information provided to me would be kept anonymous. I indicated that I was a professor at a college in the United States and that I was not working with or for any development or government organizations. I told people that the only benefit – apart from the USD 15 that the focus group participants in Medellín received – was the generation of knowledge about these issues. I stressed that people could decline to answer any question and could leave the interview, focus group, or participant drawing exercise at any time.

Re-traumatization of respondents was a constant concern. I tried to take steps to make the spaces in which interviews and focus groups took place feel safe to the respondents to reduce anxiety. For example, in the hotel meeting room where I conducted the focus groups in Medellín, I provided participants with coffee, tea, and sweet pastries. Many of them commented that they had never before been offered food during a meeting. The women in the group would always start to ask the men if they wanted coffee or tea and move to prepare it for them. At those moments I would politely intervene and serve each individual participant their drink and food myself – something which caused many smirks and raised eyebrows. I saw this as a small gesture that I hoped would indicate to participants that this was their space as much as it was mine, but, more broadly,

---

[4] Barnard College, Institutional Review Board Project #1920–1120-032.

that I respected each individual and that this was a space to treat each other with dignity.[5] When interview respondents or focus group participants shared what were obviously traumatic experiences, I always made sure to make eye contact but also paused after they had spoken instead of asking another question. I wanted respondents to be able to compose themselves if they wanted to or, in some cases, continue sharing their experiences. I cannot claim that I was always successful. In several of the focus groups people cried as they shared their stories, as also happened in interviews across the field sites. But I also believe that people appreciated the opportunity to share these stories and having an outsider interested in them. For example, one elderly woman in a focus group in Medellín told the group her name as we introduced ourselves and, before she could continue, began sobbing. Once the woman stopped crying, she explained that no one had ever asked her about herself and her experiences, and that this was why she was crying. This also illustrates how some of the data used in this project was itself coproduced (MacLean et al. 2019, 6).

To protect the information of research participants, I never wrote down names when taking down notes. I kept the notebooks in hotel room safes when available or hidden in different locations in my rental cars. At any given point in time I carried three cell phones with me in the field but stored in different locations on me or in my car – one was a personal phone with no local contacts stored on it, a second that I used to communicate with my contacts and which had anonymized codes instead of names for contacts, and a third that had basic, but no sensitive, information that I could quickly hand over if instructed to do so by state actors or other actors. Only on one occasion was I asked to do so at a checkpoint on a road in Michoacán by a group of several heavily armed men who, I later learned from an interviewee, were likely from a DTO that was trying to make inroads in the municipality that I was driving through. I only brought my personal cell phone back home with me to the United States – each time I destroyed and disposed of the other two cell phones in case they were confiscated when leaving the country where I was conducting research or upon arrival in the United States.

POSITIONALITY

Interactions with participants via interviews and focus groups in my field sites represent the empirical foundation for this project. My nationality (US-born), gender (male), sexual orientation (heterosexual) and ethnicity (Latino) each individually and in different combinations enhanced my ability to gain access to population and the types of information presented and analyzed in this book (Parkinson 2016; Thaler 2019).

I continuously made clear to research participants that the only benefit of my research and participating in the project was academic in nature. But my

---

[5] See Fujii (2017) on the "working relationships" between researchers and research participants.

nationality and professional status often raised expectations that I would either be able to help people in difficult circumstances by relating their stories and experiences directly to representatives of the US government or international aid agencies. This may have led some individuals to exaggerate or even make up aspects of their experiences of victimization. To mitigate against this, I triangulated different forms of data to ensure that the practices associated with criminal extortion that were related to me were evident in other and sometimes opposing sources.

My gender and physical appearance sometimes raised suspicions among research participants. On several occasions in each field site people indicated that I looked like a police officer because of my physical build. On one occasion an informant indicated that other people would not talk to me because I looked too much like a member of the police. I took steps to convince people that I was not a police officer, including showing them my profile on my academic institution's website. At that point most people seemed to accept that I was not a police officer. But perhaps if I had been of a different gender or different physical appearance the nature of our conversations would have been different.

I had to learn to phrase questions as nonjudgmental – something that my RAs helped me with. If someone offered an anecdote about having been part of group that engaged in extralegal violence – whether as part of extortion or as part of resistance to extortion – I had to signal in my tone, facial expression, and phrasing of my questions that I was not passing judgment but instead that I was curious about understanding the why and how of that behavior. The large number of interviews and focus groups coupled with the time spent in my field sites helps to overcome some of the biases that my positionality introduced into the research process.

During my time in the field I experienced an admittedly small amount of the fear and insecurity that characterize the everyday lives of many of the people that I interacted with in my field sites. Driving and walking by myself in these localities tended to raise my levels of stress and anxiety. Interviews and focus groups that touched on particularly difficult experiences, such as violence, disappearances, and humiliation, tended to generate within me a sense of hopelessness and symptoms associated with depression that aggravated preexisting mental health conditions and which required ongoing medical therapy. But these feelings and experiences also paradoxically helped me to better grasp the strategic contexts in which the actors I was studying operated, their incentives, and how they made decisions about what actions to take. I am not arguing that experiencing these feelings and symptoms is something researchers should aim for. Only that this was my experience.

Carrying out this study complicated and challenged my preconceived notions of all victims as "innocent" or "wronged." As I show throughout this book, victims often resist by using some of the same violent practices they were subjected to by criminal actors. I quickly learned during my field research that the boundary between a victim engaging in resistance and a criminal actor can be hazy and shift in unexpected and unsettling ways.[6] This echoes Fujii's (2010, 237) caution "against viewing victims as uniformly innocent and perpetrators as the only actors capable of violence." When I started my research, I expected that it would be hard to set aside my empathy for victims as part of advancing an objective analysis of their actions (Nilan 2002). But when sitting across from individuals that had been both the victims and then the perpetrators of different acts of violence, I found that my empathy was also linked to unease with the actions that some victims undertook as part of their resistance and how they justified them. Reflecting on this helped me to (re)think my assumptions and analysis, as well as some of the methodological choices I made. But I was able to do so only by listening to and learning from victims as part of the data collection process across multiple field sites.

Interviews

1. Agent #1 (MCN1159), member of the CUSEPT, Tancítaro, August 2018.
2. Agent #2 (MCN80), member of the CUSEPT, Tancítaro, August 2018.
3. Alan (MCN49), member of self-defense Group C, La Unión, September 2018.
4. Alejandro (IV_MDE_6010), informal vendor, Medellín, June 2016.
5. Alexandra (ESV771), civil society leader, El Pilar, July 2017.
6. Alicia (IV_MDE_911), informal vendor, Medellín, July 2016.
7. Alvaro (MCN033656), JLSV employee, Tancítaro, July 2018.
8. Amelio (MCN1200), avocado producer, Tancítaro, July 2018.
9. Amparo (MCN0316), government official, Tancítaro, July 2018.
10. Antonella (IV_MDE_899), informal vendor, Medellín, July 2016.
11. Armando (ESV67), farmer, Cienfuegos, October 2018.
12. Benjamín (MDE10), municipal government official, Medellín, March 2017.
13. Bernardo (MDE888), civil society leader, Medellín, July 2016.
14. Berry export firm representative (LU319), Guadalajara, Mexico, May 2019 (telephone).
15. Blanca (MDE12), municipal government official, Medellín, July 2016.
16. Boris (MDE320), owner of private security firm, Medellín, March 2017.
17. Camilo (MCN18), member of self-defense Group C, La Unión, September 2018.
18. Catalina (MDE13), journalist, Medellín, July 2016.
19. Community member (MCN0117), Tancítaro, July 2018.

---

[6] Krause (2018, 22) similarly argues that the boundary between civilians and combatants in communal conflicts is more fluid than much existing research acknowledges: "I distinguish between armed and unarmed civilians rather than combatants and civilians because civilian behavior can change from the adoption of unarmed to armed and back to unarmed strategies during the course of conflict."

20. Cristobal (MCN1938), avocado grower, Tancítaro, May 2020 (telephone).
21. Cynthia (MCN85001), member of the PRD municipal committee, Tancítaro, January 2019 (telephone).
22. Danilo (MDE43999), leader of private sector business association, Medellín, July 2016.
23. Dante (MDE510), civil society leader, Medellín, July 2016.
24. Diana (ESV915), FGR investigator, El Salvador, June 2017.
25. Douglas (IV_MDE_1010), informal vendor, Medellín, July 2016.
26. Edwin (MDE2097), municipal government official, Medellín, July 2016.
27. Elmer (MDE19), civil society leader, Medellín, March 2017.
28. Emilia (MDE77), community leader, Medellín, July 2016.
29. Emiliano (ESV112577), farmer, El Pilar, June 2017.
30. Emilio (MCN01), member of Leopoldo's self-defense Group A, La Unión, October 2018.
31. Emmanuel (MDE333), member of the Grupo de Acción Unificada por la Libertad Personal (GAULA), National Police of Colombia, Medellín, July 2016.
32. Esperanza (MCN201), journalist, Tancítaro, May 2018 (electronic).
33. Felipe (ESV07851), farmer, El Pilar, June 2017.
34. Félix (MCN2), berry producer, La Unión, August 2018.
35. Florencia (ESV10012), community member, Cienfuegos, June 2017.
36. Former lookout #1 for the Familia Michoacana (MCN258), La Unión, August 2018.
37. Former lookout #2 for the Familia Michoacana (MCN999), La Unión, August 2018.
38. Former lookout #3 for the Familia Michoacana (MCN131), Tancítaro, August 2018.
39. Former manager #1 at berry export firm (MCN02901), United States, May 2020 (telephone).
40. Former manager #2 at berry export firm (MCN02909), Morelia, May 2020 (telephone).
41. Francisco Javier (MCN711), JLSV employee, Tancítaro, July 2018.
42. Fredy (MCN6019), avocado producer, Tancítaro, August 2018.
43. Gabriel (IV_MDE_142), former Convivir member, Medellín, July 2017.
44. Gerardo (MCN77), berry producer, La Unión, August 2018.
45. Germán (MCN002), berry producer, La Unión, May 2020 (telephone).
46. Gladys (MCN6507), journalist, La Unión, June 2018.
47. Gustavo (ESV414563), farmer, Cienfuegos, October 2018.
48. Harold (MCN4849), municipal government official, La Unión, May 2019.
49. Héctor (MCN50), member of self-defense Group B, La Unión, November 2018.

50. Henry (MDE09), informal vendor, Medellín, May 2020 (telephone).
51. Hércules (MDE998), member of a private sector business association, Medellín, March 2017.
52. Hugo (MCN4844), mayor of La Unión (2015–18), August 2018.
53. Ignacio (MCN56), member of self-defense Group A, La Unión, September 2018.
54. Isabella (MDE11), civil society leader, Medellín, July 2016.
55. Iván (ESV9213), farmer, Cienfuegos, October 2018.
56. Jaime (ESV55), farmer, El Pilar, July 2017.
57. James (MCN3), civil society leader, Medellín, March 2017.
58. James (MCN6660), lawyer, Tancítaro, August 2018.
59. Javier (MDE56), municipal government official, Medellín, June 2017.
60. Jerónimo (MDE800), owner of private security firm, Medellín, June 2016.
61. Jesús (MCN14835), community member, La Unión, September 2018.
62. Jesús David (MCN113011), avocado producer, Tancítaro, August 2018.
63. Joaquín (ESV100), journalist, San Salvador, June 2017.
64. Jonathan (ESV3), journalist, San Salvador, October 2018.
65. José Luis (MCN030), JLSV employee, Tancítaro, July 2018.
66. Josue (ESV916), investigator in the FGR, San Salvador, June 2017.
67. Juan (MCN90), avocado grower, Tancítaro, May 2020.
68. Juan Carlos (MCN08513), municipal government official, Tancítaro, July 2018.
69. Judge #1 (ESV011), San Salvador, July 2019.
70. Judge #2 (ESV009), San Miguel, July 2019.
71. Julián (MCN2416), avocado producer, Tancítaro, July 2018.
72. Juliana (ESV40), civil society leader, San Salvador, October 2018.
73. Leo (IV_MDE_1630), informal vendor, Medellín, July 2016.
74. Lorenzo (MCN30119), JLSV employee, Tancítaro, July 2018.
75. Lucas (MCN44), member of self-defense Group A, La Unión, October 2018.
76. Luis (ESV1713), researcher, PDDH, San Salvador, June 2017.
77. Marcelino (MCN38), member of self-defense Group A, La Unión, October 2018.
78. Marco (MCN315), avocado producer, Tancítaro, July 2018.
79. Marco Antonio (MCN1900), avocado producer, Tancítaro, July 2018.
80. Marcos (ESV9092), farmer, Cienfuegos, October 2018.
81. Maria (ESV16162), government official, San Salvador, August 2020 (telephone).
82. Marta (IV_FG5_30), informal vendor, Medellín, March 2017.
83. Marvin, (MCN26), member of self-defense Group B, La Unión, August 2018.
84. Mateo (IV_MDE_141), former Convivir member, Medellín, July 2017.

85. Member of the Consejo Ciudadano de los Autodefensas de La Unión (MCN149105), La Unión, November 2018.
86. Mercedes (MCN4800), municipal official, La Unión, August 2018.
87. Miguel Angel (MCN20), member of Group B, La Unión, August 2018.
88. Moisés (MCN8002), member of Group D, La Unión, September 2018.
89. Nicolás (ESV9090), farmer, Cienfuegos, October 2018.
90. Noe (MCN7835), JLSV employee, Tancítaro, July 2018.
91. Omar (MDE53), former police agent, Medellín, July 2016.
92. Oswaldo (MCN5813), avocado producer, Tancítaro, July 2018.
93. Pablo (ESV16161), farmer, Cienfuegos, February 2020 (telephone).
94. Police agent #1 (ESV001), El Pilar, June 2017.
95. Police agent #2 (ESV303), El Pilar, June 2017.
96. Rafa (MCN1066), municipal government official, Tancítaro, July 2018.
97. Ramiro (MCN808), JLSV employee, Tancítaro, October 2018.
98. Ramon (MCN959), berry producer, La Unión, July 2018.
99. Raul (MCN950), avocado producer, Tancítaro, July 2018.
100. René (ESV1616), farmer, Cienfuegos, July 2017.
101. Representative from USDA APHIS, Phytosanitary Issues Management, Office of the Deputy Administrator, June 8, 2020 (email).
102. Ricardo (ESV12), farmer, El Pilar, June 2017 (telephone interview in May 2020).
103. Rosa María (MDE299), municipal government official, Medellín, July 2016.
104. Samantha (ESV3290), journalist, San Salvador, June 2017.
105. Samuel (ESV2020), former gang member, El Pilar, October 2018.
106. Santiago (MCN1414), berry producer and member of the Consejo Ciudadano de los Autodefensas de La Unión, La Unión, November 2018.
107. Santino (MDE103), municipal government official, Medellín, July 2016.
108. Santos (MCN20), former member of self-defense Group B, La Unión, August 2018.
109. Saul (MCN2011), avocado producer, Tancítaro, July 2018.
110. Self-defense group leader from Tepalcatepec #1 (MCN1042), Morelia, July 2018.
111. Self-defense group leader from Tepalcatepec #2 (MCN17), Morelia, August 2018.
112. Sergio (MCN8001), member of self-defense group B, La Unión, September 2018.
113. Simon (MCN200), local journalist, Tancítaro, May 2018 (email).
114. Sofia (MDE461), journalist, Medellín, July 2016.
115. Teo (MCN4848), municipal government official, La Unión, August 2018.
116. Tomas (IV_MDE_551), informal vendor, Medellín, July 2016.
117. Toño (MCN21), member of Group B, La Unión, August 2018.

118. Tony (ESV8391), participant in 2012 gang truce negotiations, San Salvador, June 2017.
119. Uriel (MCN71), berry producer, La Unión, July 2018.
120. Valeria (IV_MDE_423), informal vendor, Medellín, July 2016.
121. Vicente (MCN8003), member of self-defense Group D, La Unión, September 2018.
122. Vilma (MCN1065), municipal government employee, Tancítaro, July 2018.
123. Walter (MCN2055), avocado producer, Tancítaro, August 2018.
124. Will (ESV3223), former gang member, Cienfuegos, June 2017.
125. Yazmin (MDE9991), municipal government official, Medellín, March 2017.
126. Yolanda (MDE0021), civil society leader, Medellín, July 2016.
127. Yuri (MDE14949), civil society leader, Medellín, March 2017.

Legal Case Summaries for Chapter 4

Cases against group in Cienfuegos

- Case C: Homicide of multiple gang members engaged in extortion.
- Case F: Homicide of a gang member.
- Case P: Homicide of a gang member who kidnapped a teenage woman and engaged in extortion.
- Case J: Homicide of a gang member responsible for holding on to money collected from extortion.
- Case H: Homicide of a gang member that had engaged in extortion.
- Case T: Homicide of the relative of one of the group's members who was disliked in their community.
- Case Q: Homicide of a gang member suspected of monitoring members of the group.

Cases against group in El Pilar

- Case D: Homicide of a gang member engaged in extortion.
- Case L: Homicide of a member of the group suspected of having become a police informant.
- Case M: Homicide of a gang member engaged in extortion.
- Case E: Homicide of a gang member engaged in extortion.
- Case G: Failed homicide attempt of two relatives of one member of the group.
- Case X: Homicide of multiple gang members engaged in extortion.
- Case C: Failed homicide attempt of a gang member suspected of monitoring members of the group.

- Case J: Homicide of former gang member that had engaged in the extortion and murder of an individual that failed to pay the extortion tax.
- Case Q: Homicide of a gang member that had engaged in the extortion and murder of an individual that failed to pay the extortion tax.
- Case T: Break-in and armed robbery of a residence.
- Case P: Homicide of a gang member that had threatened a member of the community.
- Case M: Homicide of a *palabrero* engaged in extortion.
- Case B: Homicide of a gang member that worked as a lookout (*poste*) for the gang.
- Case Z: Homicide of a gang member that suspected of monitoring members of the group.

References

Abrahams, Raphael Garvin. (1998). *Vigilant Citizens: Vigilantism and the State.* Cambridge: Polity Press.

Abrahams, Ray. (2020). "Vigilantism in Comparative Perspective." In *Oxford Research Encyclopedia of Criminology and Criminal Justice.* https://doi-org.ezproxy.cul.columbia.edu/10.1093/acrefore/9780190264079.013.585

Abrahamsen, Rita and Michael C. Williams. (2010). *Security Beyond the State: Private Security in International Politics.* New York: Cambridge University Press.

Aburto, José Manuel, Hiram Beltrán-Sánchez, Víctor Manuel García-Guerrero, and Vladimir Canudas-Romo. (2016). "Homicides in Mexico Reversed Life Expectancy Gains for Men and Slowed Them for Women, 2000–2010." *Health Affairs* 35(1): 88–95.

Acevedo, Carlos, Deborah Barry, and Herman Rosa. (1995). "El Salvador's Agricultural Sector: Macroeconomic Policy, Agrarian Change and the Environment." *World Development* 23(12): 2153–2172.

Aguilar, Jeannette. (2019). *Las Políticas de Seguridad Pública en El Salvador: 2003–2018.* San Salvador: Fundación Heinrich Böll.

Aguilar, Jeannette and Lissette Miranda. (2006). "Entre la Articulación y la Competencia: Las Respuestas de la Sociedad Civil Organizada a las Pandillas en El Salvador." In *Maras y Pandillas en Centroamérica: Las Respuestas de la Sociedad Civil Organizada,* edited by José Miguel Cruz, 37–64. San Salvador: UCA Editores.

Ahmad, Aisha. (2017). *Jihad & Co.: Black Markets and Islamist Power.* Oxford: Oxford University Press.

Albarracín, Juan. (2018). "Criminalized Electoral Politics in Brazilian Urban Peripheries." *Crime, Law and Social Change* 69(4): 553–575.

Almeida, Paul D. (2008). *Waves of Protest: Popular Struggle in El Salvador, 1925–2005.* Minneapolis and London: University of Minnesota Press.

Amengual, Matthew. (2016). *Politicized Enforcement in Argentina: Labor and Environmental Regulation.* Cambridge: Cambridge University Press.

Angel, Amy. (2008). "Análisis de Mercado de Granos Básicos en Centroamérica: Enfoque en El Salvador." World Food Program. Available at: https://amyangel.webs.com/ESfinal.pdf. Accessed on April 29, 2021.

Arana, Ana. (2005). "How the Street Gangs Took Central America." *Foreign Affairs* 84 (3): 98–110.

Arias, Enrique Desmond. (2006). *Drugs & Democracy in Rio de Janeiro: Trafficking, Social Networks, & Public Security*. Chapel Hill: University of North Carolina Press.

(2013). "The Impacts of Differential Armed Dominance of Politics in Rio de Janeiro, Brazil." *Studies in Comparative International Development* 48(3): 263–284.

(2017). *Criminal Enterprises and Governance in Latin America and the Caribbean*. Cambridge: Cambridge University Press.

Arias, Enrique Desmond and Mark Ungar. (2009). "Community Policing and Latin America's Citizen Security Crisis." *Comparative Politics* 41(4): 409–429.

Arjona, Ana. (2016). *Rebelocracy: Social Order in the Colombian Civil War*. Cambridge: Cambridge University Press.

(2017). "Civilian Cooperation and Non-cooperation with Non-state Armed Groups: The Centrality of Obedience and Resistance." *Small Wars & Insurgencies* 28(4–5): 755–778.

(2019). "Subnational Units, the Locus of Choice, and Concept Formation." In *Inside Countries: Subnational Research in Comparative Politics*, edited by Agustina Giraudy, Eduardo Moncada, and Richard Snyder, 214–242. Cambridge: Cambridge University Press.

Arjona, Ana and Stathis N. Kalyvas. (2009). Rebelling against Rebellion: Comparing Insurgent and Counterinsurgent Recruitment. In *Mobilisation for Political Violence: What Do We Know?* Centre for Research on Inequality, Human Security and Ethnicity Workshop: Vol. 4, 436–455.

Arjona, Ana, Nelson Kasfir, and Zachariah Mampilly (2015). *Rebel Governance in Civil War*. Cambridge: Cambridge University Press.

Arnson, Cynthia J. (2000). "Window on the Past: A Declassified History of Death Squads in El Salvador." In *Death Squads in Global Perspective*, edited by Bruce Campbell and Arthurd D. Brenner, 85–124. New York: Palgrave Macmillan.

Arrow, Kenneth J. (1986). "Agency and the Market." *Handbook of Mathematical Economics* 3: 1183–1195.

Astorga, Luis. (1995). *El Siglo de las Drogas*. Mexico City: Plaza Janés.

Astorga, Luis and David A. Shirk. (2010). "Drug Trafficking Organizations and Counter-drug Strategies in the US-Mexican Context." Working Paper. San Diego: Center for US-Mexican Studies, University of California, San Diego. Available at: https://escholarship.org/uc/item/8j647429. Accessed on April 29, 2021.

Auyero, Javier. (2007). *Routine Politics and Violence in Argentina: The Gray Zone of State Power*. Cambridge: Cambridge University Press, 2007.

(2012). *Patients of the State: The Politics of Waiting in Argentina*. Durham, NC: Duke University Press.

(2015). "The Politics of Interpersonal Violence in the Urban Periphery." *Current Anthropology* 56(S11): 169–179.

Auyero, Javier and María Fernanda Berti. (2016). *In Harm's Way: The Dynamics of Urban Violence*. Princeton: Princeton University Press.

Ayres, Robert L. (1998). *Crime and Violence as Development Issues in Latin America and the Caribbean*. Washington, DC: World Bank.

Bachrach, Peter and Morton S. Baratz. (1962). "Two Faces of Power." *American Political Science Review* 56(4): 947–952.

Bada, Xóchitl and Andreas E. Feldmann. (2019). "How Insecurity is Transforming Migration Patterns in the North American Corridor: Lessons from Michoacán." In *New Migration Patterns in the Americas*, edited by Andreas E. Feldmann, Xóchitl Bada, and Stephanie Schutze, 57–83. Cham, Switzerland: Palgrave Macmillan.

Bagley, Bruce Michael. (2012). *Drug Trafficking and Organized Crime in the Americas: Major Trends in the Twenty-first Century*. Washington, DC: Woodrow Wilson International Center for Scholars, Latin American Program.

Bailey, John and Matthew M. Taylor. (2009). "Evade, Corrupt, or Confront? Organized Crime and the State in Brazil and Mexico." *Journal of Politics in Latin America* 1 (2): 3–29.

Bakke, Kristin M., Kathleen Gallagher Cunningham, and Lee J.M. Seymour. (2012). "A Plague of Initials: Fragmentation, Cohesion, and Infighting in Civil Wars." *Perspectives on Politics* 10(2): 65–283.

Balcells, Laia. (2012). "The Consequences of Victimization on Political Identities: Evidence from Spain." *Politics & Society* 40(3): 311–347.

Bancroft, Hubert Howe. (1890). *The Works of Hubert Howe Bancroft*. San Francisco: History Company.

Barnes, Nicholas. (2017). "Criminal Politics: An Integrated Approach to the Study of Organized Crime, Politics, and Violence." *Perspectives on Politics* 15(4): 967–987.

Barragán, Esteban. (1997). *Con un Pie en el Estribo: Formación y Deslizamiento de las Sociedades Rancheras en la Construcción del México Moderno*. Zamora, Mexico: El Colegio de Michoacán.

Bartell, Ernest and Leigh A. Payne, eds. (1995). *Business and Democracy in Latin America*. Pittsburgh, PA: University of Pittsburgh Press.

Bateson, Regina. (2012). "Crime Victimization and Political Participation." *American Political Science Review* 106(3): 570–587.

  (2013). "Order and Violence in Postwar Guatemala." PhD dissertation, Yale University.

  (2020). "The Politics of Vigilantism." *Comparative Political Studies*. Available at: https://doi.org/10.1177/0010414020957692. Accessed on April 29, 2021.

Bauer, Michal, Christopher Blattman, Julie Chytilová, Joseph Henrich, Edward Miguel, and Tamar Mitts. (2016). "Can War Foster Cooperation?" *Journal of Economic Perspectives* 30(3): 249–274.

Baumeister, Eduardo. (2018). "Entre La Persistencia y La Transformación: Los Pequeños Productores en El Salvador." *Revista Latinoamericana de Estudios Rurales* 3(6): 69–93.

Bayat, Asef. (2000). "From Dangerous Classes to Quiet Rebels Politics of the Urban Subaltern in the Global South." *International Sociology* 15(3): 533–557.

Bayley, David H. (2005). *Changing the Guard: Developing Democratic Police Abroad*. Oxford: Oxford University Press.

Becker, Anne and Markus-Michael Müller. (2013). "The Securitization of Urban Space and the 'Rescue' of Downtown Mexico City: Vision and Practice." *Latin American Perspectives* 40(2): 77–94.

Beittel, June S. (2015). *Mexico: Organized Crime and Drug Trafficking Organizations*. Washington, DC: Congressional Research Service.

Bénit-Gbaffou, Claire, Sophie Didier, and Marianne Morange. (2008). "Communities, the Private Sector, and the State: Contested Forms of Security Governance in Cape Town and Johannesburg." *Urban Affairs Review* 43(5): 691–717.

Bennett, Andrew and Jeffrey T. Checkel, eds. (2015). *Process Tracing*: From Metaphor to Analytic Tool. Cambridge: Cambridge University Press.

BenYishay, Ariel and Sarah Pearlman. (2014). "Crime and Microenterprise Growth: Evidence from Mexico." *World Development* 56: 139–152.

Bergman, Marcelo. (2018). *More Money, More Crime: Prosperity and Rising Crime in Latin America.* Oxford: Oxford University Press.

Bergmann, Adrian. (2019). "Violence, Migration, and the Perverse Effects of Gang Repression in Central America." In *Media, Central American Refugees, and the US Border Crisis,* edited by Robin Andersen and Adrian Bergmann, 36–58. New York and Abingdon: Routledge.

Berman, Sheri. (1997). "Civil Society and the Collapse of the Weimar Republic." *World Politics* 49(3): 401–429.

Bertelsen, D. (1995). "The US Strawberry Industry." *Economic Research Service, US Department of Agriculture. Statistical Bulletin* 914.

Binford, Leigh and Nancy Churchhill. (2009). "Lynching and States of Fear in Urban Mexico." *Anthropologica* 51(2): 301–312.

Blaydes, Lisa. (2018). *State of Repression: Iraq under Saddam Hussein.* Princeton: Princeton University Press.

Blok, Anton. (1975). *The Mafia of a Sicilian Village, 1860-1960: A Study of Violent Peasant Entrepreneurs.* New York: Harper Collins Publishers.

Boone, Catherine. (2003). *Political Topographies of the African State: Territorial Authority and Institutional Choice.* Cambridge: Cambridge University Press.

Boss, Pauline. (2002). *Family Stress Management: A Contextual Approach.* Thousand Oaks, London, and New Delhi: Sage Publications.

Bott, Sarah, Alessandra Guedes, Ana P. Ruiz-Celis, and Jennifer Adams Mendoza. (2019). "Intimate Partner Violence in the Americas: A Systematic Review and Reanalysis of National Prevalence Estimates." *Revista Panamericana de Salud Publica* 43(1): 1–12.

Brenneman, Robert. (2011). *Homies and Hermanos: God and Gangs in Central America.* Oxford: Oxford University Press.

Brinks, Daniel M. (2007). *The Judicial Response to Police Killings in Latin America: Inequality and the Rule of Law.* Cambridge: Cambridge University Press.

Brinks, Daniel M., Steven Levitsky, and Maria Victoria Murillo. (2019). *Understanding Institutional Weakness: Power and Design in Latin American Institutions.* Cambridge: Cambridge University Press.

Brown, Richard Maxwell. (1975). *Strain of Violence: Historical Studies of American Violence and Vigilantism.* Oxford: Oxford University Press.

Burt, Martha R. (1980). "Cultural Myths and Supports for Rape." *Journal of Personality and Social Psychology* 38(2): 217.

Buur, Lars and Steffen Jensen. (2004). "Introduction: Vigilantism and the Policing of Everyday life in South Africa." *African Studies* 63(2): 139–152.

Caldeira, Teresa PR. (2000). *City of Walls: Crime, Segregation, and Citizenship in São Paulo.* Berkeley, CA: University of California Press.

Calderón, M. (1994). *Violencia Política y Elecciones Municipales.* Zamora: COLMICH/ Instituto Mora.

Calderón, Gabriela, Gustavo Robles, Alberto Díaz-Cayeros, and Beatriz Magaloni. (2015). "The Beheading of Criminal Organizations and the Dynamics of Violence in Mexico." *Journal of Conflict Resolution* 59(8): 1455–1485.

Call, Charles T. (2003). "Democratisation, War and State-building: Constructing the Rule of Law in El Salvador." *Journal of Latin American Studies* 35(4): 827–862.

Calvin, Linda, William Foster, Luis Solorzano, J. Daniel Mooney, Luis Flores, and Veronica Barrios. (2002). "Response to a Food Safety Problem in Produce." In *Global Food Trade and Consumer Demand for Quality*, edited by Barry Krisoff, Mary Bohman, and Julie A. Caswell, 101–127. Boston, MA: Springer.

Campana, Paolo. (2011). "Eavesdropping on the Mob: The Functional Diversification of Mafia Activities Across Territories." *European Journal of Criminology* 8(3): 213–228.

Campana, Paolo and Federico Varese. (2012). "Listening to the Wire: Criteria and Techniques for the Quantitative Analysis of Phone Intercepts." *Trends in Organized Crime* 15(1): 13–30.

Campbell, Howard. (2011). "No End in Sight: Violence in Ciudad Juárez." *NACLA Report on the Americas* 44(3): 19–22.

Cantor, David James. (2014). "The New Wave: Forced Displacement Caused by Organized Crime in Central America and Mexico." *Refugee Survey Quarterly* 33 (3): 34–68.

Cano, Ignacio. (2013). "Violence and Organized Crime in Brazil: The Case of "Militias" in Rio de Janeiro." In *Transnational Organized Crime*, edited by Heinrich-Böll -Stiftung and Regine Schönenberg, 179–188. Bielefeld, Germany: Verlag.

Carey, Sabine C., Neil J. Mitchell, and Will Lowe. (2013). "States, the Security Sector, and the Monopoly of Violence: A New Database on Pro-government Militias." *Journal of Peace Research* 50(2): 249–258.

Cederman, Lars-Erik and Kristian Skrede Gleditsch. (2009). "Introduction to Special Issue on 'Disaggregating Civil War." *Journal of Conflict Resolution* 53(4): 487–495.

Centeno, Miguel A., Atul Kohli, and Deborah J. Yashar. (2017). "Unpacking States in the Developing World: Capacity, Performance, and Politics." In *States in the Developing World*, edited by Miguel A. Centeno, Atul Kohli, Deborah J. Yashar, and Dinsha Mistree, 1–34. Cambridge: Cambridge University Press.

Centeno, Miguel Angel. (2002). *Blood and Debt: War and the Nation-state in Latin America*. Penn State University Press.

Centro para la Defensa del Consumidor. (2019). *Estudio Sobre Costo de la Vida y Propuesta de Mejora para un Salario Mínimo*. San Salvador, El Salvador: Centro para la Defensa del Consumidor.

Cernea, Michael. (1997). "The Risks and Reconstruction Model for Resettling Displaced Populations." *World Development* 25(10): 1569–1587.

Chenoweth, Erica and Maria J. Stephan. (2011). *Why Civil Resistance Works: The Strategic Logic of Nonviolent Conflict*. New York: Columbia University Press.

Chollett, Donna L. (2009). "From Sugar to Blackberries: Restructuring Agro-Export Production in Michoacán, Mexico." *Latin American Perspectives* 36(3): 79–92.

Collazos, Daniela, Eduardo García, Daniel Mejía, Daniel Ortega, and Santiago Tobón. (2020). "Hot Spots Policing in a High-Crime Environment: An Experimental Evaluation in Medellín." *Journal of Experimental Criminology*: 1–34. https://doi .org/10.1007/s11292-019-09390-1.

Collier, David, Henry E. Brady, and Jason Seawright. (2004). "Sources of Leverage in Causal Inference: Toward an Alternative View of Methodology." In *Rethinking Social Inquiry: Diverse Tools, Shared Standards*, 2nd ed., edited by Henry E. Brady and David Collier, 161–99. Lanham, MD: Rowman and Littlefield.

Collier, David. (1976). *Squatters and Oligarchs: Authoritarian Rule and Policy Change in Peru*. Baltimore, MD: The Johns Hopkins University Press.

Collier, David. (2011). "Understanding Process Tracing." *PS: Political Science & Politics* 44(4): 823–830.

Cooper-Knock, Sarah Jane and Olly Owen. (2015). "Between Vigilantism and Bureaucracy: Improving Our Understanding of Police Work in Nigeria and South Africa." *Theoretical Criminology* 19(3): 355–375.

Coppedge, Michael. (1999). "Thickening Thin Concepts and Theories: Combining Large N and Small in Comparative Politics." *Comparative Politics* 31(4): 465–476.

Correa-Cabrera, Guadalupe. (2017). *Los Zetas Inc.: Criminal Corporations, Energy, and Civil War in Mexico*. Austin, TX: University of Texas Press.

Cross, John Christopher. (1998). *Informal Politics: Street Vendors and the State in Mexico City*. Palo Alto, CA: Stanford University Press.

Cruz, José Miguel. (2006). "Violence, Citizen Insecurity, and Elite Maneuvering in El Salvador." In *Public Security and Police Reform in the Americas*, edited by John Bailey and Lucia Dammert, 148–168. Pittsburgh: University of Pittsburgh Press.

(2010). "Central American Maras: From Youth Street Gangs to Transnational Protection Rackets." *Global Crime* 11(4): 379–398.

Cruz, José Miguel and Nelson Portillo Peña. (1998). *Solidaridad y Violencia en las Pandillas del Gran San Salvador: Más Allá de La Vida Loca*. San Salvador, El Salvador: Uca Editores.

Cruz, José Miguel and Angélica Durán-Martínez. (2016). "Hiding Violence to Deal with the State: Criminal Pacts in El Salvador and Medellin." *Journal of Peace Research* 53(2): 197–210.

Cruz, José Miguel and Jonathan D. Rosen. (2020). "Mara Forever? Factors Associated with Gang Disengagement in El Salvador." *Journal of Criminal Justice*. https://doi.org/10.1016/j.jcrimjus.2020.101705

Cunningham, Kathleen Gallagher, Kristin M. Bakke, and Lee J.M. Seymour. (2012). "Shirts Today, Skins Tomorrow: Dual Contests and the Effects of Fragmentation in Self-Determination Disputes." *Journal of Conflict Resolution* 56(1): 67–93.

Curry, Alexander. (2020). *Autodefensas and the Construction of Citizenship and State-Society Relations in Mexico*. PhD thesis, University of London.

Cyr, Jennifer. (2016). "The Pitfalls and Promise of Focus Groups as a Data Collection Method." *Sociological Methods & Research* 45(2): 231–259.

Dal Bó, Ernesto, Pedro Dal Bó, and Rafael Di Tella. (2006). "'Plata o Plomo?': Bribe and Punishment in a Theory of Political Influence." *American Political Science Review* 100(1): 41–53.

Davis, Diane E. (2013). "Zero-tolerance Policing, Stealth Real Estate Development, and the Transformation of Public Space: Evidence from Mexico City." *Latin American Perspectives* 40(2): 53–76.

de Souza Martins, José. (2015). *Linchamentos: A Justiça Popular no Brasil*. Sao Paulo. Brazil: Editora Contexto.

Del Frate, Anna Alvazzi. (2004). "The International Crime Business Survey: Findings from Nine Central–Eastern European Cities." *European Journal on Criminal Policy and Research* 10(2–3): 137–161.

Dewey, Matías. (2018). "The Other Taxation: An Ethnographic Account of 'Off-the-Books' State Financing." *Latin American Research Review* 53(4): 726–740.

Doner, Richard F. and Ben Ross Schneider. (2000). "Business Associations and Economic Development: Why Some Associations Contribute More Than Others." *Business and Politics* 2(3): 261–288.

Dorff, Cassy. (2017). "Violence, Kinship Networks, and Political Resilience: Evidence from Mexico." *Journal of Peace Research* 54(4): 558–573.

Dudley, Steven S. (2010). *Drug Trafficking Organizations in Central America: Transportistas, Mexican Cartels and Maras.* Washington, DC: Woodrow Wilson International Center for Scholars, Mexico Institute.

Durán-Martínez, Angélica. (2017). *The Politics of Drug Violence: Criminals, Cops and Politicians in Colombia and Mexico.* Oxford: Oxford University Press.

Durand, Francisco and Eduardo Silva, eds. (1998). *Organized Business, Economic Change, and Democracy in Latin America.* Miami, FL: North-South Center Press.

Enriquez, Elaine and Miguel Angel Centeno. (2012). "State Capacity: Utilization, Durability, and the Role of Wealth vs. History." *International and Multidisciplinary Journal of Social Sciences* 1(2): 130–162.

Epp, Charles R. (1998). *The Rights Revolution: Lawyers, Activists, and Supreme Courts in comparative perspective.* Chicago: University of Chicago Press.

Epp, Charles R., Steven Maynard-Moody, and Donald P. Haider-Markel. (2014). *Pulled Over: How Police Stops Define Race and Citizenship.* Chicago: University of Chicago Press.

Evans, Peter B. (1979). *Embedded Autonomy: States and Industrial Transformation.* Princeton: Princeton University Press.

(1989). "Predatory, Developmental, and Other Apparatuses: A Comparative Political Economy Perspective on the Third World State." *Sociological Forum* 4(4): 561–587.

(1996). "Government Action, Social Capital and Development: Reviewing the Evidence on Synergy." *World Development* 24(6): 1119.

Ewick, Patricia and Susan S. Silbey. (1998). *The Common Place of Law: Stories from Everyday Life.* Chicago: University of Chicago Press.

Fagan, Jeffrey and Tom R. Tyler. (2005). "Legal Socialization of Children and Adolescents." *Social Justice Research* 18(3): 217–241.

Fairfield, Tasha. (2015). *Private Wealth and Public Revenue.* Cambridge: Cambridge University Press.

Feder, Ernest. (1977). *El Imperialismo Fresa.* Mexico City: Editorial Campesina.

Flom, Hernan. (2016). "Police, Politicians and the Regulation of Drug Trafficking in Latin America." PhD dissertation. Berkeley: University of California, Berkeley.

Flores-Macías, Gustavo A. (2014). "Financing Security Through Elite Taxation: The Case of Colombia's 'Democratic Security Taxes.'" *Studies in Comparative International Development* 49(4): 477–500.

(2018). "The Consequences of Militarizing Anti-Drug Efforts for State Capacity in Latin America: Evidence from Mexico." *Comparative Politics* 51(1): 1–20.

Flores-Macías, Gustavo A. and Jessica Zarkin. (2019). "The Militarization of Law Enforcement: Evidence from Latin America." *Perspectives on Politics* 19(2): 519-538.

Fourchard, Laurent. (2011). "The Politics of Mobilization for Security in South African Townships." *African Affairs* 110(441): 607–627.

Fox, Jonathan. (1996). "How Does Civil Society Thicken? The Political Construction of Social Capital in Rural Mexico." *World Development* 24(6): 1089–1103.

Frühling, Hugo. (2009). "Research on Latin American Police: Where Do We Go from Here?" *Police Practice and Research: An International Journal* 10(5–6): 465–481.

(2012). "A Realistic Look at Latin American Community Policing Programmes." *Policing and Society* 22(1): 76–88.

Frye, Timothy and Ekaterina Zhuravskaya. (2000). "Rackets, Regulation, and the Rule of Law." *Journal of Law, Economics, and Organization* 16(2): 478–502.

Frye, Timothy. (2002). "Private Protection in Russia and Poland." *American Journal of Political Science* 46(3): 572–584.

Fu, Diana. (2018). *Mobilizing Without the Masses: Control and Contention in China.* Cambridge: Cambridge University Press.

Fuentes-Díaz, Antonio. (2015). "Narcotráfico y Autodefensa Comunitaria en" Tierra Caliente", Michoacán, México." *CienciaUAT* 10(1): 68–82.

Fuentes Díaz, Antonio and Guillermo Paleta Pérez. (2015). "Violencia y Autodefensas Comunitarias en Michoacán, México." *Íconos: Revista de Ciencias Sociales* 19/3 (53): 171–186.

Fujii, Lee Ann. (2010). "Shades of Truth and Lies: Interpreting Testimonies of War and Violence." *Journal of Peace Research* 47(2): 231–241.

(2017). *Interviewing in Social Science Research: A Relational Approach.* New York and Abingdon: Routledge.

Fung, Archon. (2006). "Varieties of Participation in Complex Governance." *Public Administration Review* 66: 66–75.

Gallagher, Janice. (2017). "The Last Mile Problem: Activists, Advocates, and the Struggle for Justice in Domestic Courts." *Comparative Political Studies* 50(12): 1666–1698.

Gallardo, M., F. Luna-Villanueva, R. Martínez-Barrera, R. Paz-Vega, A. García-Romero, and J. Escalante-Díaz. (1987). "El Origen de la Producción de Aguacate en el Estado de Michoacán." *Fruticultura de Michoacán* 1(12): 3–24.

Gambetta, Diego. (1996). *The Sicilian Mafia: The Business of Private Protection.* Cambridge: Harvard University Press.

Gammage, Sarah. (2006). "Exporting People and Recruiting Remittances: A Development Strategy for El Salvador?" *Latin American Perspectives* 33(6): 75–100.

Gans-Morse, Jordan. (2012). "Threats to Property Rights in Russia: From Private Coercion to State Aggression." *Post-Soviet Affairs* 28(3): 263–295.

García-Jiménez, Humberto and Bruno Gandlgruber. (2014). *Gobernanza y Acuerdos Institucionales en las Cadenas del Frijol y del Maíz en Centroamérica.* Mexico City: CEPAL/FAO.

García Pinzón, Viviana and Erika J. Rojas Ospina. (2020). "La Política de Seguridad en El Salvador: La Construcción del Enemigo y sus Efectos en la Violencia y el Orden Social." *Revista de Estudios Sociales* 73: 96–108.

García-Ponce, Omar, Lauren Young, and Thomas Zeitoff. (2019). "Anger and Support for Retribution in Mexico's Drug War." Unpublished manuscript. https://

omargarciaponce.com/wp-content/uploads/2019/09/GarciaPonce_Young_Zeitzoff .pdf.

García, Juan, Daniel Mejía, and Daniel Ortega. (2013). *Police Reform, Training and Crime: Experimental Evidence from Colombia's Plan Cuadrantes.* Bogotá: Documento CEDE.

Garland, David. (2001). *The Culture of Control: Crime and Social Order in Contemporary Society.* Chicago: University of Chicago Press.

Gauri, Varun and Daniel M. Brinks. (2008). *Courting Social Justice.* Washington, DC: World Bank.

Gaventa, John. (1980). *Power and Powerlessness: Quiescence and Rebellion in an Appalachian Valley.* Urbana and Chicago: University of Illinois Press.

Gaviria, Alejandro and Carmen Pagés. (2002). "Patterns of Crime Victimization in Latin American Cities." *Journal of Development Economics* 67(1): 181–203.

Gaviria, Alejandro. (2002). "Assessing the Effects of Corruption and Crime on Firm Performance: Evidence from Latin America." *Emerging Markets Review* 3(3): 245–268.

Gereffi, Gary, John Humphrey, and Timothy Sturgeon. (2005). "The Governance of Global Value Chains." *Review of International Political Economy* 12(1): 78–104.

Gerring, John. (2007). "The Case Study: What It Is and What It Does." In *The Oxford Handbook of Comparative Politics*, edited by Carles Boix and Susan C. Stokes, 90–122. Oxford: Oxford University Press.

Giraudy, Agustina, Eduardo Moncada, and Richard Snyder, eds. (2019). *Inside Countries: Subnational Research in Comparative Politics.* Cambridge: Cambridge University Press.

Glass, Fausto Carbajal. (2020). "Where the Metal Meets the Flesh: Organized Crime, Violence, and the Illicit Iron Ore Economy in Mexico's Michoacán State." In *Illegal Mining*, edited by Yuliya Zabyelina and Daan van Uhm, 147–183. Cham, Switzerland: Palgrave Macmillan.

Godoy, Angelina Snodgrass. (2004). "When 'Justice' Is Criminal: Lynchings in Contemporary Latin America." *Theory and Society* 33(6): 621–651.

Goldstein, Daniel M. (2003). "'In Our Own Hands': Lynching, Justice, and the Law in Bolivia." *American Ethnologist* 30(1): 22–43.

Goldstone, Jack Andrew and Charles Tilly. (2001). "Threat (and Opportunity): Popular Action and State Response in the Dynamics of Contentious Action." In *Silence and Voice in the Study of Contentious Politics*, edited by Ronald R. Aminzade, Jack A. Goldstone, Doug McAdam, Elizabeth J. Perry, William H. Sewell, Sidney Tarrow, and Charles Tilly, 179–194. Cambridge: Cambridge University Press.

González-Ramírez, María Guadalupe, Vinicio Horacio Santoyo-Cortés, José Jaime Arana-Coronado, and Manrrubio Muñoz-Rodríguez. (2020). "The Insertion of Mexico into the Global Value Chain of Berries." *World Development Perspectives.* https://doi.org/10.1016/j.wdp.2020.100240

González, Álvaro Artiga. (2004). "El Salvador: Maremoto Electoral en 2004." *Nueva Sociedad* 192: 12–22.

González, Yanilda María. (2020). *Authoritarian Police in Democracy: Contested Security in Latin America.* Cambridge: Cambridge University Press.

Grabosky, Peter N. (1992). "Law Enforcement and the Citizen: Non-governmental Participants in Crime Prevention and Control." *Policing and Society: An International Journal* 2(4): 249–271.

Grant, Wynford P. (1987). *Business and Politics in Britain*. Houndmills, Basingstoke, Hampshire and London: The MacMillan Press, LTD.

Grajales, Jacobo. (2017). "Private Security and Paramilitarism in Colombia: Governing in the Midst of Violence." *Journal of Politics in Latin America* 9(3): 27–48.

Grayson, George W. (2011). *La Familia Drug Cartel: Implications for US-Mexican Security*. Carlisle, PA: Strategic Studies Institute, United States Army War College.

Grillo, Ioan. (2011). *El Narco: Inside Mexico's Criminal Insurgency*. New York: Bloomsbury Press.

Groff, Elizabeth R., Brook Kearley, Heather Fogg, Penny Beatty, Heather Couture, and Julie Wartell. (2005). "A Randomized Experimental Study of Sharing Crime Data with Citizens: Do Maps Produce More Fear?" *Journal of Experimental Criminology* 1(1): 87–115.

Guggenheim, Scott E. (1994). *Involuntary Resettlement: An Annotated Reference Bibliography for Development Research*. No. ENV64. Washington, DC: World Bank.

Hayden, Tom. (2004). *Street Wars: Gangs and the Future of Violence*. New Press.

Heller, Patrick. (2012). "Democracy, Participatory Politics and Development: Some Comparative Lessons from Brazil, India and South Africa." *Polity* 44(4): 643–665.

Helmke, Gretchen and Steven Levitsky, eds. (2006). *Informal Institutions and Democracy: Lessons from Latin America*. Baltimore, MD: John Hopkins University Press.

Herrigel, Gary. (2000). *Industrial Constructions: The Sources of German Industrial Power*. Cambridge: Cambridge University Press.

Hidalgo, Daniel and Benjamin Lessing. (2015). "Endogenous State Weakness in Violent Democracies: Paramilitaries at the Polls." Unpublished manuscript. Available at: www.semanticscholar.org/paper/Endogenous-State-Weakness-in-Violent-Democrac ies-%3A-Hidalgo-Lessing/f2613b0459c1a514728e6ae7ffd924d30b613c41. Access ed on April 29, 2021.

Hirschman, Albert O. (1970). *Exit, Voice, and Loyalty: Responses to Decline in Firms, Organizations, and States*. Cambridge: Harvard University Press.

Holiday, David and William Stanley. (1993). "Building the Peace: Preliminary Lessons from El Salvador." *Journal of International Affairs* 46(2): 415–438.

Holland, Alisha C. (2013). "Right of Crime? Conservative Party Politics and 'Mano Dura' Policies in El Salvador." *Latin American Research Review* 48(1): 44–67.

Holland, Alisha C. (2017). *Forbearance as Redistribution: The Politics of Informal Welfare in Latin America*. Cambridge: Cambridge University Press.

Hume, Mo. (2007). "Mano Dura: El Salvador Responds to Gangs." *Development in Practice* 17(6): 739–751.

Humphreys, Macartan and Jeremy M. Weinstein. (2006). "Handling and Manhandling Civilians in Civil War." *American Political Science Review* 100(3): 429–447.

(2008). "Who Fights? The Determinants of Participation in Civil War." *American Journal of Political Science* 52(2): 436–455.

Hurst, William. (2009). *The Chinese Worker after Socialism*. Cambridge: Cambridge University Press.

Idler, Annette. (2019). *Borderland Battles: Violence, Crime, and Governance at the Edges of Colombia's War*. Oxford: Oxford University Press.

InSight Crime and Center for Latin American and Latino Studies (CLALS). (2018). *MS-13 in the Americas*. Washington, DC: American University.

Instituto de Derechos Humanos de la UCA (Iduhca). (2019). *Condiciones Laborales de la Policía Nacional Civil, Enero-Mayo 2019.* San Salvador: Iduhca.

International Crisis Group. (2018). "Life Under Gang Rule in El Salvador." November 26, 2018. Available at www.crisisgroup.org/latin-america-caribbean/central-america/el-salvador/life-under-gang-rule-el-salvador. Accessed on May 10, 2021.

Jentzsch, Corinna, Stathis N. Kalyvas, and Livia Isabella Schubiger. (2015). "Militias in Civil Wars." *Journal of Conflict Resolution* 59(5): 755–769.

Johnston, Les. (1996). "What Is Vigilantism?" *The British Journal of Criminology* 36 (2): 220–236.

Jung, Danielle F. and Dara Kay Cohen. (2020). *Lynching and Local Justice.* Cambridge: Cambridge University Press.

Kalyvas, Stathis N. (2006). *The Logic of Violence in Civil War.* Cambridge: Cambridge University Press.

(2008a). "Armed Collaboration in Greece, 1941–1944." *European Review of History —Revue européenne d'histoire* 15(2): 129–142.

(2008b). "Promises and Pitfalls of an Emerging Research Program: The Microdynamics of Civil War." In *Order, Conflict, Violence,* edited by Stathis N. Kalyvas, Ian Shapiro, and Tarek Masoud, 1–14. Cambridge: Cambridge University Press.

(2015a). "Is ISIS a Revolutionary Group and if Yes, What Are the Implications?" *Perspectives on Terrorism* 9(4): 42–47.

(2015b). "How Civil Wars Help Explain Organized Crime—and How They Do Not." *Journal of Conflict Resolution* 59(8): 1517–1540.

Kapiszewski, Diana, Lauren M. MacLean, and Benjamin L. Read. (2015). *Field Research in Political Science: Practices and Principles.* Cambridge: Cambridge University Press.

(2018). "Reconceptualizing Field Research in Political Science." In *Oxford Research Encyclopedia of Politics.* https://doi.org/10.1093/acrefore/9780190228637.013.722

Kaplan, Oliver. (2017a). "The Art of Rhetorical Traps in Civilian Self-Protection." *Journal of Peacebuilding & Development* 12(3): 111–116.

(2017b). *Resisting War: How Communities Protect Themselves.* Cambridge: Cambridge University Press.

Katz, Charles M., Eric C. Hedberg, and Luis Enrique Amaya. (2016). "Gang Truce for Violence Prevention, El Salvador." *Bulletin of the World Health Organization* 94 (9): 660.

Kearney, Kerri S. and Adrienne E. Hyle. (2004). "Drawing out Emotions: The Use of Participant-produced Drawings in Qualitative Inquiry." *Qualitative Research* 4(3): 361–382.

Kelley, Robin DG. (1993). "'We Are Not What We Seem': Rethinking Black Working-class Opposition in the Jim Crow South." *The Journal of American History* 48(1): 75–112.

Kenny, Paul D., Rashesh Shrestha, and Edward Aspinall. (2020). "Commodity Booms, Conflict and Organized Crime: Logic of Violence in Indonesia's Oil Palm Plantation Economy." Working Papers in Trade and Development, Australian National University. Available at: https://ideas.repec.org/p/pas/papers/2020-23.html. Accessed on April 29, 2021.

Kingstone, Peter R. (1999). *Crafting Coalitions for Reform: Business Preferences, Political Institutions, and Neoliberal Reform in Brazil.* University Park, PA: Penn State University Press.

Konrad, Kai I. and Stergios Skaperdas. (1998). "Extortion." *Economica* 65(260): 461–477.

Koonings, Kees and Dirk Kruijt, eds. (2015). *Violence and Resilience in Latin American Cities*. London: Zed Books Ltd.

Kramer, Roderick M., Marilynn B. Brewer, and Benjamin A. Hanna. (1996). "Collective Trust and Collective Action." In *Trust in Organizations: Frontiers of Theory and Research*, edited by Roderick M. Krame and Marilynn B. Brewer, 357–389. Thousand Oaks, CA: Safe Publications.

Krause, Jana. (2018). *Resilient Communities: Non-violence and Civilian Agency in Communal War*. Cambridge: Cambridge University Press.

Laitin, David D. (1995). "National Revivals and Violence." *Archives Européennes de Sociologie/European Journal of Sociology/Europäisches Archiv für Soziologie*: 36 (1): 3–43.

Larkins, Erika Robb. (2015). *The Spectacular Favela: Violence in Modern Brazil*. Berkeley, CA: University of California Press.

(2017). "Guarding the Body: Private Security Work in Rio de Janeiro." *Conflict and Society* 3(1): 61–72.

Lawrence, Adria. (2013). *Imperial Rule and the Politics of Nationalism: Anti-Colonial Protest in the French Empire*. Cambridge: Cambridge University Press.

Lavezzi, Andrea Mario. (2008). "Economic Structure and Vulnerability to Organised Crime: Evidence from Sicily." *Global Crime* 9(3): 198–220.

Lee, Rebekah and Jeremy Seekings. (2002). "Vigilantism and Popular Justice after Apartheid." In *Informal Criminal Justice*, edited by Dermot Feenen, 99–116. Farnham, Burlington: Ashgate.

Leeds, Elizabeth. (1996). "Cocaine and Parallel Polities in the Brazilian Urban Periphery: Constraints on Local-level Democratization." *Latin American Research Review* 31 (3): 47–83.

Lessing, Benjamin and Graham Denyer Willis. (2019). "Legitimacy in Criminal Governance: Managing a Drug Empire from Behind Bars." *American Political Science Review* 113(2): 584–606.

Lerman, Amy E. and Vesla M. Weaver. (2014). *Arresting Citizenship: The Democratic Consequences of American Crime Control*. Chicago: University of Chicago Press.

Lessing, Benjamin. (2017). *Making Peace in Drug Wars: Crackdowns and Cartels in Latin America*. Cambridge: Cambridge University Press.

Levi, Margaret. (1988). *Of Rule and Revenue*. Berkeley University of California Press.

Ley, Sandra. (2018). "To Vote or Not to Vote: How Criminal Violence Shapes Electoral Participation." *Journal of Conflict Resolution* 62(9): 1963–1990.

Lindbloom, Charles E. (1977). *Politics and Markets: The World's Political-Economic System*. New York: Basic Books.

Linz, Juan J. (1988). "Legitimacy of Democracy and the Socioeconomic System." In *Comparing Pluralist Democracies: Strains on Legitimacy*, edited by Mattei Dogan, 65–113. Boulder, CO: Westview Press.

Lipsky, Michael. (1980). *Street-level Bureaucracy: Dilemmas of the Individual in Public Service*. New York: Russell Sage Foundation.

Locke, Richard M. (1995). *Remaking the Italian Economy*. Ithaca, NY: Cornell University Press.

Lonsway, Kimberly A. and Louise F. Fitzgerald. (1994). "Rape Myths. In Review." *Psychology of Women Quarterly* 18(2): 133–164.

Loveman, Mara. (1998). "High-risk Collective Action: Defending Human Rights in Chile, Uruguay, and Argentina." *American Journal of Sociology* 104(2): 477–525.

Lukes, Steven. (2004). *Power: A Radical View*. London: Macmillan International Higher Education.

Lupu, Noam and Leonid Peisakhin. (2017). "The Legacy of Political Violence Across Generations." *American Journal of Political Science* 61(4): 836–851.

MacLean, Lauren M., Elliot Posner, Susan Thomson, and Elisabeth Jean Wood. (2019). "Research Ethics and Human Subjects: A Reflexive Openness Approach." *American Political Science Association Organized Section for Qualitative and Multi-Method Research, Qualitative Transparency Deliberations, Working Group Final Reports, Report I 2*. Available at: https://papers.ssrn.com/sol3/papers .cfm?abstract_id=3332887. Accessed on May 10, 2021.

Magaloni, Beatriz, Edgar Franco-Vivanco, and Vanessa Melo. (2020). "Killing in the Slums: Social Order, Criminal Governance, and Police Violence in Rio de Janeiro." *American Political Science Review* 114(2): 552–572.

Magaloni, Beatriz, Gustavo Robles, Aila M. Matanock, Alberto Diaz-Cayeros, and Vidal Romero. (2020). "Living in Fear: The Dynamics of Extortion in Mexico's Drug War." *Comparative Political Studies* 53(7): 1124–1174.

Maldonado, Salvador. (2010). *Los Márgenes del Estado Mexicano: Territorios Ilegales, Desarrollo y Violencia en Michoacán*. Zamora: El Colegio de Michoacán.

(2012). "Drogas, Violencia y Militarización en el México Rural: El Caso de Michoacán." *Revista Mexicana de Sociología* 74(1): 5–39.

(2013). "Stories of Drug Trafficking in Rural Mexico: Territories, Drugs and Cartels in Michoacán." *European Review of Latin American and Caribbean Studies/ Revista Europea de Estudios Latinoamericanos Y Del Caribe* 94: 43–66.

Malkin, Victoria. (2001). "Narcotráfico, Migración y Modernidad." In *La Tierra Caliente de Michoacán*, edited by Eduardo Zárate Hernández, 549–585. Zamora,: El Colegio de Michoacán/Gobierno del Estado.

Mampilly, Zachariah Cherian. (2012). *Rebel Rulers: Insurgent Governance and Civilian Life During War*. Ithaca, NY: Cornell University Press.

Mampilly, Zachariah. (2015). "Performing the Nation-state: Rebel Governance and Symbolic Processes." In *Rebel Governance in Civil War*, edited by Ana Arjona, Nelson Kasfir, and Zachariah Mampilly, 74–97. Cambridge: Cambridge University Press.

Manwaring, Max G. (2006). "Gangs and Coups D'Streets in the New World Disorder: Protean Insurgents in Post-modern War." *Global Crime* 7(3–4): 505–543.

Marston Jr, Jerome F. (2020). "Resisting Displacement: Leveraging Interpersonal Ties to Remain despite Criminal Violence in Medellín, Colombia." *Comparative Political Studies*. https://doi.org/10.1177%2F0010414020912276

Martín-Baró, Ignacio. (1989). "Political Violence and War as Causes of Psychosocial Trauma in El Salvador." *International Journal of Mental Health* 18(1): 3–20.

Marx, Gary T. and Dane Archer. (1971). "Citizen Involvement in the Law Enforcement Process: The Case of Community Police Patrols." *American Behavioral Scientist* 15 (1): 52–72.

Masullo, Juan. (2020). "Civilian Contention in Civil War: How Ideational Factors Shape Community Responses to Armed Groups." *Comparative Political Studies.* https://doi.org/10.1177%2F0010414020912285

Matanock, Aila M. and Paul Staniland. (2018). "How and Why Armed Groups Participate in Elections." *Perspectives on Politics* 16(3): 710–727.

Mattiace, Shannan, Sandra Ley, and Guillermo Trejo. (2019). "Indigenous Resistance to Criminal Governance: Why Regional Ethnic Autonomy Institutions Protect Communities from Narco Rule in Mexico." *Latin American Research Review* 54 (1): 181.

Maxfield, Sylvia and Ben Ross Schneider, eds. (1997). *Business and the State in Developing Countries.* Ithaca, NY: Cornell University Press.

McAdam, Doug. (1982). *Political Process and the Development of Black Insurgency, 1930-1970.* Chicago: University of Chicago Press.

(1986). "Recruitment to High-risk Activism: The Case of Freedom Summer." *American Journal of Sociology* 92(1): 64–90.

McNamara, Patrick J. (2017). "Political Refugees from El Salvador: Gang Politics, the State, and Asylum Claims." *Refugee Survey Quarterly* 36(4): 1–24.

McWeeney, Sean M. (1987). "The Sicilian Mafia and its Impact on the United States." *FBI L. Enforcement Bull.* 56: 1–10.

Meagher, Kate. (2007). "Hijacking Civil Society: The Inside Story of the Bakassi Boys Vigilante Group of South-Eastern Nigeria." *Journal of Modern African Studies* 45 (1): 89–115.

Medina Franco, Gilberto. (2006). *Una Historia de las Milicias de Medellín.* Medellín: Instituto Popular de Capacitación.

Medina, Leandro and Friedrich Schneider. (2018). "Shadow Economies Around the World: What Did We Learn over the Last 20 Years?" IMF Working Paper No 18/17. Washington, DC: International Monetary Fund.

Meerow, Sara, Joshua P. Newell, and Melissa Stults. (2016). "Defining Urban Resilience: A Review." *Landscape and Urban Planning* 147: 38–49.

Metelits, Claire. (2009). *Inside Insurgency: Violence, Civilians, and Revolutionary Group Behavior.* New York: New York University Press.

Meyer, David S. and Debra C. Minkoff. (2004). "Conceptualizing Political Opportunity." *Social Forces* 82(4): 1457–1492.

Michel, Verónica and Kathryn Sikkink. (2013). "Human Rights Prosecutions and the Participation Rights of Victims in Latin America." *Law & Society Review* 47(4): 873–907.

Migdal, Joel S. (1988). *Strong Societies and Weak States: State-Society Relations and State Capabilities in the Third World.* Princeton: Princeton University Press.

Migdal, Joel S., Atul Kohli, and Vivienne Shue. (1994). *State Power and Social Forces: Domination and Transformation in the Third World.* Cambridge: Cambridge University Press.

Ministerio de Economía (2009). *IV Censo Agropecuario 2007–2008: Resultados Nacionales.* San Salvador: Ministerio de Economía.

Ministerio de Trabajo y Previsión Social. (2018). *Tarifas de Salarios Mínimos Vigentes a Partir del 1 de Enero de 2018.* San Salvador: Ministerio de Trabajo y Previsión Social.

Minnaar, Anthony. (2001). "The New Vigilantism in Post-April 1994 South Africa: Crime Prevention or an Expression of Lawlessness." *Institute for Human Rights and Criminal Justice Studies,* May (2001).

Misse, Michel. (2007). "Mercados Ilegais, Redes de Proteção e Organização Local do Crime no Rio de Janeiro." *Estudos Avançados* 21(61): 139–157.

Moe, Terry M. (1984). "The New Economics of Organization." *American Journal of Political Science* 28(4): 739–777.

Moncada, Eduardo. (2009). "Toward Democratic Policing in Colombia? Institutional Accountability through Lateral Reform." *Comparative Politics* 41(4): 431–449.

(2013). "The Politics of Urban Violence: Challenges for Development in the Global South." *Studies in Comparative International Development* 48(3): 217–239.

(2016). *Cities, Business, and the Politics of Urban Violence in Latin America.* Palo Alto, CA: Stanford University Press.

(2017). "Varieties of Vigilantism: Conceptual Discord, Meaning and Strategies." *Global Crime* 18(4): 403–423.

(2019). "Resisting Protection: Rackets, Resistance, and State Building." *Comparative Politics* 51(3): 321–339.

(2020). "The Politics of Criminal Victimization: Pursuing and Resisting Power." *Perspectives on Politics* 18(3): 706–721.

Morales, Maria Cristina, Pamela Prieto, and Cynthia Bejarano. (2014). "Transnational Entrepreneurs and Drug War Violence between Ciudad Juárez and El Paso." *Journal of Urban Research* 10. https://doi.org/10.4000/articulo.2597.

Morris, Stephen D. (2012). "Corruption, Drug Trafficking, and Violence in Mexico." *The Brown Journal of World Affairs* 18(2): 29–43.

Moser, Caroline ON and Cathy McIlwaine. (2004). *Encounters with Violence in Latin America: Urban Poor Perceptions from Columbia and Guatemala.* New York and London: Psychology Press.

Moskos, Peter. (2008). *Cop in the Hood: My Year Policing Baltimore's Eastern District.* Princeton: Princeton University Press.

Mugellini, Giulia. (2013). *Measuring and Analyzing Crime Against the Private Sector: International Experiences and the Mexican Practice.* Aguascalientes, Mexico: Instituto Nacional de Estadística y Geografía.

Murillo, Maria Victoria. (2001). *Labor Unions, Partisan Coalitions, and Market Reforms in Latin America.* Cambridge: Cambridge University Press.

Nilan, Pamela. (2002). "Dangerous Fieldwork Re-examined: the Question of Researcher Subject Position." *Qualitative Research* 2(3): 363–386.

Nussio, Enzo and Govinda Clayton. (2020). *Strong Communities, Weak States. Lynching in Latin America.* Research Project. ETH Zurich.

O'Brien, Kevin J. (1996). "Rightful Resistance." *World Politics* 49(1): 31–55.

O'Donnell, Guillermo. (1993). "On the State, Democratization and Some Conceptual Problems: A Latin American View with Glances at Some Postcommunist Countries." *World Development* 21(8): 1355–1369.

Obert, Jonathan and Eleonora Mattiacci. (2018). "Keeping Vigil: The Emergence of Vigilance Committees in Pre-Civil War America." *Perspectives on Politics* 16(3): 600–616.

Ochberg, Frank. (1978). "The Victim of Terrorism: Psychiatric Considerations." *Studies in Conflict & Terrorism* 1(2): 147–168.

Olson, Mancur. (1993). "Dictatorship, Democracy, and Development." *American Political Science Review* 87(3): 567–576.

Osorio, Javier. (2015). "The Contagion of Drug Violence: Spatiotemporal Dynamics of the Mexican War on Drugs." *Journal of Conflict Resolution* 59(8): 1403–1432.

Osorio, Javier, Livia Isabella Schubiger, and Michael Weintraub. (2021). "Legacies of Resistance: Mobilization against Organized Crime in Mexico." *Comparative Political Studies.* https://doi.org/10.1177%2F0010414021989761

Osterhoudt, Sarah R. (2020). "'Nobody Wants to Kill': Economies of Affect and Violence in Madagascar's Vanilla Boom." *American Ethnologist* 47(3): 249–263.

Ostrom, Elinor. (1990). *Governing the Commons: The Evolution of Institutions for Collective Action.* Cambridge: Cambridge University Press.

   (1992). "Community and the Endogenous Solution of Commons Problems." *Journal of Theoretical Politics* 4(3): 343–351.

   (1996). "Crossing the Great Divide: Coproduction, Synergy, and Development." *World Development* 24(6): 1073–1087.

Parkinson, Sarah E. (2016). "Money Talks: Discourse, Networks, and Structure in Militant Organizations." *Perspectives on Politics* 14(4): 976.

Pasotti, Eleonora. (2020). *Resisting Redevelopment: Protest in Aspiring Global Cities.* Cambridge: Cambridge University Press.

Paz-Vega, Ramón. (1986). "El Aguacate en Estados Unidos: Un Mercado Cercano Pero Inaccesible." *Fruticultura de Michoacán* 1(3): 24–26.

Peceny, Mark and Michael Durnan. (2006). "The FARC's Best Friend: US Antidrug Policies and the Deepening of Colombia's Civil War in the 1990s." *Latin American Politics and Society* 48(2): 95–116.

Penglase, R. Ben. (2014). *Living with Insecurity in a Brazilian Favela: Urban Violence and Daily Life.* New Brunswick, NJ: Rutgers University Press.

Peritore, N. Patrick. (1990). "Reflections on Dangerous Fieldwork." *The American Sociologist* 21(4): 359–372.

Perramond, Eric P. (2008). "The Rise, Fall, and Reconfiguration of the Mexican Ejido." *Geographical Review* 98(3): 356–371.

Petersen, Roger D. (2001). *Resistance and Rebellion: Lessons from Eastern Europe.* Cambridge: Cambridge University Press.

Pfeifer, Michael James. (2004). *Rough Justice: Lynching and American Society, 1874–1947.* Urbana and Chicago: University of Illinois Press.

Phillips, Brian J. (2015). "How Does Leadership Decapitation Affect Violence? The Case of Drug Trafficking Organizations in Mexico." *The Journal of Politics* 77(2): 324–336.

   (2017). "Inequality and the Emergence of Vigilante Organizations: The Case of Mexican Autodefensas." *Comparative Political Studies* 50(10): 1358–1389.

Phillips, Everard M. (2011). "Pain, Suffering, and Humiliation: The Systemization of Violence in Kidnapping for Ransom." *Journal of Aggression, Maltreatment & Trauma* 20(8): 845–869.

Policía Nacional Civil (PNC). (2015). *Plan Estratégico Institucional, 2015–2019.* San Salvador: PNC.

Popkin, Margaret. (2010). *Peace Without Justice: Obstacles to Building the Rule of Law in El Salvador.* University Park, PA: Penn State University Press.

Portes, Alejandro and Patricia Landolt. (2000). "Social Capital: Promise and Pitfalls of its Role in Development." *Journal of Latin American Studies* 32(2): 529–547.

Portes, Alejandro and Kelly Hoffman. (2003). "Latin American Class Structures: Their Composition and Change During the Neoliberal Era." *Latin American Research Review* 38(1): 41–82.

Prado, Mariana Mota, Michael Trebilcock, and Patrick Hartford. (2012). "Police Reform in Violent Democracies in Latin America." *Hague Journal on the Rule of Law* 4(2): 252–285.

Putnam, Robert D., Robert Leonardi, and Raffaella Y. Nanetti. (1994). *Making Democracy Work: Civic Traditions in Modern Italy.* Princeton: Princeton University Press.

Ragin, Charles C. and Garrett Andrew Schneider. (2011). "Case-Oriented Theory Building and Theory Testing." In *The Sage Handbook of Innovation in Social Research Methods*, edited by Malcolm Williams and W. Paul Vogt, 150–166. Thousand Oaks: Sage.

Ramírez, Max Yuri Gil. (2013). "Medellín 1993–2013: Una Ciudad que no Logra Encontrar el Camino para Salir Definitivamente del Laberinto." Available at: www.wilsoncenter.org/sites/default/files/media/documents/publication/GilRamirez-Colombia-2013.pdf. Accessed on April 29, 2021.

Reno, William. (2006). "Insurgencies in the Shadow of State Collapse." In *Violence, Political Culture and Development in Africa*, edited by Preben Kaarshold, 85–96. Oxford: James Currey Publishers.

Rettberg, Angelika. (2008). *Explorando el Dividendo de la Paz: Impactos del Conflicto Armado en el Sector Privado Colombiano: Resultados de una Encuesta Nacional.* Bogotá: Ediciones Uniandes-Universidad de los Andes.

Reuter, Peter. (1983). *Disorganized Crime: The Economics of the Visible Hand.* Cambridge: MIT Press.

Revista Antioqueña de Economía y Desarrollo (RAED). (2019). "Una Aproximación a la Caracterización de las Empresas Informales en Medellín." 22. Medellín: RAED.

Ríos, Viridiana. (2013). "Why did Mexico Become so Violent? A Self-reinforcing Violent Equilibrium Caused by Competition and Enforcement." *Trends in Organized Crime* 16(2): 138–155.

(2014). "The Role of Drug-Related Violence and Extortion in Promoting Mexican Migration: Unexpected Consequences of a Drug War." *Latin American Research Review* 49: 199–217.

Rithmire, Meg E. (2015). *Land Bargains and Chinese Capitalism: The Politics of Property Rights under Reform.* Cambridge: Cambridge University Press.

Roberts, Kenneth M. (2002). "Social Inequalities Without Class Cleavages in Latin America's Neoliberal Era." *Studies in Comparative International Development* 36 (4): 3–33.

Rock, David. (1972). "Machine Politics in Buenos Aires and the Argentine Radical Party, 1912-1930." *Journal of Latin American Studies* 4(2): 233–256.

Rodríguez Guillén, Raúl. (2011). "Linchamientos en Zonas Urbanas: Estado de México y Distrito Federal." *El Cotidiano* 26: 27–38.

Romero, Mauricio. (2000). "Changing Identities and Contested Settings: Regional Elites and the Paramilitaries in Colombia." *International Journal of Politics, Culture, and Society* 14(1): 51–69.

Rosaldo, Manuel. (2016). "Revolution in the Garbage Dump: The Political and Economic Foundations of the Colombian Recycler Movement, 1986–2011." *Social Problems* 63(3): 351–372.

Rozema, Ralph. (2007). "Paramilitares y Violencia Urbana en Medellín, Colombia." *Foro Internacional* 47(3): 535–550.

Sabet, Daniel. (2012). *Police Reform in Mexico: Informal Politics and the Challenge of Institutional Change.* Palo Alto, CA: Stanford University Press.

Samara, Tony Roshan. (2011). *Cape Town after Apartheid: Crime and Governance in the Divided City.* Minneapolis and London: University of Minnesota Press.

Sánchez de la Sierra, Raúl. (2020). "On the Origins of the State: Stationary Bandits and Taxation in Eastern Congo." *Journal of Political Economy* 128(1): 32–74.

Sanguinetti, Pablo, Daniel Ortega, Lucila Berniell, Fernando Álvarez, Daniel Mejía, Juan Camilo Castillo, and Pablo Brassiolo. (2015). *Towards a Safer Latin America. A New Perspective to Prevent and Control Crime.* Bogota: Andean Development Corporation.

Santacruz, María, Alberto Concha-Eastman, and José Miguel Cruz. (2001). *Barrio Adentro: La Solidaridad Violenta de las Pandillas.* San Salvador: IUDOP-UCA.

Savenije, Wim and Chris Van der Borgh. (2006). "Youth Gangs, Social Exclusion and the Transformation of Violence in El Salvador." In *Armed Actors: Organised Violence and State Failure in Latin America*, edited by Kees Koonings and Dirk Kruijt, 155–171. London: Zed Books.

Savenije, Wim. (2014). "Políticas de Seguridad en El Salvador." *Cuestiones de Sociología.* 10: 1–13.

Schattschneider, Elmer Eric. (1960). *Party Government.* Piscataway, NJ: Transaction Publishers.

Schatz, Edward, ed. (2013). *Political Ethnography: What Immersion Contributes to the Study of Power.* Chicago: University of Chicago Press.

Scheingold, Stuart A. (1974). "The Politics of Rights: Lawyers." *Public Policy, and Political Change.* New Haven: Yale University Press.

Schelling, Thomas C. (1971). "What Is the Business of Organized Crime?" *The American Scholar* 40(4): 643–652.

Schmitter, Philippe C. and Wolfgang Streeck. (1981). "The Organization of Business Interests: A Research Design to Study the Associative Action of Business in the Advanced Industrial Societies of Western Europe." Discussion Paper, IIM/LMP 81-13, Berlin: Wissenschaftszentrum.

Schneider, Ben Ross. (1998). "Elusive Synergy: Business-Government Relations and Development." *Comparative Politics* 31(1): 101–122.

(2002). "Why Is Mexican Business So Organized?" *Latin American Research Review* 37(10): 77–118.

(2004). *Business Politics and the State in Twentieth-Century Latin America.* Cambridge: Cambridge University Press.

(2008). "Economic Liberalization and Corporate Governance: the Resilience of Business Groups in Latin America." *Comparative Politics* 40(4): 379–397.

Scott, James C. (1977). *The Moral Economy of the Peasant: Rebellion and Subsistence in Southeast Asia.* New Haven: Yale University Press.

(1985). *Weapons of the Weak: Everyday Forms of Peasant Resistance.* New Haven: Yale University Press.

(1989). "Everyday Forms of Resistance." *The Copenhagen Journal of Asian Studies* 4: 33–33.

(1990). *Domination and the Arts of Resistance: Hidden Transcripts.* New Haven: Yale University Press.

Secretaría de Economía. (2012). *Monografía del Sector Aguacate en México: Situación Actual y Oportunidades de Mercado*. Ciudad México: Dirección General de Industrias Básicas.

Serrano, Alfredo. (2013). *La Multinacional del Crimen*. Bogotá: Debate.

Shaw, Mark. (2016). "A Tale of Two Cities: Mafia Control, the Night Time Entertainment Economy and Drug Retail Markets in Johannesburg and Cape Town, 1985–2015." *Police Practice and Research* 17(4): 353–363.

Shelley, Louise. (2001). "Corruption and Organized Crime in Mexico in the Post-PRI Transition." *Journal of Contemporary Criminal Justice* 17(3): 213–231.

(2010). *Human Trafficking: A Global Perspective*. Cambridge: Cambridge University Press.

Shirk, David A. (2010). "Drug Violence in Mexico: Data and Analysis from 2001-2009." *Trends in Organized Crime* 13(2–3): 167–174.

Simmons, Erica S. and Nicholas Rush Smith. (2019). "The Case for Comparative Ethnography." *Comparative Politics* 51(3): 341–359.

Sinha, Aseema. (2005). *The Regional Roots of Developmental Politics in India: A Divided Leviathan*. Bloomington and Indianapolis: Indiana University Press.

Skaperdas, Stergios. (2001). "The Political Economy of Organized Crime: Providing Protection When the State Does Not." *Economics of Governance* 2(3): 173–202.

Skarbek, David. (2011). "Governance and Prison Gangs." *American Political Science Review* 105(4): 702–716.

(2014). *The Social Order of the Underworld: How Prison Gangs Govern the American Penal System*. Oxford: Oxford University Press.

Skogan, Wesley G. (2004). *Community Policing: Can It Work?* Belmont, CA: Wadsworth/Thomson Learning.

Smith, Nicholas Rush. (2019). *Contradictions of Democracy: Vigilantism and Rights in Post-Apartheid South Africa*. Oxford: Oxford University Press.

Smutt, Marcela and Jenny Lissette E. Miranda. (1998). *El Fenómeno de las Pandillas en El Salvador*. San Salvador: UNICEF.

Snyder, Richard and Angelica Durán-Martínez. (2009). "Does Illegality Breed Violence? Drug Trafficking and State-sponsored Protection Rackets." *Crime, Law and Social Change* 52(3): 253–273.

Soifer, Hillel and Matthias Vom Hau. (2008). "Unpacking the Strength of the State: The Utility of State Infrastructural Power." *Studies in Comparative International Development* 43(3–4): 219.

Soss, Joe. (2002). *Unwanted Claims: The Politics of Participation in the US Welfare System*. Ann Arbor, MI: University of Michigan Press.

Stanford, Lois. (1998). "Mexico's Empresario in Export Agriculture: Examining the Avocado Industry of Michoacán." 1998 Meeting of the Latin American Studies Association (LASA), The Palmer House Hilton Hotel, Chicago, Illinois.

(2002). "Constructing 'Quality': The Political Economy of Standards in Mexico's Avocado Industry." *Agriculture and Human Values* 19(4): 293–310.

Staniland, Paul. (2012). "States, Insurgents, and Wartime Political Orders." *Perspectives on Politics* 10(2): 243–264.

(2014). *Networks of Rebellion: Explaining Insurgent Cohesion and Collapse*. Ithaca, NY: Cornell University Press.

(2017). "Armed Politics and the Study of Intrastate Conflict." *Journal of Peace Research* 54(4): 459–467.

Stanley, William. (1996). *The Protection Racket State: Elite Politics, Military Extortion, and Civil War in El Salvador*. Philadelphia, NJ: Temple University Press.

(1999). "Building New Police Forces in El Salvador and Guatemala: Learning and Counter-learning." *International Peacekeeping* 6(4): 113–134.

Starn, Orin. (1999). *Nightwatch: The Politics of Protest in the Andes*. Durham, NC: Duke University Press.

Stephenson, Svetlana. (2015). *Gangs of Russia: From the Streets to the Corridors of Power*. Ithaca, NY: Cornell University Press.

Sung, Hung-En. (2006). "Police Effectiveness and Democracy: Shape and Direction of the Relationship." *Policing: An International Journal of Police Strategies & Management* 29(2): 347–367.

Sunshine, Jason and Tom Tyler. (2003). "Moral Solidarity, Identification with the Community, and the Importance of Procedural Justice: The Police as Prototypical Representatives of a Group's Moral Values." *Social Psychology Quarterly* 66(2): 153–165.

Superintendencia de Competencia. (2013). *Caracterización de la Agroindustria del Frijol Rojo y Sus Condiciones de Competencia en El Salvador (2007–2014)*. San Salvador, El Salvador: Superintendencia de Competencia.

Tankebe, Justice. (2009). "Public Cooperation with the Police in Ghana: Does Procedural Fairness Matter?" *Criminology* 47(4): 1265–1293.

(2013). "Viewing Things Differently: The Dimensions of Public Perceptions of Police Legitimacy." *Criminology* 51(1): 103–135.

Tarrow, Sidney. (1994). *Power in Movement: Social Movements, Collective Action and Politics*. Cambridge: Cambridge University Press.

Taylor, Michael. (1988). "Rationality and Revolutionary Collective Action." In *Rationality and Revolution*, edited by Michael Taylor, 63–97. Cambridge: Cambridge University Press.

Tellez, Juan Fernando, Erik Wibbels, and Anirudh Krishna. (2020). "Local Order, Policing, and Bribes: Evidence from India." *World Politics* 72(3): 377–410.

Tendler, Judith. (1997). *Good Government in the Tropics*. Baltimore, MD: Johns Hopkins University Press.

Przeworski, Adam and Henry Teune. (1970). *The Logic of Comparative Social Inquiry*. New York: Wiley-Interscience.

Thachil, Tariq. (2018). "Improving Surveys through Ethnography: Insights from India's Urban Periphery." *Studies in Comparative International Development* 53(3): 281–299.

Thale, Geoff and Elsa Falkenburger. (2006). *Youth Gangs in Central America: Issues in Human Rights, Effective Policing and Prevention*. Washington, DC: Washington Office on Latin America.

Thaler, Kai M. (2019). "Reflexivity and Temporality in Researching Violent Settings: Problems with the Replicability and Transparency Regime." *Geopolitics* 26(1): 18–44.

Thoumi, Francisco E. (2003). *Illegal Drugs, Economy, and Society in the Andes*. Washington, DC: Woodrow Wilson Center Press.

Tilly, Charles. (1982). *Warmaking and Statemaking as Organized Crime*. 256. CRSO Working Paper Series. Ann Arbor, MI: University of Michigan.

(1990). *Coercion, Capital and European States, AD 990-1990*. Basil Blackwell, 1990.

(2003). *The Politics of Collective Violence*. Cambridge: Cambridge University Press.

Tolentino, José Ángel, Gerson Elí Martínez, and Sherry Stanley. (2006). *El Salvador: Perspectivas de los Granos Básicos en el Tratado de Libre Comercio entre Centroamérica y Estados Unidos*. San Salvador: Fundación Nacional para el Desarrollo.

Tolnay, Stewart Emory and Elwood M. Beck. (1995). *A Festival of Violence: An Analysis of Southern Lynchings, 1882–1930*. Champaign, IL: University of Illinois Press.

Trejo, Guillermo and Sandra Ley. (2018). "Why Did Drug Cartels Go to War in Mexico? Subnational Party alternation, the Breakdown of Criminal Protection, and the Onset of Large-Scale Violence." *Comparative Political Studies* 51(7): 900–937.

  (2020). *Votes, Drugs, and Violence: The Political Logic of Criminal Wars in Mexico*. Cambridge: Cambridge University Press.

Trelles, Alejandro and Miguel Carreras. (2012). "Bullets and Votes: Violence and Electoral Participation in Mexico." *Journal of Politics in Latin America* 4(2): 89–123.

Triantafyllou, Dinara, Chong Wang, and Carol S. North. (2016). "Correlates of Duration of Intimate Partner Violence among Women Seeking Services at a Domestic Violence Support Center." *Journal of Interpersonal Violence*. https://doi.org/10.1177/0886260516647522

Tsai, Lily L. (2007). *Accountability without Democracy: Solidary Groups and Public Goods Provision in Rural China*. Cambridge: Cambridge University Press.

Tyler, Tom R. and Jeffrey Fagan. (2008). "Legitimacy and Cooperation: Why Do People Help the Police Fight Crime in Their Communities." *Ohio State Journal of Criminal Law* 6: 231–275.

Tyler, Tom R. and Jonathan Jackson. (2014). "Popular Legitimacy and the Exercise of Legal Authority: Motivating Compliance, Cooperation, and Engagement." *Psychology, Public Policy, and Law* 20(1): 78.

Tyler, Tom R., Phillip Atiba Goff, and Robert J. MacCoun. (2015). "The Impact of Psychological Science on Policing in the United States: Procedural Justice, Legitimacy, and Effective Law Enforcement." *Psychological Science in the Public Interest* 16(3): 75–109.

Ungar, Mark. (2002). *Elusive Reform: Democracy and the Rule of Law in Latin America*. Boulder and London: Lynne Rienner Publishers.

  (2007). "The Privatization of Citizen Security in Latin America: From Elite Guards to Neighborhood Vigilantes." *Social Justice* 34(3/4): 20–37.

  (2011). *Policing Democracy: Overcoming Obstacles to Citizen Security in Latin America*. Baltimore, MD: Johns Hopkins University Press.

United Nations Human Rights Council (UNHRC). (2018). *Report of the Special Rapporteur on Extrajudicial, Summary or Arbitrary Executions on her mission to El Salvador*. A_HRC_38_44_Add-2-EN.

Van der Borgh, Chris and Wim Savenije. (2019). "The Politics of Violence Reduction: Making and Unmaking the Salvadorean Gang Truce." *Journal of Latin American Studies* 51(4): 905–928.

Varese, Federico. (2001). *The Russian Mafia: Private Protection in a New Market Economy*. Oxford: Oxford University Press.

  (2014). "Protection and Extortion." In *Handbook of Organized Crime*, edited by Letizia Paoli, 343–358. Oxford: Oxford University Press.

Varshney, Ashutosh. (2002). *Ethnic Conflict and Civic Life: Hindus and Muslims in India*. New Haven: Yale University Press.

Visconti, Giancarlo. (2019). "Policy Preferences after Crime Victimization: Panel and Survey Evidence from Latin America." *British Journal of Political Science* 50(4): 1–15.

Vogel, David. (2003). *Fluctuating Fortunes: The Political Power of Business in America.* Washington, DC: Beard Books.

Volkov, Vadim. (2000). "The Political Economy of Protection Rackets in the Past and the Present." *Social Research* 67(3): 709–744.

(2002). *Violent Entrepreneurs: The Use of Force in the Making of Russian Capitalism.* Ithaca, NY: Cornell University Press.

Ward, Thomas W. (2013). *Gangsters Without Borders: An Ethnography of a Salvadoran Street Gang.* Oxford: Oxford University Press.

Weber, Max. (1946). "Politics as Vocation." In *From Max Weber: Essays in Sociology,* translated by H. H. Gerth and C. Wright Mills, 77–128. Oxford: Oxford University Press.

Wedeen, Lisa. (1999). *Ambiguities of Domination: Politics, Rhetoric, and Symbols in Contemporary Syria.* Chicago: University of Chicago Press.

Weinstein, Jeremy M. (2006). *Inside Rebellion: The Politics of Insurgent Violence.* Cambridge: Cambridge University Press.

Weintraub, Michael, Juan F. Vargas, and Thomas E. Flores. (2015). "Vote Choice and Legacies of Violence: Evidence From the 2014 Colombian Presidential Elections." *Research & Politics* 2(2): https://doi.org/10.1177/2053168015573348

Weyland, Kurt. (1996). "Neopopulism and Neoliberalism in Latin America: Unexpected Affinities." *Studies in Comparative International Development* 31(3): 3–31.

Williams, Gary W. and Dan Hanselka. (2018). "2018 Update: the US national and state-level economic benefits of avocado imports from Mexico."

Williams, Robert Gregory. (1994). *States and Social Evolution: Coffee and the Rise of National Governments in Central America.* Chapel Hill and London: University of North Carolina Press.

Willis, Graham Denyer. (2015). *The Killing Consensus: Police, Organized Crime, and the Regulation of Life and Death in Urban Brazil.* Berkeley: University of California Press.

Wilson, Ian Douglas. (2015). *The Politics of Protection Rackets in Post-New Order Indonesia: Coercive Capital, Authority and Street Politics.* London and New York: Routledge.

Wolff, Michael Jerome. (2015). "Building Criminal Authority: A Comparative Analysis of Drug Gangs in Rio de Janeiro and Recife." *Latin American Politics and Society* 57(2): 21–40.

Wood, Elisabeth Jean. (2000). *Forging Democracy from Below: Insurgent Transitions in South Africa and El Salvador.* Cambridge: Cambridge University Press.

(2003). *Insurgent Collective Action and Civil War in El Salvador.* Cambridge: Cambridge University Press.

(2009). "Armed Groups and Sexual Violence: When is Wartime Rape Rare?" *Politics & Society* 37(1): 131–161.

World Health Organization (WHO). (2005). *Multi-Country Study on Women's Health and Domestic Violence against Women.* Geneva: World Health Organization.

(2012). *Understanding and Addressing Violence against Women: Intimate Partner Violence. No. WHO/RHR/12.36.* Geneva: World Health Organization.

Worrall, John L. (1999). "Public Perceptions of Police Efficacy and Image: The 'Fuzziness' of Support for the Police." *American Journal of Criminal Justice* 24 (1): 47–66.

Yashar, Deborah J. (2018). *Homicidal Ecologies: Illicit Economies and Complicit States in Latin America*. Cambridge: Cambridge University Press.

Zald, Mayer N. and John D. McCarthy. (1987). *Social Movements in an Organizational Society*. New Brunswick, NJ: Transaction Books.

Zaluar, Alba and Isabel Siqueira Conceição. (2007). "Favelas sob o Controle das Milícias no Rio de Janeiro: ¿Que Paz?" *São Paulo em Perspectiva* 21(2): 89–102.

Zechmeister, Elizabeth J. (2014). *The Political Culture of Democracy in the Americas, 2014: Democratic Governance Across 10 Years of the Americas Barometer*. LAPOP/Vanderbilt University.

Zilberg, Elana. (2011). *Space of Detention: The Making of a Transnational Gang Crisis between Los Angeles and San Salvador*. Durham, NC: Duke University Press.

Zubillaga, Verónica, Manuel Llorens, and John Souto. (2019). "Micropolitics in a Caracas Barrio: The Political Survival Strategies of Mothers in a Context of Armed Violence." *Latin American Research Review* 54(2): 429–443.

Index

Dan Slater, *Ordering Power: Contentious Politics and Authoritarian Leviathans in Southeast Asia*

Austin Smith et al, *Selected Works of Michael Wallerstein*

Regina Smyth, *Candidate Strategies and Electoral Competition in the Russian Federation: Democracy Without Foundation*

Richard Snyder, *Politics after Neoliberalism: Reregulation in Mexico*

David Stark and László Bruszt, *Postsocialist Pathways: Transforming Politics and Property in East Central Europe*

Sven Steinmo, *The Evolution of Modern States: Sweden, Japan, and the United States*

Sven Steinmo, Kathleen Thelen, and Frank Longstreth, eds., *Structuring Politics: Historical Institutionalism in Comparative Analysis*

Susan C. Stokes, *Mandates and Democracy: Neoliberalism by Surprise in Latin America*

Susan C. Stokes, ed., *Public Support for Market Reforms in New Democracies*

Susan C. Stokes, Thad Dunning, Marcelo Nazareno, and Valeria Brusco, *Brokers, Voters, and Clientelism: The Puzzle of Distributive Politics*

Milan W. Svolik, *The Politics of Authoritarian Rule*

Duane Swank, *Global Capital, Political Institutions, and Policy Change in Developed Welfare States*

David Szakonyi *Politics for Profit: Business, Elections, and Policymaking in Russia*

Sidney Tarrow, *Power in Movement: Social Movements and Contentious Politics*

Sidney Tarrow, *Power in Movement: Social Movements and Contentious Politics, Revised and Updated Third Edition*

Tariq Thachil, *Elite Parties, Poor Voters: How Social Services Win Votes in India*

Kathleen Thelen, *How Institutions Evolve: The Political Economy of Skills in Germany, Britain, the United States, and Japan*

Kathleen Thelen, *Varieties of Liberalization and the New Politics of Social Solidarity*

Charles Tilly, *Trust and Rule*

Daniel Treisman, *The Architecture of Government: Rethinking Political Decentralization*

Guillermo Trejo, *Popular Movements in Autocracies: Religion, Repression, and Indigenous Collective Action in Mexico*

Guillermo Trejo and Sandra Ley, *Votes, Drugs, and Violence: The Political Logic of Criminal Wars in Mexico*

Rory Truex, *Making Autocracy Work: Representation and Responsiveness in Modern China*

Lily L. Tsai, *Accountability without Democracy: How Solidary Groups Provide Public Goods in Rural China*

Lily L. Tsai, *When People Want Punishment: Retributive Justice and the Puzzle of Authoritarian Popularity*

Joshua Tucker, *Regional Economic Voting: Russia, Poland, Hungary, Slovakia and the Czech Republic, 1990–1999*

Ashutosh Varshney, *Democracy, Development, and the Countryside*

Yuhua Wang, *Tying the Autocrat's Hand: The Rise of The Rule of Law in China*

Jeremy M. Weinstein, *Inside Rebellion: The Politics of Insurgent Violence*

Andreas Wiedemann *Indebted Societies: Credit and Welfare in Rich Democracies*

Martha Wilfahrt *Precolonial Legacies in Postcolonial Politics: Representation and Redistribution in Decentralized West Africa*

Stephen I. Wilkinson, *Votes and Violence: Electoral Competition and Ethnic Riots in India*

Made in the USA
Coppell, TX
18 August 2022